BIBLE CODE BROKEN!

THE TRUTH ABOUT THE CHRISTIAN SABBATH

BIBLE CODE BROKEN!

THE TRUTH ABOUT THE CHRISTIAN SABBATH

Robert B. Scott

TWO HARBORS PRESS
Minneapolis, MN

Two Harbors Press
212 3rd Avenue North, Suite 290
Minneapolis, MN 55401
612.455.2293
www.TwoHarborsPress.com

ISBN - 978-1-935097-36-5
ISBN - 1-935097-36-9
LCCN - 2009928246

Book sales for North America and international:
Itasca Books, 3501 Highway 100 South, Suite 220
Minneapolis, MN 55416
Phone: 952.345.4488 (toll free 1.800.901.3480)
Fax: 952.920.0541; email to orders@itascabooks.com

Cover Design and Typeset by Madge Duffey

Printed in the United States of America

TWOHARBORS
WWW.TWOHARBORSPRESS.COM

Table of Contents

Introduction

Shortly before my ninth birthday in 1960, my father took our family sightseeing to Washington, D.C. We brought back many good memories, immortalized by one photo of the White House lawn with a small red dot we still believe was President Kennedy's red head. But one bad memory lingered long after we returned home.

I confess. On the very spot where George Washington supposedly claimed he could not lie and that he did not chop down the cherry tree his dad thought he had felled, I lied. Probably because of the fear of rejection, or insecurity along with pride, I told a fib.

This sin took place in the Mount Vernon gift shop. I had spied a neat souvenir -- a pocketknife that fascinated me. Apparently it was more special than I thought. As I reached for the money my daddy had given me to pay for this treasure, the manager surprised me with a question: "You know how to open this special knife, huh?" Not wanting to look dumb, I said yes.

I never did learn how to open that knife. Apparently you had to know the secret to unlock its blades. Its treasures remained locked inside forever. It became something I put on my desk to look at and gather dust.

Sound familiar?

Most bibles are also gathering dust. Even for those Christians who read God's Word and endeavor to get something out of it, it remains a locked book -- a coded book few understand.

Many claim it is outdated and contradictory and doesn't apply to our modern culture. Most Christians rarely read or take seriously what they have dubbed incorrectly "the Old Testament[1]." You can't understand the New without the "Old." You can't appreciate any branches unless you have roots.

Some are beginning to seek out the Hebrew roots of the New Covenant Church. Their attempts have been superficial, at best, in most cases. Yet Paul says that we are all to become "partakers with them [the Hebrew peoples] of the rich root of the olive [anointed] tree," represented by the Hebraic roots of the church (Rom. 11:17). He added: "...it is not you who supports the root, but the root supports you" (v. 18).

My knife was a cute souvenir. But it had no blades that worked for me. It's the same sad story for most of today's believers and the Bible. They have a cute souvenir of bygone days that is either gathering dust or remains locked to their understanding as they

1 God never inspired the terms "Old Testament" and "New Testament" to refer to the Scriptures written predominately in Hebrew and Greek. Satan has cleverly used these terms to dismiss virtually three-fourths of the Bible with the phrase "that's Old Testament," as if we don't need to pay attention to it. To avoid this pitfall, we choose to use the terms "Hebrew Scriptures" or "First Testament" and "Greek Scriptures" or "Second Testament."

read it.

Many are advancing in biblical knowledge, but they haven't yet found the key to open the Bible and make it come alive as never before.

Here's what God says His Word is supposed to be: "For the word of God is living and active and sharper than any two-edged sword…"(Heb. 4:12).

Like my Mount Vernon souvenir, the power of the Bible in the lives of Christians has laid dormant because believers have not understood it. It has not become alive.

I'm sure the manager of that store would have given me a simple key to unlock the power of that knife. The key that breaks the code of the most misunderstood book of all time is also simple -- amazingly simple. Yet like me, pride has kept the church from obeying a clear and unequivocal instruction from God found in both Testaments -- a practice that would finally break the Bible code and usher Christians into a position even stronger than the early church in the Book of Acts.

This simple practice would open a door of revelation, intimacy, power, and anointing that has never been seen. The real Jesus waits at that door.

In an epistle that contains the knowledge of this powerful hammer that breaks the locks around God's Word, Paul expressed his desire for the believers: "…that their hearts may be encouraged, having been knit together in love, and attaining to all the wealth that comes from the *full assurance of understanding*, resulting in a *true* knowledge of God's *mystery*, that is, Christ Himself, in whom are *hidden* all the treasures of wisdom and knowledge" (Col. 2:2-3).

Consequently, we see that Jesus Himself is the key. He and the Father *are* love, or should we say Love (I John 4:8)? God wants us to know Him intimately and to love Him.

But how? How do we love Him? Religiosity does not like the answer, but it is Jesus Himself who gave it. We didn't write it, but you will see us repeating it and emphasizing it. Our goal is not overkill, but abundant life for all who read. This proof of our love of Jesus deserves bold type: "***If you love Me, you will keep My commandments***" (John 14:15). We will prove later in this book that Jesus is the Word who spoke all the commandments of the Bible, not only the red letter ones we read in the gospels.

Many ministries are learning more and more truth because they have grasped an important principle -- the importance of obeying what God reveals to you. They have made small steps up to now. But when they take hold of what this book reveals, we believe it will help them grow as it has us.

Wisdom and knowledge will increase when we begin to get in line with God's way of thinking, expressed in these powerful words: "The fear [margin: "reverence for," which includes love, respect and obedience] of the [Eternal] is the beginning of wisdom; A good *understanding* have all those who *do* His commandments…" (Ps. 111:10).

Many people believe you can pick and choose what you believe in the Bible. It is true that God says He plants nuggets of truth like a puzzle "...a little here, a little there" (Isa. 28:10). But all His instructions are to be obeyed (II Tim. 3:16). James clearly said that if we break one commandment, it is the same as breaking them all (James 2:10).

God tested His people Israel before the Sinai Covenant was even made with one commandment. It was His test. It is also a sign of His people that has been lost because of the pride of theologians who have reasoned around what can be amazingly simple when we grasp it. Jesus did say that we must become like little children to enter His Kingdom (Mat. 18:3).

Jesus said to His Father, "...You have *hidden* these things from the wise and intelligent and have *revealed* them to infants..."(Luke 10:21).

Only those who humble themselves like little children will understand the keys of the Kingdom. The prideful will not be able to take hold of the hammer that breaks the lock of the Bible code.

You are about to discover the key to unlock the Bible to your full understanding. You will no longer have to struggle in your Christian life because of a lack of knowledge (Hos. 4:6).

Jesus offers you the supernatural unraveling of the mysteries of the Bible that are wrapped up and hidden in Him. The best way to have the secrets of a book opened is to know the author. The Bible code breaker involves intimacy. You get to know the Author of the most important Book ever written in a way you have never known Him.

It is not important for you to know the author of this book, although I do believe the real Author behind the physical one who sometimes misses the mark is the Holy Spirit.

This physical author is seeking God's help, albeit imperfectly, to fulfill the commission of Freedom Church of God (freedomchurchofgod.com; Internet radio station freedomtruthseekers.com). God urges us to fulfill our "anointing" (our calling for which God gifts and empowers us) by saying, "Cry loudly, do not hold back; Raise your voice like a trumpet, And declare to My people their transgression And to the house of Jacob their sins" (Isa. 58:1).

In our age of political correctness and tolerance, we should recognize that even Jesus may have offended some by his words and tone. We read in Mark 1:21-22 that He taught on the Sabbath day with great force and conviction, "teaching them as one having authority, and not as the scribes." His words to the religious establishment of His day were probably viewed as more insulting than authoritative. Yet He was gentle and humble and met those who were deceived where they were, as did Paul who became a Jew to the Jew, putting himself in the place of others with compassion.

God has been merciful to us, revealing to us the truth about the blessing revealed in this book. This understanding has permitted us to grasp biblical truths that are unfamiliar to the Christian world. These revelations may seem strange to many, but we know them to be true, so we teach them unabashedly.

Please forgive us if any of these forceful pronouncements come across as condemning. While we are judging the religious establishment that Satan has used to mislead, we know that many good Christians have in all sincerity been unaware of the awesome blessing we speak about in this book.

We are simply here to point out the sin of missing out on this blessing, so that readers of any religious persuasion or none at all can be convicted by the Word of God and the Holy Spirit to make the changes that will bring about blessing in their lives. Thank you for meeting us where we are while we endeavor to meet you with love where you are.

The key He offers you in this book and in His Book is a free gift that will change your life forever. Will you accept it?

Or will you, like I did with my treasured pocketknife, let pride get in the way of unlocking the powerful blades of the sword that is the Word of God?

"Ouch" may be your first reaction to this sword. Truth sometimes hurts, at least at first. Then healing comes. Truth is controversial. Jesus lost many disciples because of powerful teachings He gave. What you are about to read may offend some who choose to cling to the pride of human and church tradition.

We hope you will approach this book prayerfully. While Elihu's words were slanted against righteous Job, the words themselves can apply to new material introduced to us: "Teach me what I do not see; If I have done iniquity, I will not do it again…" (Job 34:32). David's words are even more appropriate: "Open my eyes, that I may behold Wonderful things from Your law…Give me understanding, that I may learn Your commandments" (Ps. 119:18,73). The Holy Spirit "will guide you into all the truth" (John 16:13).

Jesus spilled His red blood on the ground to wipe out all our sins. While we are not held accountable for sins of which we are unaware (James 4:17; John 9:41), we nonetheless miss out on the blessings.

This Bible code breaker is predicated upon obedience, which opens a door to revelation, understanding, and much more. It opens a new door to intimacy with Jesus along with His blessings, anointing, and power.

No exaggeration. What God has in store for the church in these last days is available if we humble ourselves to grasp this important key to break the code of the hidden mysteries of God's Word. God said: "Indeed He will speak to this people Through stammering lips and a foreign tongue [Hebrew, Aramaic and Greek]" (Isa. 28:11) so that only a few would be called in this age, a few who would teach the many others that would be resurrected to know Him later (Rev. 20:5). The key is found in rest -- in a Sabbath rest few have known. "He who said to them, 'Here is rest, give rest to the weary,' And, 'Here is repose,' but they would not listen" (Isa. 28:12).

Will we listen? Few are called in this age. Even fewer will grasp the key that unlocks the secret Bible code. Will we?

Or will our pride cause us to refuse to listen so that we "go and stumble backward, be broken, snared, and taken captive" (Isa. 28:13) because the Bible remains a puzzle, a closed, locked Book for us.

God is so merciful that even if we choose not to accept this blessing now, He has a plan to introduce it to us later in our journey.

Before we come to the answer that will break the code and bring freedom, let's look at some of the few who have already discovered this code breaker.

Sabbath *Selah's*

The Hebrew word selah, *found often in the Psalms, has a number of meanings. Since it comes from the root, "to measure," it means to meditate upon and weigh the preceding verses. In a similar way, the Sabbath is a weekly time to pause in order to weigh and consider the words and ways of our God of love. The Sabbath is our time to cease our weekly striving, to be still and know that God is God, that He is Love. Before each chapter, we will present a fact, truth and/or Bible verse(s) regarding the Sabbath for the reader to ponder. Here is the first:*

Christians are in too much of a hurry today. They need to heed the lyrical admonition, "Slow down! You move too fast." They are in a rat race for riches, but they have forgotten to rest in Jesus.

Rush-Rush vs. Hush-Hush

Cease striving [be still] and know that I am God [Love]; I will be exalted among the nations. I will be exalted in the earth (Ps. 46:10).

So there remains a Sabbath rest [margin of KJV: "keeping of the Sabbath"] for the people of God. For the one who has entered His rest has himself also rested from his works, *as God did* from His. Therefore let us be diligent to enter that rest, so that no one will fall, through following the same example of disobedience (Heb. 4:9-11).

We live in a rush-rush society that is wrapped in busyness and business 24/7. It's time we slowed down and limited our busyness to 24/6, leaving the seventh day for resting in Jesus, meditating on His Word and doing His work. Selah

CHAPTER ONE

Breaking News! Bible Code Breaker Unleashes Earthshaking Power!

CNN doesn't report it. Few know about it. But news filters back from pastors who have returned from China.

Many know that the church is persecuted around the world. What many do not know is that many Christians die unnecessarily. Their lives are destroyed because of a lack of knowledge. Of the 100 million believers in China, about ten million have discovered a truth that most Western Christians neglect, rebel against, or simply choose to ignore.

Many Christians around the world are becoming aware of a gateway to intimacy, love, and power in Jesus that has been lost for centuries. Millions of these believers in China have discovered this key and have brought fear into government authorities because of amazing miracles God is doing through them. If you are willing to put the simple truth of God's Word over human tradition, you too can see the love and power of Jesus released in your life. When Christians begin to meet with Jesus the way He instructs, we believe the church will shake this world with the power of Jesus!

A small percentage of those ten million Chinese Christians have even gone even higher in their level of faith because of their obedience to the whole Word of God as revealed in the sequel to this book.

Armed government militia attacked this church group and murdered their pastor in front of their eyes. But these stalwart Christians didn't stand for it! In the name of Jesus, they called for the pastor to rise and be healed, and he was! He was raised to life before the incredulous eyes of the military men who looked on. Now they don't know what to do with this group. They stand in awe and fear of them. These believers walk in power!

The question is why. Why do they have such power? Why don't we have this power in the western world of Christianity? The answer will surprise you.

While the Christian world has been conditioned to resist the simple answer, it has been right there in the Bible for thousands of years. It is no secret. The Roman Catholic Church openly admits this truth. They declare that their tradition and the pronouncements of popes take precedence over what the Bible plainly says. At the end of the nineteenth century, several eminent Catholic scholars wrote to the Protestants regarding this biblical teaching. In essence, they told them: "You got your practice and tradition from *us* – not from the Bible!"

Protestant and Catholic leaders alike have gone on record to admit that their way of meeting with God is not the biblical way. No wonder we are not walking in the power Jesus said we should have (John 14:12).

The answer is so simple that it has eluded, or been explained away by, the theologians and commentators of the church.

The deceptive excuses of pastors and teachers have kept the church from this simple truth – this gateway to intimacy, love, and power in Jesus.

The apostle John knew this truth and obeyed it. History even records that his disciple Polycarp and Polycarp's successor, Polycrates, knew and kept this simple biblical instruction. Paul knew this truth and obeyed it. When he warned about the possibility of the Bride of Jesus not being ready as a pure, spotless virgin for Jesus to marry, he may not have realized that Satan would deceive the church on such a simple truth that Paul and the other apostles took for granted.

Paul warned: "For I am jealous for you with a godly jealousy; for I have betrothed you to one husband, so that to Christ I might present you as a pure virgin. But I am afraid that, as the serpent deceived Eve by his craftiness, your minds will be led astray from the *simplicity* and purity of devotion to Christ" (II Cor. 11:2-3).

It's so simple: Jesus said that if we love Him, we will obey Him.

Paul knew that the "mystery of lawlessness" (II Thes. 2:7) was already at work at that time. He had thought the end would come in his time, and was surprised to see that Jesus had more to do on earth before He came back. I think he would have been and is now surprised to see what law Christians have done away with today.

Law. What do you think when you hear that word. "Yuck?" "Bondage?" "Bad?" *Law* is a bad word for many Christians. Yet God's law is the embodiment of who He is – Love (I John 4:8). Why would Paul warn against lawlessness if he himself were against the law of God?

Know What Satan Knows

Even if Christians do not know what is important to God, Satan does! Although believers may not know the ***gateway to intimacy with Jesus***, which opens the path to His love, His righteousness, and His power, Satan does! Christians don't know why they are not walking in power and stepping on the devil's head, but Satan does!

Isn't it about time that we began to know the devices of Satan, as Paul commands us? Isn't it about time that we know what he knows – and more than he knows? As you will discover in this book, it is indeed about time. It's all about time, in a double sense. For the key to end-time power that is prophesied is a matter of time. It has to do with the time on the clock. It has to do with giving Jesus "the time of day." One of our working titles was "It's Time to Meet with Jesus!" But not our way, His way! Not on our timing, but on His!

We encourage you to read this book attentively and humbly, because Satan does not want you to know what he knows. He does not want this truth out. He will do all he can to stop it. He will do all he can to get you to call on religious prejudice and tradition to keep you from reading further.

Satan is a liar. This book which, like the Bible may seem naively simple to some, dares to speak the truth. It's a truth that Satan will try to make unwelcome. And he will succeed when it comes to the majority, who will not be lost forever as many teach but who will have the truth opened to them in a future resurrection (Rev. 20:5,12). He is about to foist the mystery of lawlessness on the whole world through a "beast" power in Europe ridden by a woman representing a false church. He has already convinced most Christians that this gateway to power is done away. Soon he will enforce that concept with a mark that will identify your acceptance or refusal of this key to intimacy and power in Jesus.

You can, however, escape the wrath of this false system if you choose to meet with Jesus the way He commanded. That's not a fear tactic. It's the truth. Even if you choose not to accept this blessing now, you will not lose out because our Father Love is merciful. He always has a plan of redemption. We hope to accentuate in this book the priceless blessings you will receive when you break the Bible code.

Rest and Relish

God saw all that He had made, and behold, it was very good (Gen. 1:31).

Ever completed a project and sat back and simple enjoyed the finished work, relishing the beauty of the work done? That's part of the Hebrew concept of rest that Jesus enjoyed when He had finished undoing the damage Satan's original rebellion had produced on the earth. By His word He created order out of confusion, light out of darkness, beauty out of an ugly mess (Gen. 1:1-3; John 1:1-18). He sat back in His Sabbath "easy chair" and relished His creation. We can do the same. The Sabbath is a day to relax and enjoy God's creation, since recognizing God as Creator is one of the purposes of the day. What do we learn from creation?

- God loves variety.
- He has a sense of humor and is full of joy (witnessed by the song of birds).
- God has made the plants and animals to teach us many lessons. They respond to love. They perform feats by their instinct that only God could produce. They sense when we are walking in love, have no fear, and respond accordingly.
- God is a God of order and loves beauty.
- The principle of interdependence reigns, as in the body of Christ.
- We look forward to the change of violent animal nature, initiated by Satan, to the lion dwelling with the lamb in the coming millennial rule of Jesus on earth.
- God is a God of seed time and harvest; the Sabbath is a day to wait on a harvest as God did when he rested.
- God is a God of detail.
- He is a God of provision.
- He is a God of seasons and timing.

Sabbath *Selah's*
A Blessing Forever

Then God blessed the seventh day and sanctified it [made it holy], because in it He rested from all His work which God had created and made (Gen. 2:3).

I have sworn by Myself, The Word has gone from My mouth in righteousness And will not turn back… (Isa. 45:23).

God is not a man, that He should lie, Nor a son of man, that He should repent…Behold, I [Balaam] have received a command [from God] to bless; When He has blessed, then I cannot revoke it"(Num. 23:19-20).

And now it has pleased You to bless the house of Your servant, that it may continue forever before you; for You, O [Eternal], have blessed, and it is blessed forever (I Chr. 17:27).

For the gifts and the calling of God are irrevocable (Rom. 11:29).

Yet He also is wise and will bring disaster And does not retract His words…(Isa. 31:2)

God blessed the Sabbath day. He cannot, by His very nature and His Word, take back a blessing once He has issued it. So the Sabbath is still blessed today and will be a blessing to those who keep it. It is one of the perfect gifts from our Father of Lights (James 1:17). *Selah.*

CHAPTER TWO

It's About Time!

Satan has done a nasty number on the body of Jesus Christ. He has deceived the church – and for that matter all mankind – into losing out on one of the greatest blessings Jesus ever offered.

Satan's rule is soon coming to an end. God's time has come to reveal to the end time church and to the world the truth about one of the greatest blessings He has given to mankind.

It's about time!

You can take that two ways. It's literally about time. It's about a special gift of time from a Father who loves His children -- a Father who wants to spend some special time with those He loves. It's about the special time Jesus instructed us to meet with Him.

It's about time! It's about time the Bride of Jesus heard this truth! It was lost to the vast majority of the church for some 1700 years. It is also a major reason why the church has not been blessed.

The first book God anointed through this ministry was *Why Doesn't God Heal Me?* It explained the blessing of healing that God promised His people and why many have missed out on that blessing. I identified personally with the subject, for I had been denied healing for twelve excruciating years. When God revealed the key to open the door to my healing, I reaped the blessing of a healing that was deemed impossible by man.

The awesome blessing revealed in this present book is one of the greatest blessings ever given to us by our Father of Love. I also identify with it in many ways. At times I related some personal testimonies in the first book. While this book is not about me, I am going to get a bit personal in this first chapter so you can understand.

A Father's Greatest Present -- His Presence

When my children were quite young, I did spend time with them. I enjoyed being with them. I enjoyed watching them, savoring their verbal jewels, their laughs, and their antics. That "quality" time, however, did not have much quantity attached to it.

I had a three-church circuit (Quebec City, Trois-Rivieres, and Saguenay), in two of these I preached every week, and a large geographical area to cover. While I was off "saving the world,", I too often left them alone and abandoned.

Struck by deadly Legionnaire's disease and the resulting organic personality disorder caused by a lack of oxygen on the brain, I was forced to live separately from my (now-ex) wife and my son and daughter. My son was only eight at the time, my daughter eleven. Daddy wasn't the same daddy they had known, and they couldn't bear him. And their daddy had a hard time bearing being without them.

As some of you know, mental illness is a great tragedy that Satan has inflicted on many in our society. But the greatest pain falls on the family members. It's hard for them to heal even if the sick one does. It can take time.

As I write these words over ten years after my healing, I look forward to seeing my children again. They're taking time to heal. Although we live only minutes apart in the same city, they aren't ready to see their dad.

I have many blessings I would like to give them. The greatest blessing I believe is time – time with their dad. Time he didn't give them enough of when they were young.

All of you who read, of course, have – or have had -- fathers. As you think about your relationship with your dad, if it was basically a good one, what was missing? Many adult children have the same answer to that question. I think both fathers and children would say the same thing: "If we could go back in time and do it all over again, we would spend more time together."

Love with a Capital L

This book is all about time. And it's all about love -- with a capital L. The Bible says, "God is love (I John 4:8)." That's who He is. He *is* Love.

All He wants to do is to lavish His love on us. To do that He needs to spend time with us. Lots of time. Every day. He wants to be with us and bless us every day.

He has set aside, however, a special day where He invites us into His presence in a way He doesn't on any other day.

Our God is offering us, His children, a special blessing. His greatest gift was His Son Jesus. And Jesus' greatest gift as well was Himself.

Yet before He even gave Himself for all mankind so they could be a part of the Family of God, He gave the gift of Himself in a day, a 24-hour day. Jesus blessed a certain day of the week and made it holy. It could not be holy unless He was in it.

One of His greatest presents is His presence.

He poured a part of Himself into that 24-hour period. The God who is outside of the realm of time gave His people who live in the zone of time and space a precious gift – the gift of time.

Paul told us that nothing we do means anything if we don't have love (I Cor. 13:1-3). The same is true with love written with a capital L. So if Love offers us His presence in a day of time and specifies the exact day, what does that mean to us? If we know about it and don't meet with Love on that day, what would Love say to us and about us? Good question. Thank God that mercy is part of Love.

Love has a day. This day of Love is a vast and virtually unknown subject to the Christian world. The chapters that explain it will overlap. And because it's new understanding, some repetition will be beneficial. Each chapter addresses the anti-Sabbath arguments in a different way, using some of the same Scriptures as they fit into the context of the chapter. The hammer of God's Word will break the Bible code bit by bit.

It's about time we heard the truth about God's gift of time with us. It's time to meet with Jesus at *His* appointed time – not ours!

Can You Handle The Truth?

If you are able to humble yourself like a little child as Jesus said in Matthew 18, and ask the Holy Spirit to guide you to understand the Word, you can understand this simple truth. God spells it out clearly in His Word.

Unfortunately, for centuries theologians have shrouded this simple truth in a fog of falseness. Parishioners have gobbled up their gobbledygook. The ruthless robber has snatched Jesus' blessed day of rest from His beleaguered bride. Tradition triumphed over truth.

A famous movie line has often rung in my head: "You can't *handle* the truth!"

Can you?

If you can, you will open up a ***gateway to intimacy with Jesus*** – a doorway to the Door Himself. You will never regret it.

If you think we're talking about lifeless legalism, think again. Please withhold judgment. Keep an open mind and an open book – and don't forget to open up the Book of books and prove in the Word everything you read (I Thes. 5:21).

Do us -- and yourself -- a favor. Don't ask your pastor. Don't see what the commentaries have to say. Go to the source. Jesus said, "Sanctify them in the truth; Your word is truth (John 17:17)." Open your bible and see for yourself.

It's Time to Enter Jesus' Rest

God's Book has much to say about the rest of Jesus and resting in Him. But before we examine the Scriptures to find rest, let's consider why it is so difficult in our modern society to rest.

We live in a harried, hurried, hectic world. We rush to and fro, doing five things at once, with cell phone in hand, wondering why we don't have time to enjoy life. We're so stuck to our Blackberry™ that we don't have time to pick the blueberries. God and family get put on the back burner of the sloppy stove of our frantic lives. We don't rest.

Author and humorist Phil Callaway is a busy man. He not only writes books about golf; he also takes time to relax and play the game. More importantly, he takes time for people. At a conference a few years ago he invited me to lunch and shared some time and ideas with me. He even allowed me to share the following excerpt from his book, *Who Put My Life on Fast Forward?* He lays groundwork for understanding the need for the Sabbath. Phil writes. . . . .

On August 13,1971 (a Friday, I believe), the devil invited millions of demons from the far corners of the Western Hemisphere to the annual Creative Chaos Convention held 300 miles beneath Texas. It was a hot day (even above ground) and attendance was mandatory.

"Fellow enemies," Satan began in his keynote address, "we have had some victories. We have split some churches and burned some Bibles, and we've got them arguing about music again like we did in the 1600s. I congratulate you on a terrible job!"

The demons began lobbing fiery darts at one another and booing loudly. Lifting his hand, Satan calmed their gleeful enthusiasm. "But let's be honest—though none of us finds it easy," he continued. "We haven't stopped these Christians from reading their Bibles, loving their neighbors, or worshiping God. It's time we tried something else."

"Like what?" shouted a particularly ugly little demon whose name tag read "Hal."

Satan emitted a long and sinister cackle, then adjusted his notes and gazed out over the darkened auditorium.

"We will gradually distract them," he wheezed. "We will keep them from God by making them too busy with other things. Oh, let them go to church, but start stealing their time. If they have no time for a relationship with Jesus, we've got 'em."

"But how?" shouted ugly little Hal, who was still trembling at the mention of That Name. "How do we steal their time?"

"Redefine success for them. It's not about people or faithfulness anymore, it's about things. Make them equate success with stuff. Keep them borrowing, borrowing, borrowing. Lower the prime rate. Replace the front porch with a garage. Convince them that they need bigger houses and more cars. Keep the husbands and wives working longer hours to get out of debt and rarely let them see their kids. I've hated the family since the beginning. This just might fix it."

"Is that all?" shouted another demon near the back.

"No, I'm just getting started," said Satan, who was met with another enthusiastic round of jeers and catcalls.

"Make them comfortable and complacent. Blind them to the needs of others. And would someone invent seedless watermelons? They're having way too much fun spitting them. I hate it when Christians laugh."

"What else, what else?" sneered Hal, just before being pelted by a rotten egg.

"Make silence a fearful thing. Create so much noise that they can't hear the still, small voice of God. Turn the music up in restaurants and supermarkets, pound their minds with 24-hour news channels, invent something better than that awful 8-track and keep the music loud. The sound systems in our cars are lousy—do something about that. There isn't nearly enough junk mail either, so have it increased. And we need more television channels. How about a shopping channel? See if you can get away with a golf channel, though I doubt you can. Offer free products and sweepstakes and trips and pyramid marketing schemes. Get them to take excessive vacations and return broke. Keep them away from nature. Let them find their rest in amusement parks, sporting events, and movies, and could someone increase the cussing in Hollywood? There isn't nearly enough cussing. Hal, you take care of that."

You could barely hear Satan now above the rising enthusiasm. But he wasn't finished.

"Speed up the world!" he yelled above the roar of the minions. "Don't give those Christians time to think. Or rest. Make them too tired to walk with God. Too weary to lift a hand to help others. Keep them busy with good things—with programs and charts and reports—but don't let them rely on Christ. Let them think they can get by on their own. Let them sacrifice their health and their family and their God on the altar of busyness. Then they will be ours."

Over Satan's sinister cackle, the demons began to stomp and chant, "We will, we will, rock them."

Some say the standing ovation is still going on.

Breaking the Yoke of Busyness

Phil's point is well taken. Someone even came up with a clever and accurate acronym for the word *busy*: Being Under Satan's Yoke. The devil has been giving us the ***business*** and the busyness for too long. He has not only deprived us of rest, but he has also substituted the anointed day for rest for a replacement that is far from restful.

While the "anointing" (presence and empowerment of the Holy Spirit) breaks yokes, Satan has cleverly deprived Christians of the day in which the anointing of the Holy Spirit is strongest. The Holy Spirit nonetheless uses the anointing to teach new truth. Truth is not new to God and has always been contained in the Bible; it is new, however, to the one who discovers it. The Divine Master of the Sabbath is calling out to every reader of this book to accept new understanding.

Jesus is beckoning to our rushed, tired generation in words similar to those etched on the Statue of Liberty. I paraphrase from my school days: "Give me your tired, your poor, your huddled masses yearning to breathe free." I also paraphrase Jesus' words in Matthew 11:28-30: "Come to me, all who are weary and heavy-laden, and I will give you rest… you'll find rest for your souls. Enter into my Sabbath rest. For My yoke is easy and My burden is light."

Are you "tempest tossed"? Are you tired out by the storms of daily life? Enter into the glorious freedom of Jesus' Sabbath rest.

Are you ready? Are you tired enough? Are you tired enough of human tradition? Are you ready to hear what God says? It may surprise you. Then again, maybe not. When you heard what pastors preached about this subject, and you looked in the Bible, deep inside you felt something was amiss. Many of you have known in your hearts the truth about the Sabbath rest. If you have read the Book from beginning to end (which I hope you will do for this book as well), you saw this truth in black and white throughout the Bible. Many of you are simply waiting, waiting for some encouragement to do what you know you should do – to do what pastors have not had the courage to do.

Foretaste of a World at Rest

The price they would have to pay to obey this truth is probably greater than the price you have to pay. The Holy Spirit is inspiring a number of TV preachers to come closer and closer to understanding this truth. We know that some are even obeying this truth without preaching it. When God reveals this truth in a greater way, we believe blessings will come.

"If you consent and obey, You will eat the best of the land," God promises (Isa. 1:19). The pastures of pastors and laymen alike can be so much greener than they have been. When this truth is understood and obeyed, the anointing will increase. Our cups will overflow. Our Shepherd will lead us beside truly quiet waters and will restore our tired souls (and bodies). His rod and staff will give greater comfort. The banquet table He will prepare before us in the presence of our enemies (who will increase when we step out and obey this truth) will be sumptuous.

We will have a foretaste of a millennial rest pictured in Isaiah: "The [Eternal] of hosts will prepare a lavish banquet for all peoples on this mountain; A banquet of aged wine, choice pieces with marrow, And refined, aged wine. And on this mountain He will swallow up the covering which is over all peoples [even the religious people], Even the veil which is stretched over all nations" (25:6-7).

Isaiah ends his book by pointing us to the time when all will rest in Jesus the way He instructs: "For thus says the [Eternal], 'Behold, I extend peace to her like a river…As one whom his mother comforts, so I will comfort you…Then you will see this and your heart will be glad, And your bones will flourish like the new grass…And from sabbath to sabbath, All mankind will come to bow down before Me…" (66:12-14, 23).

It's time Jesus lifts the veil -- the veil stretched over all peoples, especially the veil covering the Bride of Jesus.

Sabbath *Selah's*
"Connect-i-cut"? Cutting the Connector

Have we cut our spiritual umbilical cord with our Father and our connector with our siblings in Jesus? The Sabbath is a connector. It connects God's people to Him and to each other. It is a weekly, spiritual family reunion.

So there remains a Sabbath rest for the people of God . . . . . not forsaking our own assembling together, as is the habit of some, but encouraging one another; and all the more as you see the day drawing near (Heb. 4:9;10:25).

Behold, the [Eternal's] hand is not so short That it cannot save; Nor is His ear so dull That it cannot hear. But your *iniquities* have made a *separation* between you and your God, And your *sins* have hidden His face from you so that He does not hear. For your hands are defiled with blood And your fingers with iniquity; Your lips have spoken *falsehood* ...(Isa. 59:1-3).

I am the true vine...Abide in Me, and I in you...***If you keep My commandments, you will abide in My love*** (John 15:1,4,10).

Come to Me, all who are weary and heavy-laden, and I will give you rest [same Greek word used for the Sabbath in the Greek version of the Hebrew Scriptures] (Mat. 11:28). *Selah.*

CHAPTER THREE

Lifting the Veil

A murky veil is about to be lifted on one of the cleverest satanic deceptions in history. While we know as believers that Satan is a defeated foe for us and will be eliminated soon, he as done more than deceive world leaders, pagan hordes, atheists, agnostics -- even the world of religiosity -- man's puny and often counterfeit effort to worship God his own way.

The wily devil has deceived the very body of Jesus Christ – His beloved bride. He has seduced her – unwittingly for the most part – into disobeying her Husband. He has even caused her to mock God by using ways and days blemished by pagan roots to worship the holy God. He has deprived her of one of the great blessings of a loving Creator.

Our long-suffering God has patiently observed this disobedience for over 1700 years. But His time has now come to lift the veil of deception.

When Jesus lifts this veil off His beloved bride, He won't see the kind of bride for which Jacob labored for Laban seven years. Though special in God's eyes, Leah was second best in Jacob's eyes. His true beloved, whom he saw as beautiful and spotless, was Rachel. When he lifted her veil, he got no bad surprise. He looked with joy upon his spotless virgin bride. When Jesus lifts that veil of deception from His bride, He will exult over her.

Jesus Christ is soon going to call for His bride – His church. He does not want a blemished bride. He longs to behold a bride "without spot or wrinkle" and whisk her off on a thousand-year honeymoon. And He is going to be sure that she is observing the day that foreshadows their millennial reign on earth together.

Isaiah prophesied the time when the whole world would rest in Jesus according to His commandments of love. He also foretold that in these last days that a veil would cover the world, including the Bride of Jesus. She would be mixed up, confused by theologians and seers who would not speak the truth of God's Word (Isa. 8:20; 5:24). God warns (Isa. 5:20-21): "Woe to those who call evil good, and good evil; Who substitute darkness for light and light for darkness; Who substitute bitter for sweet and sweet for bitter! Woe to those who are wise in their own eyes And clever in their own sight!"

Are You Ready for Truth?

While some of you have already figured out where we're headed, others may not be ready for the punch line. Ready or not, we have a responsibility and a commission that we will fulfill (Isaiah 58:1; 59:1-3). Pointing out our sins is part of that mission. And what is sin? I John 3:4 says sin is lawlessness, or "the transgression of the law" (KJV).

Jesus puts it this way: "He who has My commandments and keeps them is the one who loves Me; and He who loves Me will be loved by My Father, and I will love him and will disclose Myself to Him" (John 14:21). Other translations render "disclose" as "manifest Myself to him, show him who I am, show him what I'm like, reveal Myself to him."

Do you want that intimacy with Jesus? You may have it to a certain degree now. Would you not, however, like to know Jesus more? As I write, the majority of sincere Christians have not accepted this intimacy. Why not start a trend?

The minority view in history has often been the true view. Winston Churchill's view at the onset of World War II was the minority view. Had we not listened to his opinion, we may not have been around to hear any more opinions. Today the "Flat Earth Society" is the minority view. Once upon a time it was the prevailing lie that passed for truth. Those who decry the prevailing lies of our society and our religion are never popular. So what's new? It's the same old story.

What may be new to you is the truth you are about to hear. Yet it is not new. It has only been covered by Satan's veil. The cloak of lawlessness covers our world and even our Bible commentaries. It covers the eyes and the fancy writings of eminent theologians.

The mystery of lawlessness is so strongly at work already that many who read the truth you are about to read have been pre-conditioned to treat it with skepticism or disdain. If you choose to do so, you may miss out on an amazing blessing.

The time that Jesus appointed for corporate worship and fellowship is today called evil – even though God calls it good (Neh. 9:13-14). The time that Satan ordained for corporate worship is called good. Those who keep the appointed times of Jesus are not usually well seen by those adopting the prevailing view.

The Shakeup before the Fill-up

God is about to shake up the church. It must be shaken up so it can be turned right side up. This book is a small part of that shaking, "so that those things which cannot be shaken may remain" (Heb. 12:27). "See to it that you do not refuse Him who is speaking..." (12:25). It was indeed not any man but Jesus Himself, the Word, who thundered out ***all*** of the Ten Commandments. Will you hear His voice?

You can choose to cling to the excuses offered by pastors and commentaries for not obeying the simple truth of God. Or you can obey the command to Israel (Deut. 6:4), which signifies the believers. "Hear, O Israel!" The Hebrew word for "hear" has multiple meanings. It commands us to listen and obey.

Jesus' words to the believers back then apply to us today: "Oh that they had such a heart in them, that they would [revere] Me and keep ***all*** My commandments always, that it may be well with them and with their sons forever!" (Deut. 5:29).

Many have been covered by the part of the deceptive veil that says, "That's Old Testament!" If that is your case, listen to the New: "For whoever keeps the whole law and yet stumbles in one point, he has become guilty of all. For He [that was Jesus!] who said, 'Do not commit adultery,' also said, 'Do not commit murder..." (James 2:10).

Which commandment of the Big Ten has been cleverly twisted to the point of omission? It is the same commandment that, if obeyed, opens the door to intimacy, love and power. It is the commandment that Satan has stolen from the church.

Do you want the fullness of the abundant life Jesus promised? Or do you want the status quo of a church sapped in strength and power by the thief that "comes only to steal and kill and destroy..." (John 10:10). Jesus said He was the Door of the sheep (10: 9). You cannot graze in the greenest pastures unless you come through the Door pictured as the true Shepherd in Psalm 23.

If you want the cup that overflows, you must go where the anointing is. You must go through the Door. Jesus blessed and made holy a certain day of the week. None of the others are called holy. That special day of fellowship and intimacy is called the Sabbath. There is only one. That day could not be called holy unless Jesus had poured part of Himself into that period of time.

Yes, it's about time -- it's about time we began to reap the magnificent blessings of the day of rest in Jesus. It's time. So, ready or not, here is the simple truth about the holy Sabbath of which Jesus is Divine Master (Mark 2:27-28).

Get Ready to Be Blessed!

What a blessing to discover a truth hidden for centuries! The Sabbath day is one of the greatest blessings ever given to man. Yet most Christians miss out on it because they don't read the Bible from the beginning. For some, the truth has to be written in red. Some Bibles put the words Jesus spoke when He was on the earth 2000 years ago in red letters. Others say that even Jesus' words were "Old Covenant" and that we must listen to the writers of the epistles to know the truth.

We hope you prefer to believe Jesus. Satan did not contradict him, as many believers have, when He said to the devil, quoting the "Old Testament," " 'Man shall not live by bread alone, but on every word that proceeds out of the mouth of God'" (Mat. 4:4). The only word available at the time Jesus spoke these words was the "Old Testament." Taking the whole Bible into consideration (Acts 24:14) is a key to unlocking the code.

Finally we've come to the code breaker -- the punch line. And some will surely feel the punch. The Word of God is sharp and it will pierce (Heb. 4:12). Our Father disciplines us for our good, "so that we may share His holiness" (Heb. 12:10). What better way to share His holiness than to meet with Him on the day He made holy. If you accept this course correction, you will taste and see that the real Jesus is good, and His day is full of blessings for His bride.

What a Day!

What a day God has given us! What a blessing! The Sabbath is the…

- Day of Revelation -- Intimacy with Jesus on this day unfolds all mysteries, which are sealed up in Jesus, who unfolds Himself into and in this day. The "here a little, there a little" puzzle is only solved by obedience to the Sabbath. The Sabbath is the key that unravels all Bible mysteries. Only obedience to the Sabbath commandment reveals the real Jesus in all His fullness.
- Day of Wisdom -- All the treasures of wisdom and knowledge and all mysteries are hidden in Jesus. You cannot, however, have access to all of this without being intimate with Jesus on His day.
- Day of Redemption – It's the day for remembering our freedom from the slavery of Egypt or sin, the day to celebrate our redemption in the cross of Jesus. It is the day He was redeemed from death, the day of His resurrection.
- Day of Freedom – We are set free from sin, free from the concerns of the week, free to relax and rest in Jesus.
- Day of Rescue --We were drowning in sin and its results and Jesus rescued us, set us free. This is a day to celebrate being rescued from the hands of Satan, who wanted to destroy us. Maybe that's why the church isn't free today – because they haven't kept the day that celebrates that freedom from Satan.
- Day of Rest – We rest from our weekly routine of work, resting in the righteousness of Jesus. It is "laid back" day. Jesus laid back and relished His creation when He rested on that first Sabbath.
- Day of Celebration – We celebrate the end of Satan's rule on earth and the establishment of the Kingdom of God on earth.
- Day of Peace – We rejoice as we look forward to the time of peace in the coming seventh millennial day. In the here and now, we leave behind a whirlwind of activities to enjoy the *shalom* of God.
- Day of Joy – The fellowship we enjoy with God and our brethren bring a joy the world cannot know. The songs of joy we sing together express and enhance that joy.
- Day of Release -- Fast food chains have apple and cherry turnovers. The Sabbath is the day for a different kind of turnover. It's the turnover to the great Caretaker of all our cares, burdens, and oppressions from Satan. And since it's a day of celebration, you can have your apple turnover too!
- Day of Revival, Renewal, Refreshing ,"Re-creation" and Life -- Jesus *is* life. Since He pours Himself into this day, we receive an impartation of His life. He also refreshes us as He was refreshed Himself when He ceased from His labor on the first Sabbath (Ex. 31:17). We are refreshed and we prophesy "times of refreshing" to come in the millennial Sabbath (Acts 3:19-21). Sometimes the Sabbath is like spiritual CPR. As Jesus renewed, completed, and perfected the *tohu* and *bohu* of

chaos into which Satan's rebellion had plunged the earth by "re-creating" it and relishing His creation on the Sabbath, so Jesus celebrates the new creation He is working in each of us on the Sabbath day. We celebrate a time when the earth will be renewed as we are renewed on the Sabbath. It is the day for corporate teaching and anointing to "re-create" us, forming in us God's character.

- Day of Sanctification -- God clearly sets the Sabbath apart to set those who keep it apart as holy unto Him. One of His very names is a part of a powerful Sabbath verse that shows the purpose of this day: "...that you may know that I am the [Eternal] who sanctifies you [Yehovah Makkadesh]" (Ex. 31:13). This day identifies the holy God is the one and only Creator and identifies and sets apart as holy His people and trains them in holiness.
- Day of Victory – This day celebrates the defeat of the devil! That's why he hates it so much.
- Day of Terror (for the devil!) -- Not keeping the Sabbath has opened the door for terror and adversity to strike the nation – and the church. Keeping the Sabbath will close the door on unnecessary adversity and will terrorize the terrorizer, Satan. That's one of the meanings of a Hebrew word that relates God's appointed times of feasting.
- Day of Eternity – This day looks forward to the time when time will not exist. It pictures the fulfillment of God's plan of love when we enter into His eternal joy.
- Day of Hope – When things in the world look bleak, this day points to the sure hope of a better day to come.
- Day of Kingly and Priestly Training – We are given special instructions on this day to teach us to be kings and priests in our sphere of influence today and in a much larger way in the Kingdom of God on earth.
- Day of Remembrance – The only commandment God tells us to remember is the one that reminds us that God is Creator. He remade the earth in six days and rested on the seventh day. It is a memorial day to commemorate the most important Being in the universe. We specifically remember Jesus as Creator and Deliverer/ Redeemer.
- The Day of Intimacy – This day is the gateway to intimacy with God the Father, Jesus, and the Holy Spirit. In spirit we sit on our Father's knee. The Bride of Jesus has her weekly date with the Bridegroom. And because of the powerful presence of the Holy Spirit, the Sabbath is also the...
- Day of the Anointing – The Holy Spirit anoints us with fresh oil on this day. His presence can be sensed, felt, and seen more than on any other day of the week. Many healing ministries, without realizing why, hold their healing meetings on the Sabbath. They get greater results on that day because the Sabbath is the...
- Day of Healing – Jesus did great and numerous healings on the Sabbath. He saw the appropriateness of the healing of the woman with the issue of blood on the Sabbath. Why, he asked those around him, should she not be set free from Satan's oppression on this day of freedom from sin and sickness?

- Day of Provision – The manna miracle reveals the Sabbath as the day of provision.
- Day of Fellowship – This is the appointed time that we are commanded to meet with Jesus and with our brothers and sisters in Jesus. And what a joy it is to obey that command!
- Day of Rapture – We are "raptured" up into His presence as we praise Him on the Sabbath day. The Sabbath also pictures and prepares us for that intimate communion we will have with Jesus when He brings us up to enjoy His presence. We will then descend to earth to rule with Him and revel in intimacy with Him forever.
- Day of Glory – God's glory is all that He is. It is the most infinite word in the Bible. He releases His glory on that day. We stay stuck at a certain level unless we keep the Sabbath. It pictures the government of God, which is to be ever increasing (Isa. 9:7) throughout eternity. So the Sabbath pictures eternity – going from glory to never-ending glory. Putting Himself in this day meant Jesus was pouring His glory into it -- a glory that is infinite. That's why the angels cry Holy, Holy, Holy every few seconds. Moreover, He has given *us* His glory. It is in us and will also rise in greater strength in us and will be revealed around us. The fullness of God's end time glory will be revealed only on those who keep the Sabbath.
- Day of Belonging -- The Sabbath sets us apart as belonging to God (Ex. 31:13). Assembling together on His day gives us each week freedom from the feeling of homelessness that attacks so many today and that wonderful feeling of belonging (II Cor. 6:16-18).
- Dominion Day (Kingdom Day) -- One of the most important aspects of the Sabbath is the dominion power it gives us. It is the day that prophesies Jesus' reign on the earth. It also assures our dominion over the earth as ambassadors of God's Kingdom in this world today (Isa. 58:13-14).
- Day of Excellence -- The excellencies of Jesus are released in the Sabbath. When we choose the higher road of obedience by keeping this test commandment, God says we will ride on the heights of the earth, leading the way in excellence. Keeping only nine of ten laws of love is not excellence.
- Day of Love – Love poured Himself into this day. When we meet with Him on his day, we receive His love and grow in love. It is the day to soak in God's love and celebrate it, to rejoice that He has set us apart as special to Him, to rejoice that the Father sent Jesus to die for us and save us. On this day we individually and corporately express our love to God in prayer and song. This day also prophesies the time when the whole world will experience God's love and we will all bask in His love forever.

Sabbath *Selah's*
Christians Playing "Who Am I?"

Many Christians can't see who they really are in Jesus. They have no identity. Too many churchgoers feel invisible and useless because they can't see themselves as special to God.

The [Eternal] spoke to Moses, saying, "But as for you, speak to the sons of Israel [the believers], saying, 'You shall surely observe My sabbaths;' for this is a sign between Me and you throughout your generations, that you may know that I am the Eternal who sanctifies you [sets you apart as holy] (Ex. 31:12-13).

The two truths Christians have the hardest time understanding are: they are the righteousness of God (Heb. 10:2; II Cor. 5:21), and they are set apart as special to God (Mal. 3:17). The Sabbath teaches and affirms both of these truths. It ends the "who am I" game believers play. When they sit on Abba Father's knee in the Holy of Holies on His day of love, they will know to whom they belong. As they keep the day that celebrates the Kingdom or Family of God (Love), they will know they are loved. They will know they belong to the Family of Love. Selah.

CHAPTER FOUR

The Bountiful Blessing Satan Stole from the Bride

When you begin to obey one of God's commandments -- His test commandment -- the blessings He offers will overtake you. Satan has stolen from the Bride of Jesus one of the greatest blessings He gave her. He has convinced her that this blessing is not a blessing but a curse. He has gotten her to call it "bondage" and "Jewish" and "evil" and "cultish."

Enough of what Satan says. What does God say about the Sabbath rest most church people have never known? Where in His Word does God reveal the truth that, if obeyed, would break the seemingly "uncrackable" Bible code -- the code that has kept the church from the breakthrough knowledge that would finally set it free.

Are you ready for the answer?

The Bible Code is Broken! Blessings Can Now Come

The time has come to give the answer. If it is heeded, we believe God will pour out His blessings on you and your family.

In Genesis 2:1-2, God blessed the seventh day (Friday night sunset to Saturday night sunset – Gen. 1:5, Lev. 23:32) and made it holy. He made it for the first man Adam and for all mankind as a blessing (Mark 2:27-28).

We shall describe briefly some of the blessings you may have missed.

The Sabbath is the day of Love (I John 4:8). Love poured *Himself* into the seventh day, making it holy by virtue of His presence. Moses was on holy ground for a simple reason: God was present (Ex. 3:5).

The Sabbath is the New Covenant day of celebration. It's the celebration of God's love for us – of our redemption by the blood of Jesus. It's the day of joy and rejoicing over our freedom in Jesus. One of the reasons God gave to His people for keeping it was to remember that He had freed them from the bondage of Egypt or sin by the blood of the Passover Lamb (Deut. 5:15).

How could Jesus have done away with one of the Ten Commandments (Ex. 20:8) – a commandment that celebrates the very core of the gospel – Jesus' blood shed to redeem us from all sin, sickness, and poverty?

Jesus, who is Love and Life, poured Himself into this day. He infuses His life into us on this day every week. It is the day of refreshing and revival. We shall see that the seventh day of a thousand years will bring times of refreshing when Jesus comes to refresh the whole world with His rule of peace (Acts 3:19-21).

Do you feel tired and run down? It may not be an iron-rich elixir that you need. You need a weekly day of rest. Science has proved it. But not just any day will do. Jesus wants you to rest in Him on the day He invites you to feast at His table and rest in His arms. He didn't put His very presence into any day but the Sabbath. If you need a little spiritual CPR, Doctor Jesus offers to revive you on His day to give you strength for another week.

Isaiah, in a prophecy for our day (58:13-14), says that if you keep your feet off God's holy Sabbath, you will find your joy in Jesus (NIV). That's a promise! It's the day in which Jesus wants us to express our praise and our joy to Him. What's more, because of the powerful anointing of that day and the collective praise and worship, the Holy Spirit releases new joy to us. Jesus' joy is our strength, a phrase written in the context of an annual Sabbath day (Neh. 8:10).

Because of the presence of Jesus, a special Sabbath anointing blesses and empowers believers on that day. Why do you think some of the major healing ministries have their greatest manifestations of healing on Friday night and Saturday? It's no coincidence.

What freedom! A day where you need not be in any rush – a day of rest and relaxation. A day of family unity – oneness and harmony with the family of God and your own family. Bondage? No. The Sabbath is the opposite -- release from bondage.

I speak from forty years of personal experience: this day is not a burden!

You can keep *any* commandment like a Pharisee, but Jesus has set us free from legalism. What a joy to keep the Sabbath in the grace and freedom of the New Covenant! The Comforter leads us away from the strict straightjacket. He eases us into our comfy recliner to truly enjoy His day of comfort and peace.

Try it! You'll like it! You'll taste and see that God is good – and ***all*** His commandments are good for us (I John 5:3; Deut. 5:29). You will see what the enemy – the killjoy – has stolen from you and from most of the body of Jesus Christ. Those ten laws are like a wall around us – ten boundaries that protect us from the enemy. Why do you think Satan has caused a breach in that holy barrier?

You can begin to repair the breach in that wall and keep the enemy of your soul out. You will destroy his blinders and bask in the sunny smile of the light and warmth of God's love. It is His day to shower His love on you, His precious loved one -- His day of love par excellence.

It is indeed the day of excellence – the day that enables us to attain to God's glory and excellence.

It is the day Jesus was raised in glory and took off our coat of sin and put upon us His coat of righteousness. We bathe in His love and rest in His righteousness.

All the major redemptive themes are tied together in the Sabbath day. You can claim sevenfold return from what the thief has stolen from you. Time is short, but Jesus is the Redeemer.

You Call This a Burden?

One Friday evening as the Sabbath began I enjoyed a lovely Sabbath stroll in a beautiful Edmonton ravine, communing with God, even singing some enjoyable songs of praise beside a peaceful stream. I was headed to buy myself some gourmet ice cream as a Sabbath celebration, when I encountered a couple of religious acquaintances.

We somehow got on the subject of the Sabbath, and they began to lambaste me. "You're under the curse of the law!" I thought, "If this is a curse, then 'more, Jesus'– give me more, Jesus!'" A curse?

Satan has masterfully deceived the whole Christian world. He has convinced Christians that the seventh-day Sabbath is a Jewish burden. Absurd! Jews void of the Holy Spirit may keep it as a burden – full of silly legalism. But that's not the way Jesus kept it.

That's not the way even the few who had the Holy Spirit under the Old Covenant kept it. For David, for instance, the holy days were days of joy and thanksgiving (Ps. 42:4). He was a man after God's own heart – a balanced man who knew how to enjoy the Sabbath day.

The Pharisees had a law that you couldn't carry anything bigger than a dried fig on the Sabbath! David didn't worry about figs. He knew how to rejoice! And so did Jesus.

Jesus had the great joy of healing people on the Sabbath. Nothing in the Old Testament forbade healing on the Sabbath, only Pharisaical laws, not God's laws.

Those laws are love (Rom 13:10). Jesus said He would know His people by their love for one another (John 13:34). The virgin Bride of Jesus, represented in one parable by ten virgins, five foolish ones and five wise ones, will be flowing in that love. Why? Because they are like branches connected to the Vine. They connect with Love on His day. They fellowship with their siblings in Jesus on His day of love.

The Bride at Her Best is a Bride at Rest!

Don't be a virgin who lacks oil. Allow Jesus to pour His precious and abundant Sabbath oil of anointing on you and your family. Be blessed by keeping the weekly appointment Jesus has given you – on ***His*** day. Bask in the Sabbath freedom and joy. Above all, enter the gateway to true intimacy with the Divine Master of the Sabbath Day. Bride of Jesus, come into the secret place of the Bridegroom. Reap the blessing of His day of love.

Don't let Satan keep you away from this blessing any longer. But please ... don't feel condemned for not having kept it. God understands. Satan is the one who has kept you from this blessing. On the other hand, you don't need to wait another week to start receiving the blessing of God's true Sabbath rest.

Satan wants you to be like him and his demons – restless. He surely doesn't want you to know what this day portends for him. The devil knows – better than most Christians – that the day most call "Jewish" is the day symbolizing his defeat – the day he will be mincemeat under the feet of the saints. It is the day that prefigures the thousand-year day when he will be bound – unable to deceive anyone. The Bride will be rejoicing with the Bridegroom, resting from the onslaught of a now-defeated enemy.

Sincere Deception

Lest some be offended by the forthright tone of this book, we need to make something clear from the start. Ignorance and deception do not mean that sin is not involved. The Bible makes it clear, however, that we are not held accountable for a sin until we know it is wrong (James 4:17). Jesus told the religious leaders of his day that they were on dangerous ground because they knew He was teaching the truth (John 9:41).

Some of the religious leaders today know which day God made holy. They know they would lose their finances and their flock if they obeyed God. Most, however, have been sincerely deceived. That is the case for the vast majority of their flocks.

God is probably more sad than mad that the Christian church has trampled on His day. He is not pleased with theologians and pastors who have hoodwinked His precious sheep. His real anger is aimed at Satan and the demons for pulling the wool over the eyes of His sheep.

Many powerful Christians have gone to their reward without knowing they were worshipping God on the wrong day. Their pristine character is admittedly more important than a day. That day is nonetheless quite important to God. It is His day. It is holy and precious to Him. It should be holy to us. He made it for all mankind -- as a weekly proof of His love.

We're not here to heap condemnation on anyone for being ignorant of the Sabbath. God doesn't condemn you. His heart is grieved, however, that the church has missed out on one of His greatest blessings (Ezek. 18:31; 20:11-26; 22:8,26; 33:11).

You'd Be Surprised How Many Know About This Day

You would be surprised how many preachers know about the Sabbath. They know it is the day the Bible says is holy to God. They simply don't have the courage to buck the established tradition. And admittedly, it does take a lot of courage. After all, their livelihood is at stake – and their reputation.

At the 2004 National Religious Broadcasters' Convention in Charlotte, N.C., one of the rare Sabbath-keeping TV preachers took me aside at his display booth. He told me that a number of prominent church leaders had come to him in private. They admitted they knew they were supposed to keep and preach the Sabbath but said their parishioners would never go along with the change.

Yet more and more Christians are getting in touch with their Jewish roots. More Christians keep the Feast of Tabernacles in Jerusalem today than Jews!

Many believers have had their minds opened to the Sabbath. They hear what their pastors preach, but they also read the Bible. The two don't match. Something's fishy. The slippery seduction of Sunday justification doesn't reel in these faithful fish. They have begun to realize they've swallowed betrayal's bait, hook, "lie," and sinker. They need a little encouragement to be set free.

If you have taken the Sunday bait and are comfortable in the Sunday boat, you may need more than encouragement. You need proof. You will find it in this book and in *the* Book. You can relish one of God's greatest gifts of love.

Religionists have enveloped the Sabbath in an ugly, "Judaizing" package with a distasteful ribbon of legalism tied around it. They have marked it as a gift you don't want -- the kind you would take back to the store unless your Dad gave it to you.

Well, your Father *did* give it to you. Are you going to refuse a special gift of love from your Heavenly Father without even opening it – without examining it? It's the pastors and theologians who have given it a bad "wrap." God wants you to unwrap His gift. Will you refuse His love?

It's your choice. We hope you will leave this book open and open God's Book of Love to prove if what we say is true (Acts 17:11; I Thes. 5:21). It's up to you.

Blessed Rest of Intimacy With God

The Sabbath is the day when Father God has the joy of "sitting His children on his knee" and having intimate fellowship with them. We enjoy and worship Him and He enjoys us.

Where two or three Christians are gathered any day, Jesus is among them. He is present in a special way, however, on the Sabbath since it is the day He made holy. It is His day. It has always been that way.

It began with Adam. One Jewish tradition says that Adam and Eve walked with God for 40 years before God allowed Satan to test them. The Sabbath was that holy time of special fellowship and intimacy with God. How many a wonderful Sabbath they must have shared with their Creator!

We can, of course, fellowship with God any day of the week – and we do. But the Sabbath is special. It is not called holy for nothing, since God doesn't waste His words. He means it.

The Sabbath is holy for the same reason we are holy – for the same reason the ground near the burning bush on Sinai was holy. The presence of God was in it. The other ground was not holy. Other people that are not Christians are not called holy. They do not have God – the ***Holy*** Spirit – in them.

God made man in His image, pouring a part of His own breath of life in him (Gen. 1:26-27; 2:7), and He has chosen some in this age to receive the seed of spiritual life in Jesus in the form of the Holy Spirit. These gifts of divine life are not complete, however, without the Sabbath. Jesus poured Himself into the Sabbath when He made it holy. Whereas He gave only part of Himself to mankind and gave Himself to the believers to dwell inside the holy ones, it is only in the Sabbath where Jesus meets with His saints that they can attain to the fullness of His likeness and holiness.

God put a strong emphasis on distinguishing what was holy from what was not (Lev. 10:10). He wants us to learn to revere and hallow that which is holy so we can be holy as He is.

Satan Hates This Day of Blessing

Satan hates God's holy day, for good reason. He wants Christians to shrug their apathetic shoulders and say. "What's the big deal? What's the difference? Saturday? Sunday?" Some say: "Any ole day'll do." Others swear by Sunday and say keeping a Saturday Sabbath is Jewish bondage.

Satan hates the Sabbath because it represents the summum bonum, the summit, the apex of God's intimate fellowship with man. That is a fellowship he never had.

One of the main reasons he rebelled is that he was jealous of man. Angels were not sons. They were servants. They were not the apple of God's eye – His pride and joy – as we are. If you are a parent, you know no one can ever have the special place in your heart as your own flesh and blood – your sons and daughters. The maid who may help you with some of your housework just doesn't have the same fellowship with you. Your family pet doesn't have that special intimacy with you.

Lucifer had a high position, but he wasn't a son. He saw a man and woman who had a special intimacy with God that he never had. The Sabbath was the epitome of that intimacy. Satan realizes that the Sabbath is a special ***blessing*** made for mankind. It is a weekly blessing that gives man sweet communion with his Creator – a communion Satan feels he should have enjoyed.

But there's more. Not only is the Sabbath a physical blessing for man; it is also a powerful spiritual blessing. The Sabbath gives the intimacy with God that will lead man to eventually be counted worthy to share eternal intimacy with Him. Satan hates that idea. He wants to keep as many as possible from being eternally in God's Family.

What's more, Satan knows how important the Sabbath is to God. God reserves special blessings for those who hallow that which is precious and holy to Him. It is one of the ways we humans have to touch the heart of our loving God. When we keep His day holy, He can't resist blessing us. And one of the greatest blessings is the blessing of His manifest presence in a special way that justifies the word He uses regarding that day – ***holy.***

Entering God's Rest Brings a Greater Blessing

We are not about to say that our Spirit-filled brothers and sisters who keep Sunday are not blessed. We have seen some powerful anointings on Sunday and other weekdays as well. The Holy Spirit and Jesus are definitely present in those meetings. But what anointing would these people experience if they understood God's holy day and kept it?

Not keeping the Sabbath, even due to being sincerely deceived, deprives us of a colossal ***blessing*** of God. That day is the day our Father in heaven has a special fellowship with His children. His presence is especially in that day. God doesn't say anything in vain. *Holy* is not just some "nicey-nice," syrupy, spiritual word. *Holy* means the presence of the Holy God is in that day like it is in ***no other.***

We yearn for the day when powerful, Spirit-filled men and women of God whom we respect are going to understand, where they were sincerely deceived before, the awesome truth about the Sabbath. The powerful anointing we see on them is going to increase dramatically.

This truth about the Sabbath – found abundantly in the "Old Testament" – is confirmed in the New. It is there – in the gospels, in the epistles' teaching about the importance of obeying God's law, and especially in Hebrews. It is there and has always been there. But Satan has not wanted us to see it, and God has let him succeed – until now. Satan knows the Sabbath is a gateway – a door to intimacy with Jesus and great blessing.

A Prayer to Open the Door of Blessing

To say that this is a controversial subject is an understatement. Satan brings in opposition to deprive the church of the Sabbath blessing. This will be one of the major tests of the body of Christ in this time of the end. Many will refuse this blessing until in a time of persecution they will be forced to make a choice.

Most of us Christians have kept Sunday for as long as we can remember. Our parents did. Our grandparents did. Our pastor preaches it. Most of us don't know any Christians who keep another day as their day of worship. In fact, 99.9% of the Christian world keeps it. Bible commentators and theologians believe it. Anybody who is anybody in the Christian world teaches it. Everybody couldn't be wrong, could they?

Once upon a time a man built a big boat. Except for him and only seven other family members, the rest of the whole world was headed to a watery grave. They were all evil. The whole world was wrong.

The body of Christ has been wrong before. It took the church years before realizing that God fully accepted Gentiles and that they did not have to be circumcised to be in the church.

Aside from a few needed revelations, the early church started out a pristine mountain spring. Alas, over the centuries the pure little stream of living waters became in all too many cases a large polluted river. Those who accepted doctrines of men persecuted, even murdered, those who held to biblical teachings. At one point bibles were confiscated, and only clergy were allowed to read God's Word.

Even with the recent propagation of the Bible, true believers have unwittingly accepted traditions they have never really seriously and prayerfully examined in the light of God's Word.

So before we begin, we respectfully request that you pray first. Ask the Holy Spirit to guide you into all truth. Ask for a humble attitude. Be willing to admit you may be wrong. Ask for help to be totally honest with the Word of God. Allow the Holy Spirit and His ink-stained sword to be your guides. Be willing to put God's Word ahead of tradition. Ask for the strength to obey what you find to be the truth. Ask Jesus, "Which day is *Your* day? And does it really matter to You?"

We invite you to receive the gift of blessed rest, the present of Jesus' presence in a special way. Receive Abba Father Agape's gift of love to you.

An Open Invitation to Receive God's Gift of Love

The Sabbath is about love -- and passion -- more passion than a romance novel. It's about the passion Jesus has for His bride. It's about His love for her and her love for Him. It's about intimacy -- the best date with the best Date in the world – Jesus.

It's a weekly rendezvous of love -- a secret hideaway from the terrible turbulence of our times. It's a time to relax, to reflect. A time to rejoice in Jesus. A time to rejoice as a family. A time when you can take your time. No rush. No fuss. No stress. No routine work!

Since many diseases are stress-related, what a blessing the Sabbath is – an aid to spiritual health and physical well-being!

A popular country song's lyrics portray our stressed society and its anxiety addiction: "I'm in a hurry to get things done… rushin', rushin' till life's no fun; all I really gotta do is live and die, but I'm in a hurry and don't know why…" That's the refrain of the harried, hurried people – even Christians! – in the modern maze called civilization. It's hard to be civil in such a mad rush.

To quote author Phil Callaway: "Even if you win the rat race, you're still a rat!"

Yes. A dirty rat – soiled by the world and its ways. The world is indeed too much with us – and the things we collect in our ratty race can't go with us when we die.

We're chasing "stuff" – not relationships.

Alas, the most important relationship of all slides to the side as we speed down the highway of life. We're leaving our Father Love in the dust. We're missing the peace, joy, intimacy, revelation, love, and power Jesus offers us.

Our God of love offers all that to you! Jesus offered it to Adam and Eve 6000 years ago when this world was a paradise. Today it is not paradise. We need this gift of love more than ever before.

It's not too late. But it's time! Love is patient. Love is kind. And Love is opening His arms of love to receive and bless you on His day of celebration.

Resting in God's Day of Love Casts Out Fear

We are living in the very last days. Jesus must purify His bride. Every wrinkle must be removed. Every sin. Yes, even the sin we have not recognized. Even the sin we have committed sincerely -- or because of fear. Remember, there is no fear in love.

Fear has gripped even Christians since the beginning of the days of sorrow on September 11, 2001. God wants to shelter us from fear in His love, but that umbrella of love cannot open fully over a bride who is not keeping the appointed times Jesus commanded – His feasts of love.

Fear not! Bride of Jesus, hear the words of God's Book of Love. Open your heart to what His Word says about His day.

"Read All About It!" -- God's "Press Release" on the Sabbath

Evil reports about the Sabbath may have influenced you. If you want to hear what God's Word says, read on. We don't have all the answers, but we want to bless you by sharing the truths God has given us. You will discover that the Sabbath is God's day of love, redemption, and freedom. It celebrates His love in blessing us with the beautiful creation that surrounds us. It celebrates His love in sending Jesus to shed His blood to set us free from sin and all the bondages of Satan, including the bondage of blindness to His Word -- the coded book whose secrets have remained locked.

This day is His gift of Himself. It's His appointed time to meet with us. It is Jesus' weekly "date" with His bride – His intimate time to pour out His love to her. It's that holy period when our Father of love invites us to share a special time of closeness with Him. He invites us -- His sons and daughters – to bask in the warmth of His love, sitting on His knee and looking adoringly into His eyes of love.

It's also His day to give us, His people, the opportunity to express our love to Him in corporate praise and worship. As we gather to express our appreciation to Him, we also encourage one another in love and good works.

Unfortunately, the Sabbath has gotten a lot of bad press. It is nevertheless the day of liberation for those enslaved in the chain gang of the fast lane. The Sabbath is the chain breaker and the Bible code breaker.

Sabbath *Selah's*
Sabbath versus Sunday

Six days shall you labor and do all your work… (Ex. 20:9).

Part of the fourth commandment is that Sunday is to be a normal workday. Setting Sunday aside as a day of rest is a direct violation of God's command. No other day of the week except the seventh, called the Sabbath, is ever called by name in the Bible. That name has roots in some one hundred languages as the name for Saturday, as in the Spanish word for Saturday, sabado, *and the Italian,* sabbato, *which is also the English transliteration of the modern Greek word for Saturday*, sabbaton *in the Greek New Testament. In one of Ghana's languages, the literal translation of the day for Sunday is "white man changed this day"!* [1]*Nowhere in the Bible is Sunday called the Sabbath or the Christian Sabbath. The Sunday tradition is pure invention, but there's nothing pure about it. The Catholic Church readily admits that Saturday is the Sabbath and that it is only by church, not Bible, authority that Sunday has replaced it in both Catholic and Protestant churches. Subtle twists of the truth are nothing but lies. Selah.*

1 Steve Wohlberg, White Horse Media, "Can We Know Which Day is the Christian Sabbath? http://www.whitehorsemedia.com/articles/details.cfm?art=86

CHAPTER FIVE

Break the Code - Break the Chains

Our church and ministry emphasize freedom and identity in Jesus. The Sabbath day offers both. In fact, it is impossible to fully know the real Jesus and your identity in Him without resting in Him on that day.

Remember also what God says about freedom. He says that only the truth can set or make you free (John 8:32). The Sabbath covenant is a most important nugget of truth in our quest for freedom.

When you break the code, you break the chains.

We are a church called to fast for the breaking of yokes over God's people (Isa. 58:6). We are also called to repair the breach, raising up the age-old foundations and restoring the way in which Christians were designed to walk (Isa. 58:12). The arbitrary and clever substitution of Sunday for the real Sabbath is part of the breach in the Ten Commandments and also part of the breach between God and man. The restoration of the Sabbath is clearly an important pathway to freedom (Isa. 58:13-14), so it is no coincidence that God has called and anointed us to write this book.

Break the code -- break the chains. Why is that statement true?

Have God's people not been destroyed, imprisoned for lack of *knowledge*? Is it not true that freeing knowledge is only available in Jesus (Col. 2:3)? How can we expect to receive that knowledge and understanding if we don't obey (Ps. 111:10)? How can we be sure to know the full truth that sets us free if we don't meet with Jesus on the day He commands us to meet with Him?

How can the Holy Spirit lead us into all truth (John 16:13) if we don't show up when the anointing is most powerful? The apostle of love who kept the Sabbath, the day of love, said it well: "But you have been anointed by [you hold a sacred appointment from, you have been given an unction from] the Holy One, and you all know [the Truth] *or you know all things*" (I John 2:20, AMP.)

A powerful anointing for revelation permeates the Sabbath day.

The words for rest in Matthew 11:28-29 are the Greek words used for Sabbath rest in the Greek version of the Hebrew Scriptures at the time, the Septuagint. Jesus beckons His people to come to Him at the end of a weary week and rest in Him. He doesn't offer that special rest on Sunday, or even on a mid-week Bible study.

"Take My yoke upon you," He says. The Sabbath, which pictures the yoke of Kingdom rule that Jesus put upon His shoulders (Isa. 9:6), is not a heavy yoke at all (I John 5:3).

What else does Jesus say? He says: "... *learn* from Me." Jesus knew when the anointing for teaching was strongest: "...as was His custom, He entered the synagogue on the Sabbath, and stood up to read" the passage that spoke of Him being anointed "to proclaim release to the captives" (Luke 4:16-18).

Our cover shows two locks over the coded Bible, one representing the First (wrongly called "Old") Testament and the other representing the Second. It was on the Sabbath day that Jesus "unlocked" the coded understanding of Isaiah 61:1-2.

It's Code Breaking Time

Daniel did not understand the book he wrote. God told him, "But as for you, Daniel, conceal these words and *seal up the book* until the end of time; many will go back and forth, and *knowledge* will increase...those who have insight will understand" (Daniel 12:4,10). God was thus prophesying between the lines that the Sabbath would be restored to the church in the end time. Only the Sabbath breaks the Bible code.

God also prophesies that only those who keep the Sabbath will decipher the code and solve the puzzle. In a puzzle you have pieces all over the place, "a little here, a little there," as the Bible describes itself (Isa. 28:10). The Sabbath unravels all Bible mysteries.

The French use the English word *puzzle* for that kind of game whereas the more common term in Quebec is *casse-tete*. The latter literally refers to breaking your head (or brain) over the dilemma of an unsolved puzzle. That's exactly what the Christian world is doing today. They are beating their heads against a brick wall, as it were, because they don't understand the Word that would set them free.

The time has come to stop breaking our heads by finally breaking the code.

But who will heed? Or as Isaiah puts it, "To whom would He teach knowledge, And to whom would He interpret [or unlock] the message [of the Bible]? Those just weaned from milk?" Both baby Christians and mature ones are soon going to be faced with a choice: will you obey God's Sabbath commandment and see the secret code of His Word unlocked to your understanding, or will you be lost in a maze, perplexed by the Bible puzzle?

While it is true that one of the meanings of verse 11 is the foreign tongues of invading armies, this is also a prophecy that translations from the original Bible languages would cause those who don't obey to go astray. An example we will see later is the title "Lord," a blatant mistranslation that demeans Jesus and robs the church of the power of His name. As we shall see in the sequel, this title is also associated with the days celebrated by "churchianity" today, days that are not the ones God made holy. They are not the "unlockers"; they are the blockers to understanding.

"Here is rest, give rest to the weary," and "Here is repose," but they would not listen" (Isa. 28:12). Jesus has spoken of His Sabbath rest to His people for 6000 years. He gave the Sabbath to Adam. Later He tested Israel (Exodus 16) to see if they would enter His rest by obeying the Sabbath manna instructions. Manna was symbolic of Jesus, the Word from which we eat spiritually, as well as the Word He gives us on His Sabbath day. Later on Sinai He commanded us to remember His day of rest. He reaffirmed this day of rest in the gospels (Mark 2:27-28; Mat. 11:28-30).

Sad to say, the history of the believers from the time of Israel and from the second century A.D. until now reveals a people who have not listened to God's invitation to enter His Sabbath rest. They have not come to Jesus on His day to learn from the One who possesses all knowledge.

Consequently, what do God's people get today from Sunday pulpits before they rush off to their weekend frenzy of activities? Do we graze tranquilly in pastures green, or is the fare rather lean? The Bible remains, for pastor and laymen, a coded Book, a puzzle with "a little here, a little there," and so they "stumble backward [into scandal and struggles], [and are] broken, snared and taken captive" (Isa. 28:13).

Break the Chains -- of *Believers*

Why do unbelievers laugh at Christians today? They see all the scandals, the sins, the hypocrisy, the adulteries, and the divorces (more *inside* the church than outside) and respond to the obnoxious soul savers: "None of that for me, thanks."

The sad truth is that it is the *believers* who need to be set free! But if the chains are to be broken, the Bible code must be broken. Only the Sabbath can make that happen.

Being established in the righteousness of Jesus (Isa. 54:14) is the only "hail [that] will sweep away the refuge of lies" and cause "the waters [of refreshing of the Holy Spirit to] overflow the secret place [the Sabbath access to the Holy of Holies, to a holy God we meet on His holy day]" (Isa. 28:17).

Perhaps we should heed the next chapter of Isaiah, which warns the ancient city of Ariel to keep God's "feasts on schedule" (Isa. 29:1). Sunday is not on God's schedule. Because we have bowed to deception, God has allowed us, especially the pastors, to be blinded with "a spirit of deep sleep" (Isa. 29:10). "The entire vision will be to you like the words of *a sealed book*, which when they give it to the one who is literate, saying, 'Please read this,' he will say, 'I cannot, for it is sealed'" (Isa. 29:11). The same goes for the illiterate, and God reveals the reason: His people have given him only "lip service…And their reverence for Me consists of tradition learned by rote [in seminaries and Bible schools?]." And God predicts the day will come when those "who err in mind will know the truth, And those who criticize will accept instruction" (Isa. 29:13,24).

Will we be among those who accept instruction? Will we obey the command to keep the seventh day as a day of rest and corporate worship (or even two or three gathered together)? Will we allow God's hammer to unlock His coded Book? Will we allow Jesus to break the seal of His sealed Book?

Will we rest with Jesus in His day, allowing Him to prepare a table of abundant spiritual food before us (Ps. 23:5)? Will we allow Jesus to be our Shepherd, to hear His voice, especially on His day? Will we allow Him to make us lie down in green Sabbath pastures, to lead us beside quiet waters? The word for "quiet" in Psalm 23:2 is the same word used for "rest" in Isaiah 28:12.

Once again God bemoans the believers' refusal to rest in His Sabbath in Isaiah 30:15. But He declares that Sabbath rest is the way to the fullness of salvation. Another piece of the puzzle lies in Paul's words to Timothy, "that from childhood you have known the sacred writings which are able to give you the wisdom that leads to salvation" (II Tim. 3:15).

"In repentance [or returning, *shubah*] and rest you will be saved…" (Isa. 30:15). The word "repentance" is linked etymologically to the same root word that is a part of the word *Shabbat. Shabbat,* when you grasp the breakdown of this word in Hebrew picture language, means *shoov* (return to the *tav*, cross or Sabbath covenant). It is a clarion call for repentance in the last days, a return to the Sabbath covenant with the refreshing and redemption it brings.

The Sabbath points us to the cross of Jesus and the redemption from slavery in the sin pictured by Egypt (Deut. 5:15). It is the day of revelation -- the day of the release of the knowledge and the anointing that breaks yokes. It is the day of freedom.

The church is an *ecclesia* or called-out crowd of "huddled masses yearning to breathe free." Jesus is crying out a much surer call than that inscribed on the Statue of Liberty. He is waiting "on high to have compassion on you" (Isa. 30:18). He is saying, "Come unto Me. Meet with Me and rest in Me on My day. Learn from Me -- and be free!"

Recovering our Stolen I.D.

Identity theft is a modern plague. The biggest identity thief of all is Satan. He has succeeded in depriving many Christians of their identity in Jesus. His main method is the deception that has stolen the Sabbath day from God's people. That's because our identity can only be fully discovered and affirmed in the Sabbath day.

It is only meeting with our Creator, on the day commemorating Him as the only One who made the earth and us, that we can know who we truly are. The reason is simple. In keeping that day we get to know the real Jesus who makes us who we are (Ex.31:13). It is the only sign that identifies the true God who made all things. It is also to be reestablished in these last days as the sign of a true believer. Love is the sign. The test, however, as it was from the beginning, is: "Who will show they truly love Me by keeping all My commandments, especially the one that represents the very first covenant I made with man (Gen. 2:2-3; Isa. 56:1-7; Ex. 19:5; John 14:15)?"

Only by keeping our feet from trampling on holy time will we be able to see ourselves as the kings and priests God calls us to be, riding "on the heights of the earth" (Isa. 58:13-14).

A Gathering of Saints to be Taught by Jesus

God holds great promises in store for those who obey Him fully by keeping His Sabbath: "Who is the man who [loves, respects and obeys Jesus]? He will instruct him in the way he should choose. His soul will abide in prosperity…the *secret* of the [Eternal] is for those who [love and obey] Him, And He will make them know His *covenant*" (Ps. 25:12-14).

Those who humble themselves like little children to stand in awe of God and His commandments, who take the first step of resting on the seventh day, will know the fullness of the Sabbath covenant. It is a covenant of sacrifice. To those who make that commitment of love to Jesus, He says, "Gather My godly ones to

Me" (Ps. 50:5). They will meet with Jesus on His day, and the day will come when He will gather them to Him to escape the times of trouble to come (Ps. 91:14-16).

The Sabbath is the day the real Jesus meets with His people to teach us His Word and His ways of love. It is a day of provision, feasting on physical and spiritual food as we fellowship with Him and each other. The priests in Israel would gather and fellowship with each other around the table of showbread in the tabernacle. Food and fellowship go hand in hand.

Moreover, eating in biblical times was, as it is in reality today, a covenant matter. When you broke bread with someone, you were making a covenant of loyalty to each other. Judas broke that covenant with Jesus (Ps. 41:9). We renew our covenant of loyalty with Jesus and with each other as we listen intently to the messages given on the Sabbath day.

While the meanings of the manna miracle are manifold, one aspect is that of the provision of spiritual food in abundance on the Sabbath. We don't have to go out and gather our spiritual manna. Jesus provides it through the Sabbath anointing through His servants in the five-fold ministry and others called upon to teach that day.

This is good food. No worms. Jesus does not give stale leftovers on His day of instruction. As the priests in the tabernacle removed the showbread of that week and replaced it with fresh bread on the Sabbath day, so Jesus gives us fresh spiritual bread every Sabbath. As the priests gathered around the fresh aroma of that bread, we are refreshed and renewed in fellowship and spiritual sustenance.

Adam was probably in the garden for forty years (the most plausible of the two Jewish traditions), thus sustained with the freshest manna possible every Sabbath, Jesus Himself teaching the first man and woman. Jesus continued the manna miracle for forty years for Israel in the wilderness, supplying their needs daily and a double portion on the Sabbath.

A special anointing for the preaching and hearing of the Word permeates the Sabbath day. Psalm 92, a Sabbath psalm, shows that every Sabbath we are anointed with fresh oil to learn more of Jesus. The Sabbath anointing sensitizes our spiritual senses: we smell the fresh bread of His presence, the exciting newness of the Word and the heavenly aroma of *the* Bread of heaven, the Rose of Sharon. We are strengthened and nourished for the coming week. As Jesus commanded a weary Elijah to rest and eat, so He commands us to rest and eat of Him and His Word on the Sabbath day. Since Jesus *is* the Word, we eat of Him on the Sabbath, both in communion and by digesting the Word.

Mysteries Demystified

While the promise of eating the "hidden manna" is mainly futuristic (Rev. 2:17), the principle applies today. As we show our willingness to overcome and obey God's commandments, He reveals to us the mysteries wrapped up in Jesus, our Manna, whose spiritual food is hidden in large part from those who do not meet Him on His day.

Jesus told His disciples, "To you it has been granted to know the mysteries of the kingdom of heaven, but to them it has not been granted" (Mat. 13:11). Jesus' disciples, like their Master, kept the weekly Sabbath and all the holy days of Leviticus 23. This is why Jesus could make that statement. Only the believers who enter His presence on the Sabbath day see the door opened to understand the mysteries of the Kingdom of God.

The Sabbath is the day that prophesies and proclaims both the rule of the Kingdom today and especially its establishment over the whole earth when Jesus' millennial Sabbath presence will be manifested bodily. This is why the mysteries of the Kingdom can only be revealed as we keep "Dominion Day," the Sabbath day that reveals and proclaims the mysteries of the King.

The "mystery which has been kept secret for long ages past" (Rom. 16:25) can only be revealed to those called from all nations by those who are stewards of those mysteries (I Cor. 4:1). They must have the knowledge to break the Bible code, since that mystery "now is manifested, and by the Scriptures of the prophets [the "Old Testament" must be decoded], according to the commandment of the eternal God [stewards must keep the commandments, especially the Sabbath, or test commandment]..." (Rom. 16:26).

This Kingdom mystery "for ages has been hidden *in God* who created all things; so that the manifold wisdom of God might now be made known through the church...." (Eph. 3:9-10). How can we decode the mystery if we don't meet with God on the day He convokes us? This mystery is defined as "Christ in you, the hope of glory" (Col. 1:27). Yet we cannot have Jesus strong in us, being "complete in Christ" (Col. 1:28) unless we, like Paul, meet with Jesus on His appointed times.

In order to understand the Holy Bible, God's holy ones must begin to meet with the Holy One on His holy day. There is no other way. The special code that opens up God's Book, the Book of Love, is surprisingly simple: ***the day of Love opens up the secrets of the Book of Love***.

Why? Because God, who *is* Love, poured Himself into the Sabbath. Jesus is in this day. Yes, Jesus, "in whom are *hidden* all the treasures of wisdom and knowledge " (Col. 2:3). Yes, Jesus, "who became to us wisdom from God, and righteousness, and sanctification, and redemption..." (I Cor. 1:30).

Sabbath Sound Bytes

We live in an age of brief sound bytes. Here's a brief resume of the Sabbath truth. Reading the selected verses aloud will allow God's Word to be internalized in your heart.

Jesus said in Mark 2:27-28, "The Sabbath was made for ***man*** [mankind, not just the Jew, as a blessing, not a legalistic, Pharisaical burden], and not man for the Sabbath. So the Son of Man [Jesus] is [Divine Master] even of the Sabbath." [That's one of His names. If we deny His name, we deny Who He is. We deny Jesus. So "the Lord's day" or day of Jesus the Divine Master is not Sunday, but Saturday, or more precisely Friday sunset to Saturday sunset (Gen. 1:5, Lev. 23:32). See "Saturday" and "Sabbath" in dictionary and look at a monthly calendar]. God gave the Sabbath to the first man, Adam, who was not Jewish, later repeating that first covenant with Israel, calling the weekly and annual Sabbaths "*My* feasts" (Lev. 23:2). God had blessed ***seventh*** day [not Sunday and not just any day of the week] and made it ***holy*** (Gen. 2:2-3 -- NIV). Something or someone is holy when the Holy God is present (Ex. 3:4-5; I Cor. 3:16-17).

When we love God, we will keep ***all*** His commandments and "make a distinction between the holy and the profane" (Lev. 10:10; Eccl. 12:13; Gen. 26:5, Deut. 5:29; James 2:10-12, I John 5:2-3; Rom. 13:10; John 14:15). If keeping the fourth commandment is being "under the law," then so is refraining from idolatry, images, blasphemy, adultery, or murder. The Sabbath is a test commandment, defying human logic. As with tithing, which is also illogical without divine revelation, it is binding today since it was given before the Old Covenant and is confirmed in the New (Gen. 14:20, Ex. 16:25-30, Mat. 23:23, Heb. 7:1-17).

Many twist Paul's teachings on the law (II Pet. 3:16-17), not understanding that he upheld the law when it came to moral conduct but condemned those who sought to be saved and justified by keeping the law. Certain physical and ceremonial aspects of the law were rendered unnecessary by Jesus' sacrifice and by the circumcision of the heart (Heb. 9:8-15; 10:1-18). Paul contrasted circumcision with the importance of keeping the "commandments of *God* " [thus distinguishing them from Jesus' commandments in the gospels" (I Cor. 7:19).

Jesus summed up the commandments when He said to love God and neighbor (Mat. 22:37-39; Lev. 19:18; Deut. 6:5). Love does not destroy, but fulfills or completes the law (Mat. 5:17-20; Mat. 19:16-19; Rom. 13:8-10, Rom. 6:1-2, 7:16). If the Holy One lives in us, He who is the personification of the perfect law and character of God will keep the law in and through His holy ones by His empowering grace, respecting that which is holy to Him (Tit. 2:11-14).

Those who say the Law is done away will agree they should still keep the letter and spirit of all the Ten Commandments — except the fourth! They say it doesn't matter how and when we worship God. But what about Cain (Gen. 4:5), Nadab, and Abihu (Lev. 10:1-4), and ark-bearer Uzzah who suddenly perished for simply touching a holy ark (II Sam. 6:6-7) -- or Israel, whom God sent into captivity because they didn't keep His Sabbaths (Ezek. 20:11-21)? The Sabbath was a *sign* of His covenant people to show who He was (the Creator who rested on the Sabbath) and who they were (Ex. 31:12-18).

One of the ten cardinal moral laws of God (part of the first four which show how to love and worship Him *His* way) says to keep the seventh day holy. You can't *keep* ice hot. God never made Sunday holy. Constantine imposed it on the Christian world three centuries after Jesus to make Christianity palatable to the pagans who worshiped on the day of the "Invincible Sun," replacing the commandments of God with tradition (Mark 7:7-9).

If one of the very Ten Commandments were to be abolished, Jesus would have made it abundantly clear. Instead, He kept it as His day of worship (Luke 4:16), and we are commanded to follow His example (I John 2:6). Hebrews 8:10 is a direct quote from Jeremiah 31:31-33, which clearly shows that the moral laws spoken by the Word, Jesus, in the First Testament (including number four) are now to be written in our hearts. Take away one and you take away all (James 2:10).

Isaiah 56 is an end-time prophecy that predicts a restoration of the Sabbath in our day and in Jesus' millennial rule (Isa. 66:23; Zech. 14:16-19).

Jesus' faithful disciples kept the Sabbath after His death (Luke 23:56). In a prophecy clearly for the last days, Jesus commands His followers to pray to avoid fleeing on the seventh day, still a day of rest in our day (Mat. 24:20-22).

The apostles kept the weekly and annual Sabbaths in the Acts (2:1; 13:13,42-44, where we see Gentiles keeping it too; 20:6,16; 27:9, which refers to "the fast" or Day of Atonement). Paul commanded Christians to keep the Feast of Unleavened Bread (I Cor. 5:7-8).

Satan hates the Sabbath! It is at the beginning of the seventh "day" of 1000 years when Satan will be bound (Rev. 20:1-3). A prophetic day can be one year or 1000 years (Ezek. 4:6, II Pet. 3:8-13). The millennial Sabbath or 1000-year "day" of rest from sin and Satan, is typified by the seven-day week, ending in the Sabbath day of refreshing and intimacy with God (Acts 3:19-21, NIV).

The weekly Sabbath is a special, anointed, and holy time when the Father has the joy of intimately fellowshipping with and enjoying His children. When kept in the freedom of the Holy Spirit, it is a day of joy, rest, celebration, and church worship. We observe it as New Covenant believers, following the example of the priests who "profaned" the Sabbath by doing their priestly work (Mat. 12:5). We can perform our New Covenant ministries as kings and priests by doing God's work on the Sabbath (John 5:17), exempting us from a legalistic observance -- but not changing the day.

The Word who spoke the Ten Commandments (John 1:1-18; I Cor. 10:4), was the One who said: "***If you love Me, you will keep My commandments***" (John 14:15).

The eight-pointed star (sun), as we will explain more fully in the sequel, was the mark God put upon Cain; it has been perpetuated in the world's major religions. This star in its linear form also later represented Ishtar (Astarte), the Babylonian goddess known as the queen of heaven. The eight-pointed star surrounded by a circle represented the sun god. The deception surrounding this mark has locked the Bible from the understanding of the secular and religious world. The truth revealed in this book is the "lock-buster" that dispels the falseness and opens the door to the true knowledge hidden in God's Word. The lack of this knowledge has brought destruction and bondage upon God's people (Hos. 4:6).

Sabbath *Selah's* Sabbath Sandwich

When you take the Hebrew wording, the Sabbath is sandwiched right in the middle of the Ten Commandments. This commandment to remember *Shabbat*, whose picture meaning is "return to the covenant or cross," is placed in the middle of the covenant as with all ancient treaties. The day of Love into which Love poured Himself is situated in the middle of the law of Love. The word for love in Hebrew is *ahav*, whose letters express this thought: "the Father revealed." The fourth Hebrew letter *dalet* (meaning "door") denotes the fourth commandment. While Satan is the thief that came to steal the day of Love from God's sheep, Jesus is the Door (John 10:7-10) that leads to knowing Father Love, *Agape*, and the abundant life God wants for His sheep. That abundance includes financial blessings with which to preach the gospel in these times of economic turbulence. Since we can only learn fully who Jesus is in the Sabbath (Mat. 11:28-30; Ex. 31:13), we can only become intimate with our Father, sitting on His knee, by observing the day of Love. *Selah.*

CHAPTER SIX

The Day of Love

Have you ever given someone a gift they obviously did not appreciate? I have. It hurts, doesn't it? You may have spent quite a bit of time and money searching for that gift, and to have them turn their nose up at it is painful.

Perhaps we can then understand how our God feels when He sees how His people react to one of His most beautiful love gifts. The church, and all mankind, have rejected one of God's greatest gifts of love.

While we cannot pretend to know God's exact feelings on the matter, the Bible gives us a good indication that He is grieved when we disobey.

Can you imagine this scenario? A father approaches his five-year-old boy and says, "Daddy is going to start spending Saturdays with you! We'll go out for your favorite food and dessert and enjoy being with each other all day! Whad'ya say, my boy?"

"I don't wanna. I've got other stuff to do," replies the boy.

I don't know of any five-year-olds who would turn down such an offer. Do you?

Yet almost the entire church composed of God's "chillun" have been "chillin' out" in the face of the warmth of their Father's love – turning a cold shoulder to the sunshine of His love.

All Day with Daddy!

Adam was like a son to Jesus. Genesis 3:8 indicates that Jesus met with Adam and Eve on a daily basis, at certain specified times such as "in the cool of the day." What made the Sabbath special and holy was that Jesus gave them more attention than He did on weekdays. The Sabbath was special: ***He spent all day with them!***

What is the gift most children crave most from their parents? If you ask most children – both when they are young and when they are adults – what they would most like to have or to have had from their parents, they will not talk about money or presents money can buy. They will say, "I would have loved to have had more time with my dad." And when a wife is at the end of her life, she would say, "I would have loved to have spent more time with my husband."

The church has misunderstood this precious gift and rejected it. God gave us one of his most precious gifts – time in His very presence. It's His gift of Himself – His special time with His children. It is Jesus' weekly date with His bride.

We may have times of communion with God all during the week. But on the Sabbath He spends the whole day with us!

It is His day of love. Jesus poured Himself into a 24-hour period. He created it in order to have special fellowship with us. That special gift of Himself, His time, and His love He called the Sabbath. He called it holy, set apart for special use – sacred use.

Stand Up for Jesus? Or "Stand Jesus Up?"

Ever been stood up on a date? Doesn't feel good, does it?

Jesus is the Bridegroom of His bride, the church. He doesn't like to be stood up any more than we would. He is rightly jealous of our time. We should in turn be jealous of our time with Him.

Millions innocently sing "Stand Up for Jesus" on Sunday, while they stand Him up on His date with them on Saturday. We know Jesus honors their love and praise. He would prefer, however, that they stand up for Him by keeping His day.

Actually, Jesus' perfect will was to have this special time with Adam and all His descendants – all mankind. He made the Sabbath for man, as a gift for all mankind (Mark 2:27-28). The first man Adam kept it for a while but then rejected all fellowship with God. So Jesus then gave it as a sign to His people that He was the God of love and they were His beloved people who obeyed Him. They rejected it as well and He had to send them into captivity because of it.

Later He demonstrated its importance to His disciples – the foundation of

His New Testament church – showing them how to keep it. Like Adam, they kept it for a while, but the wily serpent Satan slithered into the ranks of the church and deception gradually crept in. History opens on a large church in the fourth century that traded God's day for Satan's day – the "venerable day of the sun," as Constantine called it. They did more than reject His day. They rejected His love. They rejected His day of love.

Fathers, would you not be grieved if your children rejected one of your most heartfelt gifts? The Bible does tell us that God does experience grief (Gen. 6:6; Eph. 4:30). As we will learn a bit later in this book, it was Jesus who was grieved at mankind's sin before the flood. Why would He not be grieved when His bridegroom is a no-show on the day He invites her for their *rendezvous d'amour*, a date to celebrate their future marriage?

Deuteronomy 5 gives one of the major reasons for His grief. Verse 15 says, "You shall remember that you were a slave in the land of Egypt, and the Eternal your God brought you out of there by a mighty hand and by an outstretched arm; therefore [the Eternal] your God commanded you to observe the Sabbath day.'"

This is Jesus' day for us to celebrate our freedom from slavery -- the slavery of sin under the taskmaster Pharaoh, the devil. Jesus ardently desires for His bride to celebrate the demise of the killjoy who tries to destroy the love between Jesus and the church.

Jesus' plan is simple: exit Satan and fear -- enter Love.

The Sabbath is the day when God wraps us in his arms of love. Satan has convinced Jesus' gullible bride to leap out of the arms of Jesus into his arms on his unholy day. Jesus' bride is actually denying Him and cuddling with the deceiver. It's the day to cease the fast forward week in which the deceiver has tried to oppress us, pushing God's pause button instead. It's the day to be still and soak in the hot tub of God's love. It's the glorious time of feeling the massaging jets of the Comforter's waters – letting go and letting God refresh us.

In Exodus16 Jesus revealed Himself to His bride as her Provider: He gave her a double portion of manna on Friday. She rested in the Sabbath in Jesus, her Provision. Although she may not fully realize it, Jesus' bride today has gone after Satan as her lover and provider.

For those who have missed the Sabbath blessing unknowingly, no sin is accounted to them. After all, they are walking in Jesus in the knowledge they possess, and God says "...there is now no condemnation for those who are in Christ Jesus" (Rom. 8:1). So please don't take our strong words as condemnation. We are simply speaking God's Word as a call to repentance -- not condemnation. I know from personal experience that God often gives us abundant "time to repent" (Rev. 2:21). I shall now allow a prophet of old to make this plea for change.

Hosea says it best: "For their mother has played the harlot; she who conceived them has acted shamefully. For she said, ' I will go after my lovers, Who give me my bread and my water, My wool and my flax, my oil and my drink.'... She will pursue her lovers, but she will not overtake them; And she will seek them, but will not find them. Then she will say, 'I will go back to my first husband, For it was better for me then than now!' For she does not know that it was I who gave her the grain, the new wine, and the oil, And lavished on her silver and gold, which they used for Baal... I will punish her for the days of the Baals When she used to offer sacrifices to them... (2:5,7-8,13a)." This is not only referring to the days in a figurative sense but also in a literal sense. She kept "the days of the Baals," as does the modern church – more than Sunday, as we shall see in the sequel.

"Give me a break!"

How many times have you heard someone or even yourself say in frustration and disgust, "Give me a break!" Rather than a literal break, the phrase refers to a respite or rest.

Sometimes we do address those words heavenward. As tired runners in a rodent race against time, hurried and harried, we scream, "Stop the world, I wanna get off!"

If the world and the church knew the real meaning behind "TGIF – Thank God it's Friday," they could read God's road sign that He puts up every Friday at sunset: Stop! He wants to stop our mad Monopoly mess with "Do not pass Go and do not collect $200!" But His children go on with their little games, mired in their money-go-round, house of horrors, dizzy-land circus and never stop to smell the sweet Rose of Sharon. They leave Jesus and His day behind on the asphalt, further blackened by their screeching tires on their road to nowhere.

When you take a break with Satan on his day, you don't get a real break. As you rush out after a pitiful pit stop with the devil, and you realize your tires are still flat and your working parts have not been anointed, he hollers mockingly, "That's the breaks!"

The vast majority of Sunday keepers don't really put their week on pause that day. They stay in fast forward, when they really need to rewind.

For the few who do actually pause on the wrong day, they may get some anointing from Jesus. It does not compare, however, to what they would receive if they quit trying to feast at two tables at the same time, mixing paganism with the real thing. Deuteronomy 12 is clear on that kind of cowardly compromise.

It's almost as if church leaders have read the Bible and decided to do exactly the opposite. I'm sure that is not their intention, but it does appear that way. God says, "Don't say this!" – and we say it. "How do these nations serve their gods, that I also may do likewise?" (Deut. 12:30). He says, "Don't do this!" And that's exactly what we do! "Whatever I command you, you shall be careful to do; you shall not add to nor take away from it" (12:32).

We have been extremely careful to avoid keeping the seventh day. I have a French catechism of the universal church which even changes the word "Sabbath" to Sunday in quoting Exodus 20:8 and totally eliminates the second commandment against images. This kind of mockery does not please God.

Day of Eternal Love

Jesus is possibly saying, if we judge from His condemnation of Sabbath breaking in various parts of the First Testament, "Give me a break (rest), and take the break (rest) I have given you. Stop your fussin'. Stop your rushin'. Rest in Me. Rest on the day that prophesies and celebrates the eternal rest."

Hebrews 3 and 4 speak of that eternal rest and tell us we are to rest as God did, meaning we cannot fully understand the eternal rest unless we keep the weekly Sabbath rest. It's the day we picture, the time when time will be no more – infinity, eternity. We will inhabit eternity as God does. Actually, we already are eternal, but we haven't yet tapped all the indescribable joys of eternal life with our Father, Brother, and Comforter of Love.

Jesus is telling us in the Sabbath day, as the song says, "Slow down, you move too fast, you gotta make the [Sabbath] last..." "Take it easy – no rush. Relax. Enjoy. Smell the roses." That can even be literal since the Sabbath is the day to enjoy God's creation as He did when He rested, sitting back and relishing what He had made.

As a pastor and worship leader I should sing another tune to qualify the first one: "Get me to the church on time!" Presently we have long afternoon services with snacks, meals, and fellowship. So it's possible to enjoy a good sleep and a family brunch and still show up on the Sabbath -- one of Jesus' appointed times – at the appointed time. The hour of praise and worship we enjoy prepares us to receive the spiritual food from the Word.

Unlike the picture painted by many who have never kept it, the Sabbath is fun! It's family time. Time to be intimate with our Father, Brother-Bridegroom, and Comforter of Love. Time to enjoy our physical family and worship God together. Time even to do fun things together as a family in the context of Sabbath rejoicing. After all, it is a day of celebration – a glorious gift from our Father. And He is fun! He created fun and joy and humor. He created smiles and laughter.

Our God is good. He wouldn't have given us the Sabbath unless it was good for us. It is good for what it does for us spiritually, emotionally, mentally, and physically. It is also good for what it pictures – God's eternal love.

It is the day that foresees the time when all mankind will love and worship the true God in the Millennium. What's more, it prophesies the eternal rest the whole earth and all the inhabitants it has ever had will experience. They will know Jesus and have the opportunity to bask in His love forever.

What a blessing God has given us – a day to celebrate His love – and to show Him how much we love Him!

The Day of Excellence

Before one of the most famous chapters of the Bible, Paul said, "And I show you a still more excellent way" (I Cor. 12:31). The love chapter follows.

We live in a society of the mediocre, the half-baked, half-done, incomplete, slipshod, almost, "kinda sorta," okay I guess, more or less, "not up to snuff," "so-so" -- the quick and cheap fixes that keep us broken. Even the Christian world is lounging lazily in lukewarm mediocrity.

God is not fond of Christian excuses. We shrug our shoulders with a wimpy "Nobody's perfect." We mock Jesus' words: "Therefore you are to be perfect, as your heavenly Father is perfect (Mat. 5:48)."

How perfect is our heavenly Father? "Kinda sorta" perfect? No, sir. Jesus is saying, "Don't settle for mediocrity. Walk in the way of excellence. Seek to imitate the perfect love of your Father."

God calls us to proclaim His excellencies (I Pet. 2:9). And His Excellency is Love. That's who He is and who He wants us to be.

The Sabbath is a test commandment. One reason is that it defies human logic – just as tithing does[1]. "What's the big deal? Why does it matter which day we keep?" is the human and even Christian logic today.

It doesn't matter if we want mediocrity. It does matter if we seek God's excellence. He is love. His law is love (I John 5:3). What part of Him do we not want? If we reject one of His laws (James 2:10), we reject part of His way of love and excellence – part of Him.

Moreover, since the law is a wall of protection around us – God's boundary of protective love – we have a serious breach in that wall when we break the fourth commandment.

Furthermore, this test commandment and sign of God's people (Ex. 31:13) is placed, as was the custom in contemporary covenants between kings and their subjects, in the middle of the covenant agreement. That's no accident.

---

1 Because of space limitations, we decided to save the chapter, "'Stop! Thief!' – Tithing and the Sabbath Stand or Fall Together," for the sequel(s). You will find a brief resume in the Appendix.

The Sabbath was the first covenant God made with mankind, and the first covenant He brought to His people's remembrance. Exodus 19:5 refers to the Sabbath covenant, for it was the only one that God had made (Gen. 2:3) and reestablished with Israel (Ex. 16:28). It was the centerpiece and sign of the covenant.

This day of love and excellence was and is a test. Will we settle in mediocrity for any day? Will we choose to love God our way – or His way? Will we annul what human logic would call "one of the least of these commandments" (Mat. 5:19)? Will we devise our "own interpretation" (II Pet. 1:20) of a scripture like Exodus 20:8? Do we decide to contradict God when He commands us to keep a certain day? Will we choose to water down to an acceptable level of mediocrity His perfect law of love?

In most schools, C is average. Do we want to be average? Or do we want to be one of God's A students? How about A+? Do we settle for second best?

If we do, we are not seeking His way of excellence. If we do it knowingly and willfully reject the Sabbath, we are telling God we don't want to be excellent like He is. We are not respecting our Father of love. He will be then eventually be forced to meet out some corrective, tough love so we can come into harmony with His way of excellence.

Jesus wants a bride who is a "10" – not a "3 or 4" on the beauty scale. She needs Sabbath sin surgically removed. He is calling her to repentance. He is saying, "Shape up, grow up – or you won't go up!" He won't rapturously lift up His bride and carry her over the threshold of the Holy of Holies if she dilly-dallies about showing up for His dates. It's high time Jesus' bride began to lift Him high by keeping His holy time. It's time she exchanged her "holey," hand-me-down, bedraggled dress for His holy robe of righteousness and excellence. That's not condemnation, but elevation -- an exhortation to raise our standard to meet God's high standard.

When Jesus' bride begins to respect her Groom enough to keep His day of love, her limitations will be removed. When she decides to rise from the mire of mediocrity into His way of excellence, His glory can rise upon her (Isa. 60:1). A glorious bride without spot will not be keeping Satan's day of the sun when she grasps the Sabbath truth. She can't be glorious until she's keeping the day of the Son – the Son of love.

Path to Perfection

This day of God's love, however, is more than the expression of our active desire to walk perfectly in our Father's love and excellence. It is the pathway to excellence – and perfection.

In His wisdom and in His love for mankind, Jesus made the Sabbath as a day of spiritual creation. The physical creation (or recreation) took six days – the number of man. Seven is God's number of completion and perfection. How appropriate. The seventh day was to be God's tool for creating His perfect love and excellence in His children.

The Sabbath was to be a key to growth in grace and knowledge. Obedience to it would unlock all Bible mysteries (Ps. 111:10; Col. 2:3). The whole Bible, the plan of God and the vast concept of righteousness begin to make sense. The hidden code is broken. Rather than being destroyed for lack of knowledge, God's people are instructed in God's way of perfection.

The Day of Love Unlocks the Book of Love!

This concept is the crux of this book. This "bottom line" will put you and your family on the heights of the earth because of your newfound intimacy with Jesus, in whom you will greatly delight (Isa. 58:13-14). If you see that as an overstatement, recognize that it comes from God. How could we have missed this truth that unlocks the code -- the Bible code that hides the Word of Love from our understanding?

The key that unlocks the Bible code is the Day of Love, the Sabbath. Yes, ***Keeping the Day of Love opens up the Book of Love!***

This simple truth explains why the church today is mired in confusion, with competing denominations that will not forgive one another. Satan has succeeded in getting the Christian world to see the Sabbath as something disdainfully "Jewish," a burdensome remnant of a bygone covenant. On the contrary, it is the very first covenant of ***love*** that God made with mankind. Many know the Sabbath is not Sunday, but Satan has made it difficult for pastors to step out in faith because of losing sheep and their tithe money.

Whether or not your pastor has the courage to step out in love and faith to keep God's Day of Love, you can. You can begin to know intimately the Jesus who poured Himself into the Sabbath day. Jesus the Revelator (Rev. 1:1) is waiting on you to meet Him on His day to receive the revelation that will open the coded Book of Love to you. Only then can you come to the "true knowledge of God's mystery, that is, Christ Himself, *in whom are* ***hidden all the treasures of wisdom and knowledge***" (Col. 2:3).

The high and mighty of the world and even highly respected church officials have so far missed out on this blockbuster (and "lockbuster"!) understanding. God may have to go into the highways and byways to call the "base things of the world" (I Cor. 1:28) who can humble themselves to keep the day of Love in order to summon them to a marriage supper with the Bridegroom Jesus (Mat. 22:1-10), who as Divine Master of the Sabbath requires obedience to prove our love for Him.

Will you be part of the system of tradition and religiosity that will refuse to accept Jesus by keeping His day of Love? Or will you perhaps be among the humble ones who read the simple words of Exodus 20:8 and begin to enter Love's Sabbath rest every Friday night after a productive week? It is these "weak things of the world" who will in these last days of testing be truly and completely "in Christ Jesus, who became to us wisdom from God, and righteousness and sanctification, and redemption" (I Cor. 1:26-30).

The Sabbath contains all of those gifts from God, since the Sabbath contains Jesus. The day of Love is also the day of wisdom, righteousness, sanctification, and redemption. Redemption, indeed, for Jesus is the crux of the matter, and His cross of redemption is a major part of the meaning of the day. As we show in this book, the picture meaning of the letters in Shabbat is return (by destroying the house of lies Satan has built to keep us from the day of Love) to the covenant, *tav*, the last letter of the Hebrew alphabet, which also means "the cross."

In teaching about the Sabbath, we are preaching "Christ crucified, to Jews a stumbling block and to Gentiles foolishness" (I Cor. 1:23). Will Jesus offend you in revealing Himself as "Divine Master of the Sabbath" (Mark 2:28)? Will you not allow yourself to see the cross of Jesus in *Shabbat*? Will you miss out on the way God said to celebrate your redemption from sin (Deut. 5:15)? Will you, in these ominous last days when "most people's love will grow cold" (Mat. 24:12), miss out on the hugs of Father Love on His Sabbath day, on the special love date with Bridegroom Jesus? Will the Book of Love remain a closed, locked book for you?

Jesus is calling you to the love, joy, peace, and revelation embodied in Him on His Day of Love. He beckons you in Matthew 11:28-30: "Come to Me, all who are weary and heavy-laden, and I will give you rest [same word used for Sabbath rest in the Greek version of the Hebrew Scriptures in the time of Jesus]. Take My yoke upon you and ***learn from Me***...."

This concentrated time of fellowship with Jesus on the day He set aside for sharing His love and truth with His people is His time for premarital counseling. He gets to know His bride and she gets to know Him.

Dates are fun when you're in love. Are you in love with Jesus? You can't truly and fully know and love Him if you're showing up for a date on a day when He didn't even invite you. And when you come into the full realization of the Sabbath truth, you're standing Him up on the day He *did* invite you! That's not love, not in its fullness. Not even fickle infatuation!

So few have been blessed to understand how powerful this holy day is – the day we rest in Jesus' righteousness and love. All God's commands are important, but the fourth one brings forth something special.

It is God's weekly educational, inspirational retreat to create us spiritually in His image. It reminds us every seven days of the importance of all God's commands and ways. It's an insurance plan for eternal rest in Jesus. Properly observed, it solidifies our relationship with God. It is the key to intimacy with Jesus – the invaluable key to walking in the excellence of our Excellency.

Virtually every truth of God's Word is tied into the Sabbath. It is the fulcrum upon which the plan of God revolves. It is not optional.

The infinity sign, resembling the figure eight, originates from a covenant walk around the split sections of a sacrificed animal. And do you know who walked through the bloody sacrifice in a figure eight formation in Genesis 15 with Abraham? It was Jesus – the Alpha and Omega Himself. The Infinite One walked through the infinity sign to make an eternal covenant with the father of the faithful. Jesus thus vowed, as the custom went, that He and all the Godhead would have to die eternally if He did not give eternal rest in the Promised Land to Abraham and to us, His faithful, obedient children.

Here was the picture of the Sabbath rest on the earth in the abode of the kings and priests in the area of Jerusalem for those who would be faithful in obeying all God's commands. Both partners in the covenant vowed by their figure eight walk through the pieces of the animal that they would fulfill their part of the covenant -- or die.

Abraham showed Himself faithful by keeping all God's laws (Gen. 26:5). That of necessity included the Sabbath Jesus gave to Adam. Although a separate covenant, it was part of Abraham's faithfulness to the covenant of obedience to receive the eternal inheritance.

The eternal, infinite figure eight is the picture of the Alpha and the Omega. It is God's eternal plan for all mankind. In the center of the figure a cross is formed. Jesus, both our Passover and our Sabbath, and His cross are thus the center around which the plan of God turns. Since the Passover and the Sabbath are both celebrations of Jesus' redemptive blood and the freedom it brings, they are also central in that plan.

The two oval parts of the figure eight have multiple meanings. The first represents the first fruits of God's harvest and the second the great harvest of those resurrected after the Millennium (Rev. 20:5,12). Also, the first oval pictures the "first" of the First Testament – Israel – becoming the "last" (resurrected later for a lesser reward) and the last – those called in this age – becoming the first (the bride of Christ with the double reward of the firstborn).

The Sabbath unfolds the awesome plan of love through Jesus' blood shed on the cross. As the Sabbath was made for man, so the Sabbath includes all mankind one day in the arms of our Father -- Love Himself. What the world needs now, as the song says, is love. What the church needs now is love. Jesus offers it in His day of Love. When you embrace it, you embrace Jesus.

About the Covers

The Bible has been locked from the understanding of even most Christians. God foreknew that Satan would be the god of this present world (II Cor. 4:4) and that he would deceive the whole world, even the religious world (Rev. 12:9). The system of religiosity started by Cain -- represented by his mark, the eight-pointed star -- and Baal or lord worship introduced by Nimrod have put padlocks around God's Book. God made His plan accordingly, calling very few in this age and writing the Bible in conceptual languages difficult to translate. Only a called-out few at this time would grasp the only key to breaking the secret Bible code: doing and speaking the very Word we are seeking to understand. The Bible itself, which is also like a hammer when spoken and obeyed (Jer. 23:29), declares that only those who are doers of the Word will understand it (Ps. 111:10). An important test of obedience has been totally overlooked by the Christian world. It is the only key that breaks the special code. In these pages we challenge today's believers to make the courageous change that will turn a weary Bride of Jesus into the spotless Sweetheart who will walk in an intimacy and power in Jesus never seen before.

The two locks have several meanings. In addition to the star of Cain and Baal worship, they can also represent the First and Second Testaments, more commonly and erroneously called the Old and New Testaments. The First Testament has been locked and sealed because people have not known the God of the Hebrew Scriptures who spoke to and dealt with those in that time period, Jesus, the Word (John 1:1-18). The Second Testament has been locked because Christians have not known nor have they been intimate with the real Jesus, and because they have not met with Him to come to know Him in His Sabbath day into which He pours Himself (Mark 2:27-28). When we keep the Sabbath without truly connecting with Jesus, we keep it legalistically. When we don't keep it at all, we keep ourselves from knowing Jesus intimately, since He reveals Himself in His Sabbath fellowship with us.

While the Sabbath is a figurative key to unlock the Bible code, we use the powerful and biblical analogy of the hammer, since the powerful hammer blow represented by obeying the whole Word of God, including the Sabbath, leaves no doubt about a reopening by a key. The lock is smashed. The code is broken without a doubt.

Sabbath *Selah's*
Breaking News! Mankind and Millennium Cancelled -- And Jesus Isn't Coming Back!

Truth: the Sabbath was made for man (Mark 2:27-28). Fact: many religious people say that the Sabbath has been done away. Conclusion: If the Sabbath has been done away, that means that mankind has also been done away.

Truth: the seventh-day Sabbath represents the seventh thousand-year period of human history on Earth, what the Bible refers to as the Millennium, or millennial Sabbath. Fact: Some say the Sabbath has been cancelled. Conclusion: If so, so has the Millennium. And so has Jesus' return to earth to be present with mankind as He is in a similar way on the Sabbath.

The crux of the gospel of the Kingdom of God, the only gospel Jesus preached, is that Jesus is coming back to rule over all mankind on the earth. If we cancel the Sabbath, we cancel mankind and we cancel the Kingdom. If we deny the Sabbath, we deny the gospel of the Kingdom. We also deny the King of the Kingdom, Jesus.

But whoever denies Me before men, I will also deny him before My Father who is in heaven (Mat. 10:33). *Selah.*

CHAPTER SEVEN

Beginning at the Beginnnig

Bible truths are often easier to grasp when we start at beginning. We begin with Genesis 2:2-3: "By the seventh day God had finished the work he had been doing: so on the seventh day he rested from all his work. And God ***blessed*** the ***seventh day*** and made it ***holy***, because on it he rested from all the work of creating that he had done (NIV)."

Finding which day is the seventh day is as easy as consulting a dictionary and a wall calendar. ***Saturday*** is the seventh day of the week.

We see, however, in reading Genesis 1, that god starts His days at evening. That means this ***holy day*** begins on Friday night at sunset and ends Saturday night at sunset.

When we look up "evening" in the concordance, we the word relating to an *annual* holy day called the Day of Atonement (Lev. 23:32). It calls this day a "sabbath" as well and says, "…on the ninth of the month [Tishri or September-October] at evening, from evening until evening you shall keep your sabbath."

Jesus' Words Explain Genesis Account

It is important to read the "New Testament" or Greek Scriptures to understand the "Old." We therefore read Mark 2:27-28 in its context. The self-righteous Pharisees, spokesmen of the "Old Testament" teaching along with a lot of tradition never given by God to Israel, criticized Jesus for the *way* He and His disciples kept the

Sabbath.

We know from history an indisputable fact: today's Jews keep the same day as they did 2000 years ago: Friday sunset to Saturday sunset. So Jesus was keeping the ***seventh*** day of the week.

What we read in verse 27 is amazing, if we believe Jesus meant what He said: "The Sabbath was made for ***man,*** and not man for the Sabbath." Man in this verse obviously refers to mankind. Jesus does not say the Sabbath was meant for the Jews, and that He kept the Sabbath because He was a Jew. He kept the Sabbath because He was the "Son of Man" and had to keep His own law perfectly in order to be the unblemished sacrifice for our sins.

This is Jesus' own commentary on Genesis 2:2-3. Jesus is saying that when He made man, He also made the Sabbath for him – for his benefit.

He is clearly countering the Pharisee's approach of laying unnecessary burdens on man – especially regarding the Sabbath. Their rules included picky rules about carrying nothing bigger than a dried fig. It was their theology that was dried up!

Jesus was simply saying that He gave the seventh day to man as a blessing – not a burden. And He knew that His words would be written down for all people for all time.

Jesus was plainly showing that although He was dead set against *legalism,* He was all for *law – His* law. He was all against keeping the law by mere human effort – in a self-righteous attempt to gain God's favor apart from His grace and empowerment. But He was all for keeping the law by the power of the Holy Spirit in him and in us.

Jesus never changed the Sabbath day! He said nothing about observing a different day. He only changed the ***way*** to keep the ***day.*** Nor did He somehow prepare His disciples for the time after His death when the law would supposedly be done away.

How could God make the seventh day for man, and yet not expect man to benefit from what He made for him? God obviously made the seventh day holy ***so man would keep it holy!***

Exodus 20:8-11, was, of course, addressed to Israel. This fourth of the Ten Commandments says: "***Remember*** the ***Sabbath*** day, to ***keep*** it holy. Six days shall you labor and do all your work, but the seventh day is a sabbath of the [Eternal] your God…[Jesus] blessed the sabbath day and made it holy."

Sabbath Existed from the Beginning

God made the ***seventh*** day ***holy – from the beginning.*** He made it holy for man to keep holy, beginning with Adam. He made it holy long before the first Jew – Judah, son of Jacob or Israel – ever took a breath of air.

In addition, God said to ***remember*** the Sabbath. It existed before the giving of the Ten Commandments in tablet form. It was given in tablet form, but it was a pill Israel didn't want to swallow. Some Christians don't want to swallow it today. They don't want to admit this law existed before Sinai.

God wasn't only referring to the Exodus 16 test involving manna and the Sabbath. Genesis is clear: God made the Sabbath, i.e. the commandment that became the fourth of the ten given at Sinai, in the beginning. People were aware of *all* of the Ten Commandments long before Sinai. One prominent example is Joseph resisting Potiphar's wife's advances. He obviously knew about the commandment against adultery that became the seventh of the ten.

Abraham obeyed all God's commandments and laws (Gen. 26:5). Abraham was a man. The Sabbath was made for man. It was definitely made for Abraham, the father of the faithful. *All* of God's laws were for the benefit of man.

Furthermore, God didn't forbid adultery and murder only for the people of Israel. All His laws were intended eventually to spread to all people. God told Israel to obey His laws so all the nations around would stand in awe of such a righteous nation with such *good laws* (Deut. 4:6-8). This did not exclude the fourth commandment!

Jesus: "Divine Master of the Sabbath!"

For these incredibly arrogant religious leaders who were telling Jesus how to keep the day He Himself made for mankind, the next words of Jesus probably exploded in their self-righteous faces. It was dynamite.

"Therefore, the Son of Man is also ***"[Divine Master]*[1] *of the Sabbath*** (Mark 2:28, NKJV)." Did you catch that?

Some Christians cannot swallow this Sabbath pill when they see it in tablet form in the Ten Commandments – that ancient "Old Testament" law. Stone doesn't sit too well on their stomachs. They think this law is done away because it was Old Covenant, written on stone.

The problem was not with the stone tablets -- but with the stony heart of a rebellious people who, for the most part, did not have the Holy Spirit. In describing the ***New*** Covenant, God said He would put His into their minds and hearts (Heb. 8:10).

---

1 As we will show later in this book, the word "Lord" is a deceptive translation that does not faithfully render the Greek *kurios*, which translates the Hebrew *adonai*, properly translated as "Divine Master." Satan cleverly introduced in the King James Bible the title "Lord" for Jesus to keep the end-time church from unleashing the power of His name.

In case some "greasy grace, sloppy *agape*" Christian would like to suggest that these laws are only the "law of Christ" expounded in the New Testament, notice that this is a ***direct quote*** from the "***Old*** Testament," describing the *same* laws that were the basis of the Old Covenant or agreement (Jer. 31:31-33). Surprise!

We hope and pray that it will be a pleasant surprise, as Christians embrace – not the Jewish – but the ***Christian*** Sabbath. Yes, it is the Sabbath that the Word, Jesus, blessed by His words in Genesis and shouted from Sinai. It is the day He Himself kept (Luke 4:16), the day he reaffirmed by His life and His teachings.

Jesus is "*[Divine Master] of* ***the Sabbath***" (Mark 2:28) -- ***not Sunday.*** The "Lord's" day may indeed be Sunday, but the day Jesus made holy is ***the*** **seventh *day – the Sabbath.***

The same Yahweh or Eternal One (the Word, Jesus) who spoke the Sabbath law from Sinai says emphatically to His people, "I change not" (Mal. 3:6, KJV). The writer of the book of Hebrews, who makes a clear reference to the seventh-day Sabbath in his book, says of that same Being, that He is "the same yesterday and today and forever" (Heb. 13:8).

Sabbath Intimacy

It is true that some have put an undue emphasis on "the *Sabbath* of the Divine Master" rather than on "the *Divine Master* of the Sabbath." Without Jesus the Sabbath is nothing. Without the Sabbath, however, our knowledge of Jesus is not complete. Both are necessary.

In fact, keeping the Sabbath is a gateway to knowing and being intimate with the real Jesus. We get to know Him better and better as we, His holy ones, enjoy His presence on His holy day. He offers a special intimacy with Him only on the day He calls holy.

So it was in the beginning, when Adam and Eve walked with God and fellowshipped with Him in a special, intimate way on the Sabbath day.

That Sabbath intimacy has opened for us a door of understanding that we now share with you. The Bible is a coded puzzle with "a little [truth] here, a little there" (Isa. 28:10). As we obey the simple and clear biblical command to keep the Sabbath, the puzzle is solved, and we begin to see the Sabbath principle throughout the Bible[2].

So many verses apply to the Sabbath that we had originally planned fifty pages of the manuscript of this book in the Appendix containing expositions of Scriptures relating to the Sabbath. We hope to include these in some format in the sequel(s) to this book.

---

2 So many verses apply to the Sabbath that we had originally planned fifty pages of the manuscript of this book in the Appendix containing expositions of Scriptures relating to the Sabbath. We hope to include these in some format in the sequel(s) to this book.

Sabbath *Selah's*
WWJD: What Would Jesus Do?

And He came to Nazareth, where He had been brought up; and as was His custom, He entered the synagogue on the Sabbath, and stood up to read (Luke 4:16).

The real Jesus, who is the same forever (Heb. 13:9), would keep the same day today that He kept 2000 years ago. Two truths are indisputable: Jesus kept the same day as the Jews of His day, and the Jews have never changed the day they kept. It's still Friday sunset to Saturday sunset. Those who wear a WWJD bracelet should do what Jesus did -- keep the only day of the week called by name in the Bible, the Sabbath. In His 33 years on Earth Jesus kept 1700 seventh-day Sabbaths as an example for us. That's one Sabbath He remembered for every year the church has forgotten His day, thanks to "Lord" Constantine. Paul said He followed Jesus' example (I Cor. 11:1). Will we? Selah.

CHAPTER EIGHT

The New Covenant Sabbath: Misunderstood Blessing

As we have seen, the "Old Testament" (in reality "Part One of the words of Jesus, the Word") makes it eminently clear that the seventh day Sabbath is God's day. It is the day He made holy by putting His presence in it. It is a day of rest from a person's normal work and a day of corporate worship.

God gives absolutely no indication in the "New Testament" ("Part Two of the words of Jesus, expounding the New Covenant") that He changed the day He made holy. He certainly never de-sanctified it – or somehow made it unholy.

Those who say there is no such thing as holy time are mistaken. Since the Sabbath is a period of time, and since God made the Sabbath holy, the seventh day of the week is therefore holy time.

The fourth commandment is clear. God commands us to keep that period of time holy, by our thoughts, actions, and attitude – and by ceasing our normal weekly work on that day.

If the letter of the fourth commandment had been changed in the Greek Scriptures we call the New Testament, Jesus would have told us. He would not have left us in doubt about such an important point.

The law is a whole. All its commandments must be observed (James 2:10). They stand or fall together.

If Jesus were to nullify the letter of the fourth commandment, He would also have to render void the letter of every other commandment. In forbidding even an attitude of hate in Matthew 5, He goes beyond the simple letter of the sixth commandment, which forbids committing actual murder. Because we cannot hate, that obviously doesn't mean we are now allowed to murder under the terms of the New Covenant.

The fact that Jesus did not amplify the fourth commandment in Matthew 5 is not a valid argument for annulling the letter of the commandment, which says we are to keep the seventh day holy. If that were so, you could break the first commandment.

The meaning of the fourth commandment is simple. We are to keep the seventh day holy, not Sunday, which is the first day of the week. The commandment does not say to keep the first day, second day, or simply any day holy. God specifies the seventh day.

No one would seriously suggest that we should change the letter of the law relating to the sixth commandment against murder. Yet many believe we have biblical authority to change the letter of the fourth commandment by changing the day God specified from Saturday to Sunday.

The Catholic Church understands this. They have told the Protestants that the Bible never advocates Sunday worship. They believe basically that the pope has greater authority than the Bible and that the Protestants are following Catholic authority and tradition rather than the Word of God.

We either keep the Sabbath or we don't. Keeping Sunday is not keeping the Sabbath. To pretend we are keeping the Sabbath holy under the New Covenant by changing the day and thus the letter of the law is not biblical. It is just as illogical as saying we are not allowed under the New Covenant to hate our mother-in-law, but we can feel free to murder her! We cannot lust after our neighbor's wife, but we can have sex with her!

We do not have the authority to change God's law. Our modern Christian world has changed the fourth commandment according to tradition – a tradition started by a worldly emperor 1700 years ago.

As Jesus did, we speak with authority because we base what we say on God's Word. Please do not interpret this as condemnation. God meets us where we are. He is patient with us. He gives us time to change, time to understand truths that have been robbed from us by church leaders. We have been blessed to understand the Sabbath. Jesus judges us more severely, however, because He has given us more revelation at this time. Our words may be strong, and we may write them with emphasis, but we say them in love as well as with authority -- at least that is our goal.

Burden or Blessing?

Why would God make the Sabbath for mankind – for the first man, Adam – if He didn't intend for Him to be blessed by keeping it? In the context of Mark 2, Jesus was talking to the Pharisees, who had their own version of the Sabbath, and who made it a *burden*. God intended it as a ***blessing***.

Mankind was not made for the Sabbath – in other words, to worship the Sabbath day. The Pharisees had a long man-made list of do's and don't's that put the Sabbath on a higher plane than God intended. They worshiped Sabbath legalism but refused to worship the ***Divine Master*** *of the Sabbath* that stood among them!

He was telling them in essence: "You have the gall to tell *Me* how to observe ***My*** day! I'm the Master, the Boss of that day. I made it! Who do you think you are?" They were telling God Himself how to observe His day. Even worse, they were saying He was breaking the fourth commandment!

Come on, fellows! Jesus Himself was the Creator who rested on the seventh day (Heb. 1:2; Gen. 2:1-3). He was the One who thundered it from Mount Sinai. He was the *Logos*, the Word, who spoke the will of God in the "First Testament" (John 1:1-18). You're telling the Divine Master of the Sabbath how to keep His own day? Talk about self-righteousness!

Many religionists today claim the Sabbath is a harsh, Jewish, Old Covenant burden. If they had ever kept it, guided by the Holy Spirit, they would know it is a day of *freedom*. It is not a day of Pharisaical legalism, even though there are those who may keep it that way.

Not so with David. He knew how to rejoice on the Sabbath days (Ps. 42:4). So did Jesus.

Jesus Taught the Sabbath

The Divine Master of the Sabbath was not doing away with the day. On the contrary, He was showing ***how*** to keep it.

Some say Jesus did not confirm the Sabbath commandment in the New Testament. What Bible are they reading? More teaching is found in the gospels about how to keep the fourth commandment than any of the other nine! Jesus taught the Sabbath by His words and by His example. The gospels are full of Sabbath teaching.

People do not see the Sabbath in the New Testament because they have accepted a false tradition. As we will further prove, Jesus was resurrected on the weekly Sabbath – not on Sunday. Even if He *had* been resurrected on Sunday, no New Testament authority exists to do away with one of the "*Big Ten*" in order to celebrate the resurrection on a weekly basis.

How many Christians have ever dared check up on what their church teaches – what their pastor tells them? The Bible commands us to prove all things and only hold on to what is true (I Thes. 5:21). Truth is not tradition. Truth is not a pastor's opinion -- including mine. Jesus said to His Father, "**Your *word* is truth** (John 17:17)."

You cannot find *one* word in the Bible that commands us to keep Sunday. Nowhere does the Bible tell us to observe any other day than the seventh.

Since when do we believe the tradition of ***man*** above the word of ***God***? Listen to what Jesus said to those who worshiped religious tradition in His day. Unlike those tradition worshipers today, at least they kept *His* **day** – only the wrong way. "'You are experts at setting aside the commandment of God in order to keep your tradition'" (Mark 7:9).

We have many experts today as well – too often experts in tradition, not experts in rightly dividing the word of truth. As Peter said, many twist Paul's writings. They paint him as one who dares contradict a multitude of plain scriptures, including the words and example of Jesus Himself.

Actually, they picture him as contradicting *himself* – since we see him always keeping the Sabbath and holy days in the Acts (Acts 13:42-44; 16:13; 18:4,11; 20:6,16) and commanding the observance of the Feast of Unleavened Bread (I Cor. 5:8).

How could Paul contradict Jesus? How could he contradict his own teaching and practice? He didn't.

Jesus – Messenger of the New Covenant

Although the New Covenant came into effect only when the blood of Jesus was shed, Jesus came to explain during His ministry the terms of that covenant. He is called in Malachi 3:1 the Messenger of the covenant, meaning the New Covenant, based on the same law as the previous covenant (Heb. 8:10; Jer. 31:31-33).

It is true that two First Testament passages refer to the Ten Commandments as synonymous with the Old Covenant (Deut. 4:13). God says: "And he wrote on the tablets the words of the covenant, the Ten Commandments" (Ex. 34:28).

The Hebrew word for *commandment* is *dabar*, the same word as the word for *word* earlier in the verse. Mind you, these were quite forceful words. They were also laws, constituting the basis of the covenant. A covenant is an agreement. Israel agreed to obey these "words."

Although the agreement and the terms of what was to be agreed upon were considered synonymous, an obvious distinction exists that common sense would dictate. An agreement is one thing; what is *agreed to* is another. The Ten Words were the words or terms of the covenant – not the covenant itself.

Using one verse to establish a doctrine that would do away with the Ten Commandments under the New Covenant, as some have done, is dangerous and unethical. A multitude of verses proves the contrary.

Two Covenants – One Law

Even a casual reading of Matthew 5 clearly shows that Jesus, in explaining the terms of the New Covenant, was not changing the moral laws that were the basis of the Old Covenant.

In a sense, He was simply changing their "location." He was writing these laws on the *hearts* of His people, as we have seen.

Some have misread Hebrews 8:13. It does not say the moral *law* of the Ten Commandments on which the Old Covenant was based is now obsolete. It says the *covenant* is obsolete. The *law* Israel agreed to is not obsolete. It is the *agreement* based on that law that is obsolete.

Why would Jesus do away with the Ten Words that describe the very character of God? Why would He who never changes (Heb. 13:8) change the law He Himself gave to Israel – a law He calls good in both testaments?

The failure of the Old Covenant was not the fault of the law given by the perfect God. It was the fault of the carnal *people* who disobeyed it (Heb. 8:8). Why do we persist in throwing out the good with the bad? Dirty bath water is expendable. Babies are not. God's law is good. It always has been and it always will be. To say the law is done away because of grace is a satanic lie!

Jesus' Teaching on the Law

Paul never taught against obeying God's law, even though many Christians think he did. Before getting entangled in the convoluted phrases of the former pupil of Gamaliel, it would behoove us to ask a simple question: Would Paul's teaching on the law of God contradict the teaching of Jesus? The answer is an obvious, resounding no. We shall see what Jesus taught.

In Matthew 5:17-18, Jesus plainly said He did not come to do away with the Hebrew Scriptures. Lest some think that statement does not apply to the Ten Commandments or any other statement of moral law, read verse 19: "Whoever then *annuls* one of the *least* of these *commandments*, and *teaches* others to do the same, shall be called least in the kingdom of heaven; but whoever *keeps* and teaches them, he shall be called great in the kingdom of heaven."

What an indictment against those who teach that the law is done away! Remember that Jesus is speaking in the context of the "*Old* Testament." So what is He saying?

He plainly says we are supposed to *keep the commandments* (excluding, of course, the sacrifices fulfilled in Jesus' death on the cross) of what men call **the "*Old* Testament!"** Not with a legalistic mindset – mind you. Not by our own strength, but by the *grace of God!*

Jesus even adds this in verse 20: "For I say to you, that unless your *righteousness [i.e. obedience to God's law] surpasses* that of the scribes and Pharisees, you will not enter the kingdom of heaven."

The Pharisees had a carnal, legalistic approach to the law. But we're not talking about a different law than what Jesus commands us to keep under the New Covenant.

What commandment did the Pharisees keep with the greatest, albeit misguided, zeal? The fourth! The Sabbath! This means we are to ***keep the Sabbath under the New Covenant!*** If we are to ***surpass*** the obedience of the Pharisees, we must ***at least*** keep the letter of the fourth commandment, which says to observe the ***seventh day!***

The Jews have not changed the day in 2000 years. This is an historic fact no one can dispute. It cuts through all the excuses people give for not keeping the Sabbath, including their muddled understanding of the calendar changes that never changed the seven day weekly cycle. When you are questioned about keeping the Sabbath on Saturday, remember this important truth: ***Jesus kept the same day as the Jews kept 2000 years ago and today!*** Saturday is still Saturday!

The Calendar Concoction

Has time been lost, as some say, to get around keeping the Sabbath? They claim the calendar was changed, which made it impossible to determine the seventh day of the week. Truth is, a calendar change did indeed take place. It did not, however, involve days. It was a matter of dates being changed -- merely another lame excuse to avoid a date with Jesus.

The facts refute this clever argument. The calendar was changed once in October of 1582 in order to keep up with the solar cycle. This change in no way altered the weekly cycle. Ten dates were omitted from the calendar following October 4, 1582. What would have been Friday, October 5, became Friday, October 15. Absolutely no change occurred in the order of the days of the week. Friday remained Friday. Saturday remained Saturday. It's that simple.

Moreover, a U.S. Naval Observatory document sent in 1932 verifies that no change has taken place in the weekly cycle. In response to a question in a letter dated March 12, 1932, an observatory official wrote: "...we have had occasion to investigate the results of the works of specialists in chronology and we have never found one of them that has ever had the slightest doubt about the continuity of the weekly cycle since long before the Christian era...There has been no change in our calendar in past centuries that has affected in any way the cycle of the week."

After all, would God have given a commandment that would be impossible to keep, especially when He said it was to be kept forever and given as a blessing for all mankind (Mark 2:27-28; Ex. 31:17)? And in case detractors want to throw another red herring, the church today bears the name of Israel, which means "believers." God calls us by the name of His physical people, "the Israel of God" (Gal. 6:16). While believers no longer need to sacrifice animals and do numerous rituals that have been fulfilled by Jesus and the Holy Spirit, God still requires us to obey the commandments (I Cor. 7:19).

Had Jesus failed to keep the right day as the Sabbath, He would have sinned and sabotaged His effort to save us. Had He kept Sunday, the Pharisees would have surely pointed that out to Him. Not only did Jesus keep the seventh-day Sabbath, but the Jewish people have also faithfully kept it since the time of Jesus. Even if a calendar change had occurred that mixed up the order of the days of the week, the Jews would still know which day to keep. And they have kept it throughout the last two millennia. The only doubt that exists regarding the right day to keep is in the minds of those who have been sincerely deceived to believe a lie.

Will you allow a deception about dates to keep you from the weekly date Jesus commands you to have with Him? Why not begin this coming Friday sunset to get intimate with the real Jesus?

Not Nit-picky Legalism

Now, that doesn't mean that we have to figure out how many figs we can lift on the Sabbath! People who are quick to condemn Sabbath keeping as legalism are confusing apples with oranges, and they surely don't understand the Pharisaical fig law. They confuse legalism with obedience to the law of love. Picky, carnal legalism is not superior to Spirit-led righteousness! Jesus Himself blew their legalistic bubble. He healed people on that day. He let his disciples eat some grain when they were hungry on that day, which did not break *God's* Sabbath law.

For a Spirit-led Christian, the new Covenant Sabbath is not a straightjacketed day of do's and don't's. It is a joyous day of ***freedom and celebration!*** We obey the fourth commandment in a *spiritual* way – a way far superior to the way most observed it under the Old Covenant, and far better than the Pharisees observed it. Not stricter – simply better!

Sabbath Silliness

When Jesus did miracles of compassion on the Sabbath, the Pharisees accused Him of breaking the Sabbath commandment (John 5:17-18; Luke 6:2). Some Christians believe they were correct. Since He was Master of the Sabbath, they reason, we can break it too. Claiming to be friends of Jesus, in reality they are agreeing with His enemies! It was Jesus' enemies who made this accusation, and it was false.

The traditional Sabbath laws or *melachot* the Pharisees cited were later expounded in the Jewish *Mishnah,* but they are not part of the Bible! In fact, they were disobeying the Word by adding to the Scripture (Deut. 4:2; 12:32) and burdening the people (Mat. 23:4). Jesus created the Sabbath in order to relieve people of burdens, not put more on them. They even considered their laws to be superior to the Scripture.

Here is an example of the absurdity: If a hen laid an egg on the Sabbath day, you could not eat it. If the hen had been kept for fattening rather than for laying, however, you could eat the egg. They considered the egg a part of the hen, a part that had fallen off.

These laws forbade picking grain out of a field, as the Pharisees caught Jesus' disciples in the act of doing. But if a man wanted to move a sheaf of wheat on his field, all he had to do to be within the law was to lay a spoon on it. Since he then had to remove the spoon, which was permitted, he was also allowed to remove the sheaf under it.

Jesus Did Not Change the Day

The Pharisees went to church on the ***seventh*** day. Jesus went to church on the ***seventh*** day (Luke 4:16). How can we follow Jesus' own example and ***surpass*** the righteousness of the Pharisees if we don't even do the minimum? How can we say we obey when we don't even keep the right day?

We don't even need this verse, of course, to prove that Jesus taught obedience to the fourth commandment. He plainly taught the Sabbath by word and deed. He told and showed the Pharisees the *right* way to keep the Sabbath.

Nowhere did Jesus say to his followers, "I'm showing you how to keep the seventh day now since you're under the Jewish law, but after I die I'm going to change the day to Sunday." He could have said that, couldn't He? He *should* have said that if He were going to *change* one of the *Ten Commandments*! He would have had to make such a monumental change clear. He didn't.

Moral or Ceremonial Law?

Jesus taught the Sabbath by word and deed. It is clear, however, that His death ended the need for laws regarding animal sacrifices and strictly ceremonial purity.

He had to fulfill these laws – to obey them – since He had not yet shed His blood and since the purifying waters of the Holy Spirit had not yet been released after His ascension. They were good laws – but they were only temporary.

God makes a clear distinction between the moral laws and the ritual, sacrificial, ceremonial laws under the Old Covenant. Hebrews 8:10 says the moral laws of the Old Covenant will be the *same* laws that will be written in the *hearts* of believers filled with the Holy Spirit under the New Covenant.

But what does Hebrews 9:9-10 reveal regarding the ceremonial laws? "… both gifts and sacrifices are offered which cannot make the worshiper perfect in conscience [only Jesus obeying the moral laws in us can make us perfect in conscience], since they relate only to food and drink [offerings is the context] and various washings, regulations [rules, laws] for the body [not the spirit] imposed *until* a time of reformation."

Verse 11 shows the time of reformation referred to is Christ's coming as atoning sacrifice and High Priest. We have seen that He did not do away with the commandments of the First Testament (Mat. 5:17-19). But we can obviously see that the laws of Hebrews 8:10 – Old Covenant laws written in our hearts under the New Covenant – do not include the ceremonial laws. The ritual laws dealing with the temporary tabernacle and subsequent temple were *temporary.*

After all, under the New Covenant we *are* the temple of God. Jesus "tabernacles" with us and in us. Temple rituals are no longer necessary in Christ. Paul showed they are not *sin*, per se, in performing a Nazarite temple vow (Acts 18:18).

But they are not necessary.

What *is* necessary is to become like our Father in heaven, to be holy like Him. The weekly and annual holy days of God, a complete list of which is given in Leviticus 23, are all important days commanded by God to enable us to be holy as He is holy. Nowhere in the Word, contrary to the teaching of some Sabbath keeping churches, does God call ceremonial any of the days He declares to be holy, whether they are weekly or annual holy days. Even the weekly Sabbath involves some form of ceremony, but that does not make it ceremonial and thus expendable. The holy days are statutes that fall under the moral law of the fourth commandment. We don't choose; God decrees what is holy. The Day of Atonement, for instance, is called a "sabbath" and involves a "*holy* convocation" (Lev. 23:27,32). We will explore this in depth in the sequel.

God tells us, "Pursue peace with all men, and the sanctification [holiness] without which no one will see [Jesus]" (Heb. 12:14). And Jesus said, "Therefore you are to be perfect, as your heavenly Father is perfect" (Mat. 5:48). That's a tall call. And that's why God created the Sabbath. It's the day we learn to be like Him. We grow into His perfection.

The Holy Day for Perfecting the Holy Ones

The moral laws of God are permanent, not temporary. Jesus lived them perfectly and He *commands* ***us*** to be ***perfect*** by His power in us (Mat. 5:48; Phil. 2:13).

God has been patient in regards to the church's disobedience to the fourth commandment because we have been sincerely deceived. I myself kept Sunday until I discovered the Sabbath at age 16. Like many of the teens reading this book, I realized pastors had lied to me about this Sunday business. I hope these young people will have the grace to forgive those who lied to them as I was able to do.

It was by the grace of God that I found out about the Sabbath and the wonderful blessing it has been in my life. I never considered myself in bondage to it, although I believe God has rid me of its legalistic observance.

Powerful men and women of God have lived and died without knowing about the Sabbath. It was not required for their *salvation.* It is required, however, for ***perfection.*** But alas, sometimes legalistic or cultic Sabbath keepers are much farther from perfection in other ways than some Christians who are mightily walking in the Spirit. Their imperfection does not minimize the importance God places on His holy day.

The day is fast coming when God will reveal clearly to all Christians the importance of keeping His day holy. When the Holy Spirit reveals this truth to them, they will then be responsible for walking in obedience to it. It will prove to be a crucial test for Christians in these last days. Jesus' bride must be without spot – holy.

The Quest for Holiness

We applaud the emphasis some Christians are putting on holiness -- not the exaggerated, legalistic holiness, majoring on externals that some have espoused. We refer to an emphasis on obedience from the heart. Holiness is Torah teaching as well as an important emphasis under the New Covenant, and the Sabbath is a means to that end.

A most eloquent expression of the emphasis on holiness is John Bevere's book, *A Heart Ablaze*. While not agreeing with every word, we applaud Bevere's courage in explaining the true meaning of grace.

It is encouraging to see Spirit-filled men and women of God emphasize God's holiness and the importance He places on us walking in holiness. Joy Dawson's little book *Intimate Friendship with God,* is a powerful portrayal of the proper reverence for God and obedience to Him.

It is also heartening to hear from Christians who do not fall into the trap of the heresy that says the law is done away. Without realizing the full implication of their emphasis, many influential Christians are teaching and elevating the Ten Commandments.

Kenneth Copeland has emphasized that God gave all the Ten Commandments to us out of His profound love for us – to protect us from harm. He heard this from the Holy Spirit: "My commandments are love letters from heaven to you."[1] Sin and other "blessing-blockers" keep us from God's blessings. Copeland realizes that the commandments Jesus said to keep if we wanted to abide in His love include the Ten Commandments.

He writes: "Keeping God's commands is not difficult for us because sin no longer has dominion over us. We have been completely set free from it by the abounding grace of God!" He also says that "the commandments are not harsh and heavy burdens that are impossible to bear. They are wonderful and precious guidelines from God…." He explains that the commandments show us how to stay close to God. What better way to stay close to Jesus than to meet with Him on His day?

It won't be long before some anointed men and women of God realize that the Sabbath is as much New Covenant as it was Old Covenant.

1 Quoted from article, "Love Letters from Heaven," *Believer's Voice of Victory* magazine, May 2004.

Who is Our Shepherd?

Jesus is the Good Shepherd (*Yehovah Raah* or *Ro'i*) who rests His flock (Jer. 31:10; 33:12). He does that on the Sabbath. *Raah* is connected to the word for friend. Jesus said: "You are My friends if you do what I command you" (John 15:14). The shepherd always rests with his flock and they rest with him. Do you rest with the Shepherd or with the enemy? Jesus keeps His flock by sitting down to rest with them at the time He appoints. What a sad thing to see a modern flock who tells their Shepherd when *they* want to rest, refusing to be led by the Good Shepherd! They even contradict one of their favorite verses, one of the few in the "Old Testament" they accept, Psalm 23.

"I shall not want" cannot have its true fulfillment for them, because they do not keep the day of manna provision of *Yehovah Yireh*, Our Provider and *El Shaddai*, the All-sufficient One. They let Satan lead them into a day of restlessness. They do not allow Jesus our Peace (*Yehovah Shalom*) to make them lie down in green pastures of *Shabbat shalom*. The waters are troubled, not quiet. Sunday churchgoers miss out on the peaceful anointing of the Holy Spirit on the Sabbath day. They don't allow Jesus to restore their souls on the day of restoration, picturing the millennial "restoration of all things" (Acts 3:21).

"He restores our soul" in a special way each Sabbath. The word "restore" here comes from the same root as *Shabbat*, the root *shoov*, meaning to return or repent. The letters of *Shabbat* picture a return to the covenant of the cross, laying down on Jesus' cross our weekly cares so *Yeshua Rapha* can restore and heal us.

Satan is guiding the Sunday crowd, sincerely deceived, into paths of unrighteousness, of disobedience to God's laws of love, for *his* name's sake and for the sake of the name of the "lord" Baal. They are unwittingly keeping the days of Baal and thus honoring his name, not the name of Jesus, the Divine Master of the Sabbath and *Yehovah Tsidkenu*, our Righteousness.

Today's Sunday-keepers go through many a valley of the shadow of death, being only partially protected within the boundaries of ten laws of love. They fear evil because they are not keeping the day of love, opening a door for Satan to fill them with the spirits of religiosity and doubt. They often feel Jesus is not with them because they are not meeting with Him when He convokes them. While He is always with us, always there for us as evidenced in His name *Yehovah Shammah*, He gathers His sheep for special nourishment on the Sabbath.

Those who do not meet with the Shepherd on His day do not have access to the rod of Jesus since He gives it out on the Day of Trumpets they disdain as Jewish. They prefer the staff of betrayal wielded by the religious leader of a great false church and its protesting daughters (Isa. 14:5). They cannot wield full Kingdom authority with King Jesus because they don't keep Dominion Day.

They miss out on their table of provision in the presence of their enemies. The enemy has triumphed over them by convincing them that the day that symbolizes and confirms his defeat is not really important to keep. They prevent Jesus from fully performing His role as *Yehovah Nissi*, our Banner around whom we rally and in whom we take refuge.

The Bible calls Jesus our Ensign or Standard, giving us identity in face of the foe. In fact, Jesus is our Sabbath, and the day He calls the Sabbath establishes our identity in Him (Ex. 31:13).

Sunday worshippers miss out on the Sabbath anointing oil, the fresh oil spoken of in the Sabbath psalm (Ps. 92:10). They only receive a dab of the soothing oil of the Comforter, the Holy Spirit that He pours out abundantly when His people meet in unity with the High Priest (Ps. 133:1-3). Oil is often applied for physical, emotional, and spiritual healing. Our Shepherd and Healer *Yehovah Rapha* anoints hurting sheep for healing on the Sabbath.

Those who persist in Sunday keeping once they see its falseness cannot know the fullness of God's loving kindness because they will be spurning the day into which Love pours Himself. And if they persist in their disobedience with full knowledge, they will not dwell in the house of the Eternal forever (an extremely small minority will be in this category because of God's abundant mercy). Those who keep His covenant will always know Jesus as *Yehovah Shammah* and *El Olam*, the Everlasting God.

The last two phrases can also mean in Hebrew that Jesus is relentless in His love for sheep that are not walking fully in His love. He pursues them as a hunter his prey with His unfailing love until they return (the word "dwell" actually comes from *shoov* or return) to His covenant of love. That covenant is based on the Sabbath, the day in which He pours out His love more than on any other day.

Most of Jesus' sheep today have gone astray from the Shepherd's love poured out on the Sabbath. They have strayed by deception. But Jesus wants them -- He wants you -- to *Shabbat*. He wants you to return to the covenant of the cross. He wants to take your burdens with which you are "heavy laden" and put them on His cross, laying them at the feet of your Burden-bearer, your Shepherd who binds up your wounds.

Jesus understands why we have been sincerely misled and missed His Sabbath rest. He is meek and gentle and patiently beckons beleaguered believers to come and rest in Him on His day (Mat. 11:28-30). Will we hear His voice?

Are we hearing the voice of the Good Shepherd who wants us to lie down with Him in green pastures of Sabbath rest reserved for His people (Heb. 4:9)? Or are we listening to a thief and a robber who wants to deprive us of the abundant life Jesus has for us (John 10:7-10)? It's not too late to forsake tired tradition for what Jesus offers: "I came that they may have *and* enjoy life, and have it in abundance (to the full, till it overflows)" (John 10:10, AMP.)

Sabbath *Selah's*
Decalogue Destruction? Doing Away with Love? Why Forget the Only Commandment God Said to Remember?

Do *not* think that I came to *abolish* [Webster: do away with wholly; annul; destroy completely] the Law or the Prophets; I did not come to abolish but to fulfill [complete; fill to the full]...Whoever then annuls one of the *least* of these commandments, and teaches others to do the same, shall be called least in the kingdom of heaven; but whoever *keeps* and teaches them, he shall be called great in the kingdom of heaven (Mat. 5:17,19).

I shall delight in Your commandments, Which I love. And I shall lift up my hands to Your commandments, which I love...O how I love Your law! ... I do *not forget* Your commandments (Ps. 119:47-48,97,176).

And I commanded them to respect the Sabbath as a way of showing that they were holy and belonged to me. But the Israelites rebelled...They refused to obey my laws and teachings, and they treated the Sabbath like any other day...I told them to respect my Sabbath to show that they were my people and that I was the [Eternal] their God... They refused to obey my laws and teachings, and they treated the Sabbath as any other day... (Ezek. 20:12-13,20-21, CEV)

Remember the sabbath day, to keep it holy (Ex. 20:8).

Is the Sabbath commandment one of the least *of the commandments? No! It's one of the Big Ten. Whatever the word "fulfill" may mean, it cannot signify "abolish." The Law is love (I John 5:3). Has love been abolished? If we are to keep and teach even the least of the commandments, we are surely called by Jesus to keep and teach the fourth commandment of the ten. Why has the church not done this? We have instead distorted the Word of God (Jer. 23:36; II Cor. 4:2; II Pet. 3:16, all NIV). Strange, isn't it? We have forgotten the only commandment God said to remember. Selah.*

CHAPTER NINE

Only Nine Commandments?

The *Spirit Filled Life Bible* has an interesting note on Exodus 20. "These 10 **words** [emphasis in Bible notes] (the Ten Commandments) are absolute law, principles that are all-encompassing and allow for ***no exception*** [emphasis ours]. Jesus confirms their ***timeless application*** [emphasis ours] (Mat. 5:21-37)." The editors of this version believe, then, that the Ten Commandments – with no exception – are thus valid under the New Covenant.

But there's a twist. The note on the verse stating the Sabbath commandment is as follows: "…One who is in a covenantal position with God is to stop his everyday activities of life and honor God with rest every seventh day." The phrase "every seventh day" gives leeway to ignore the command to keep ***the*** seventh day. Is that not an exception? The "timeless application" of the Ten Commandments seems to be limited to only ***nine*** of the Ten Commandments.

While some lambaste a certain church that has conveniently eliminated the second commandment against using images in worship [which they do use] and has artificially broken up the tenth into two arbitrary parts to retain the number ten, some of them do the same. Being sincerely deceived for the most part, they deny the clear meaning of the wording of the fourth commandment and thus do not obey it.

If you're going to take it – take it like it is. Take it like God says it. Unlike me, God needs no editing. And I'm sure He doesn't appreciate it. After all, the seventh day is holy to Him. He is sad to see us depriving ourselves of the special blessing of His presence on His day. Nine out of ten sounds good in baseball. That's a .900 bating average. But when it comes to the Ten Commandments, nine out of ten is not perfection. You miss the blessing. And you miss the training in holiness this holy day provides.

Two Errors: "All Nine" or "None"

We can readily see the error of those who preach, in effect, "*all nine commandments.*" Perhaps they mixed up one of God's numbers of completion with the expression, "the whole nine yards." No one knows for sure where this term came from, but two possibilities fit well with this discussion -- the length of a hangman's noose and the size of a double grave at the time of Henry VIII. Both meanings are about death, and that's what will eventually happen in a spiritual sense to those who, once enlightened about the Sabbath commandment, keep only nine of the Big Ten. The wages of sin is death (Rom. 6:23). Sin is breaking the law (I John 3:4) and if we break one point of the law, we break all (James 2:10).

The "all nine commandments" heresy gives us the result of the above definitions of "the whole nine yards." Death. Those who cling to this excuse may not admit it yet, but they are rendering void the commandment of God by their worship of tradition. In effect, they put the word of a worldly emperor before the Word of God. At best, they have swallowed Satan's lie that Jesus was resurrected on Sunday morning and we should thus keep that day.

Those, on the other hand, who say the Ten Commandments were Old Covenant laws that are not binding on us today are equally wrong. If the Ten Commandments are not binding on Christians today, then I can pull out a gun and shoot their heads off! And that is *not* a silly argument. If I don't have to obey the fourth commandment, then I don't have to obey the sixth – against murder. Why would the word "binding" be different for the fourth commandment than for the sixth? Binding means binding.

The commandments against murder and adultery are binding on Christians today. Either **all** are binding or all are ***not.*** As one of our former presidents caught in sin, some don't know what the meaning of the word "is" is. And some like to play on words when it comes to the Bible.

God doesn't play around with words. He is not a man that He should lie. He means what He says. And He says – yea, commands -- us Christians today to keep holy the ***seventh day!***

By clever deception Satan has blinded some of the best adult Christian minds in the world to what should be obvious. Satan is clever. He has made it sound intelligent to believe a lie and infantile and naïve to believe the truth.

Letter Versus Spirit

Many Christians, sincerely deceived, led into a ditch by mostly sincere, blinded teachers, believe a strange teaching. They believe God gave ten major laws or commandments in the Old Testament. Then – in the New Testament – this God Who says He never changes took away one and there were only nine. New math? It is strange New Testament math and agrees with neither Testament.

Some believe Jesus came and changed His Father's law. Even if you don't understand the biblical truth that Jesus *was* the God of the First Testament, the Word Who spoke the Ten Commandments, this idea is still illogical. Jesus plainly said He and the Father were one. He said what He spoke was what the Father told Him to speak.

So that leads us to wonder about the Father. Does He play the role in people's minds of a forgetful granddad? Did He forget one of His ten main laws? Would He forget something that important? He counts the number of hairs on our heads and the number of the stars, but He forgets what He says? What kind of absent-minded God is that?

That God doesn't exist. The God of the Bible is a God who means what He says. He says not to murder, which is the strict "letter" of the law. But He also says that under the New Covenant we must not even hate our brother.

This is reminiscent of the expression "going above and beyond the call of duty." The call of duty is the strict minimum requirement. God only punished Old Covenant Israelites for breaking the strict letter of the law. You didn't get stoned to death for hating someone. You had to physically commit murder.

The only exception to the letter-spirit connection of the Ten Commandments – no doubt a foreshadowing of the spiritual expansion of the law in the New Testament – was the tenth commandment against coveting. Coveting is a mental sin. Leaders could only punish Israelites who somehow physically manifested their covetousness. They must have shown their sin by their words or their actions. So even here we see the limited physical obedience to the law by a people who did not have the Holy Spirit to elevate their obedience to a spiritual plane.

Israel only obeyed the letter of the fourth commandment as well. They clearly kept the ***seventh*** day – not Sunday or any other day. Basically, all they did was to stop working and rest. They had not been to the "mountaintop" like Moses. They did not know God intimately. How could they keep the spirit of the law?

Praying, meditating on God's principles and other spiritual activities were not in their limited paradigm. The Sabbath was a physical blessing to them, but not much of a spiritual blessing. They lacked the Holy Spirit. The spirit of the law thus eluded most of them.

The first four commandments show us how to love and worship God. Many Christians today keep the *spirit* of the fourth commandment. The Holy Spirit inspires them to praise and worship and love God in a beautiful, spiritual way. And God appreciates that. He loves His people, whatever day they keep.

But there's a catch. God cannot ***bless*** them with the special Sabbath blessing. That's all. He loves all His children. But He can't bless them all to the same degree unless they are walking in His perfect will expressed through His perfect law.

We shall put it another way. They are "going above and beyond the call of duty." The problem is: they are ignoring the "call of duty," like those who give offerings but don't pay the tithe God commands. They are students who are doing extra credit assignments – but they are, without realizing it, ignoring their regular, required homework.

They are keeping the advanced spirit of the law without obeying the literal letter of the commandment. It's elementary. We have graduated from high school without going through elementary school. Is that a well-rounded education?

A Golf Analogy

A golf commentator remarked that Tiger Woods had mastered the basics better than any other golfer. Maybe that's why he is so successful.

My basketball coaches always loudly preached, "Fundamentals, fellows, fundamentals!" That's what wins ball games. Players that come up with those "fancy-dancy" plays are almost always those who have mastered the fundamentals of the game.

God the Holy Spirit is a gentle Teacher in this game we call life. He is extremely patient with us. He realizes that other teachers have gotten between Him and us. They have blinded us to certain important fundamentals. They told us it didn't matter to God.

We may have done fairly well without some of the basics. I have seen golfers that simply hit the course with no lessons. They may do fairly well. But when the pro sees their strange grip, he is going to correct it. When the "V's" of the fingers point to the right shoulder, the results are measurably better.

God has a plan. Our Teacher has a master plan that has allowed Satan and the demons to lead the church astray with over 9000 doctrines of demons. One of those is the keeping of God's "Sabbath" on the wrong day and mocking God by keeping Baal's day and calling it "the Lord's Day." We may think we're playing pretty good "Sunday" golf, but when God corrects our "grip" by revealing His Sabbath blessing, our game will shine.

What God Allows

My South Carolina mama would often interrupt our childish fights with this song: "Mama don't 'low no fightin' 'round here. We don't care what Mama don't 'low. We're gonna fight anyhow!" Because of the double message, it didn't always lessen or stop the pandemonium.

The message of church officials has been equally unclear. Most admit that God did command the Sabbath – but only for Israel. And then they take a couple of verses written by the man Peter said was hard to understand and teach that these wipe out all the other words of God. Some have raised clear voices to reveal the Sabbath, but we have preferred to be deceived by the voices of confusion.

God hasn't changed. He still "don't 'low" Sabbath breaking. Oh, He won't – under the covenant of grace – kill you for it as He once did. He "'lows" a lot under the covenant of freedom and grace. He gives us rope to hang ourselves if we like. He allows demons to have sway over His church.

His ways are higher than ours, and without being intimate with Him on His day we will not be able to understand His ways. He has allowed the demon directly under Satan – the spirit of betrayal – to divide the body of Christ and introduce thousands of doctrines of demons. God has even allowed some in His church to preach that a little adultery is okay, that homosexual acts, which break God's sex commandment are alright -- even for pastors.

Has God not "allowed" the world's largest Christian organization, some of whose members are true believers, to pretend the second commandment doesn't exist? Has He not "allowed" Christians to worship TV, ungodly entertainment, smut on the Internet, and commit a myriad of other sins, after having accepted Jesus as their Savior? Has He not allowed pastors to approve the calculated murder of unborn babies? Oh yes, he has. Unbelievers are not the only ones with free will.

Jesus has even allowed deception, numerous false doctrines to invade His body. One of those deceptions is widely accepted. Virtually no one has seen it as a deception. No voice has cried out to correct it – at least in a way that has been heard.

But Isaiah prophesies that voices will indeed cry out (Isa. 58:1). You are hearing one of those voices.

He goes on to describe a people who strangely resemble our modern Christian nations. They seek God and they even fast. They worship God. They go to church. But their lives are full of sin, known and unknown.

It is interesting that the last two verses of this chapter emphasize the great blessing of obeying the fourth commandment. This is an end-time prophecy. The omniscient God knew all along that this would be a problem in the end time. He said that if we kept the Sabbath, we would "delight" in Jesus (58:14).

Satan knows that verse. He doesn't want us to take delight in the Divine Master of the Sabbath. He knows that it would open a door of intimacy that would thwart his plans.

But God has other plans. We don't always understand why He waits. "How long, O [Eternal]?" was David's fervent plea. Jesus has waited 1700 years to make this sin plain.

God's Time to Reveal the Sabbath Has Come

Sin is the breaking of the law (I John 3:4). And Sabbath breaking constitutes the breaking of one of the ten major laws of God.

Why has God waited? Remember that He did make the Sabbath a test commandment for His Old Covenant people. He will again make it a test.

The Holy Spirit's love in us is the proof we are Christians (John 13:35). God does, however, define love and the keeping of the commandments (I John 5:3; Rom. 13:10). The Sabbath is one of His commandments. It is not a casual suggestion. And it is not, as some have falsely portrayed, a Jewish burden. It is a Christian rest – a glorious day of freedom!

Our Instructor – our Teacher in the game of life – is finally going to show us the correct grip. And wow is it going to change our game!

While He may be tougher on the pastors, He will not chide His sheep for their ignorance of His Sabbath. But He will make it clear – in no uncertain terms – that it *is* important to Him. That grip is sacred to Him. He knows it is a must if we are to be ready for the big tournament. The stakes are high.

Once He shows us the grip, and we understand it, our Pro will expect us to put it into practice. It may feel funny at first. When I learned golf at the age of nine, the "Vardon grip" seemed unnatural at first. But the results proved it was the right thing. Now I don't even think about it.

The Sabbath will be a major adjustment for most of us. But when we "get in the swing" of the Sabbath thing, we will begin to reap the bountiful spiritual and physical blessings God has always intended for us. And we won't look back. Our spiritual joy will overflow as we walk in God's perfect will.

It's Jewish!

When we present God's holy law,
And arguments from scripture draw,
Objectors say, to pick a flaw,
'It's Jewish'.
Though at the first Jehovah blessed
And sanctified His day of rest,
The same belief is still expressed,
'It's Jewish'.
Though with the world this rest began,
And thence through all Scriptures ran,
And Jesus said 'twas made for man' -
'It's Jewish'.
Though not with Jewish rites, which passed,
But with the moral law 'twas classed,
Which must exist while time shall last,
'It's Jewish'.
If from the Bible we present
The Sabbath's meaning and intent,
This answers every argument -
'It's Jewish'.
Though the disciples, Luke and Paul,
Continue still this rest to call
The 'Sabbath day', this answers all,
'It's Jewish'.
The gospel teacher's plain expression,
That "Sin is of the law transgression,"
Seems not to make the least impression -
'It's Jewish'.
They love the rest of man's invention,
But if Jehovah's day we mention,
This puts an end to all contention,
'It's Jewish'.
O ye who thus God's day abuse,
Simply because 'twas kept by Jews,
The Saviour, too, you must refuse,
'He's Jewish'.
The Scriptures, then, we may expect
For the same reason you'll reject;

For if you will but recollect,
'They're Jewish'.
Thus the apostles, too, must fall;
For Andrew, Peter, James, and Paul,
Thomas, Matthew, John, and all
'Were Jewish'.
So to your helpless state resign
Yourself in wretchedness to pine;
Salvation, surely you'll decline,
'It's Jewish'.
Author: Unknown

Sabbath *Selah's*
Far More Righteous than the Pharisees

For I say to you that unless your righteousness surpasses that of the scribes and Pharisees, you will not enter the Kingdom of heaven (Mat. 5:20).

Therefore you are to be perfect, as your heavenly Father is perfect (Mat. 5:48).

The Pharisees kept the Sabbath. While they obeyed legalistically and self-righteously, we are to keep both the letter and spirit of this law. We can only do that by the empowering grace God offers under the New Covenant. Selah.

CHAPTER TEN

The Sabbath Under "Grace"

The Sabbath is not a burden. It's the day for laying down burdens, including legalism. It is a day of rest, rejuvenation, refreshing, intimacy with God – a day of celebration!

We are not "under the law." We are keeping a Sabbath of "grace." The Sabbath is a gift of God to man. He made it for all time.

We chose initially to put the word "grace" in quotes, since it is such a misunderstood term and is used with such gratuitous abandon. The Greek word for grace – *charis* -- is also the word for gift. The Sabbath represents grace – both in the way we receive it from God as His gift to us, and in the way we keep it. The New Covenant Sabbath is a graceful observance. The Holy Spirit inspires us to emphasize what we *can* do to enjoy our God and our family – not what we *can't* do. A legalistic mindset can make anything a burden. But that is not what God intended the Sabbath to be.

God's grace is not only unmerited pardon. It is His unmerited favor. It is most importantly His ***enabling power*** to do for and in us what we cannot do of ourselves. It is Jesus' righteousness in us (II Cor. 5:21, Phil. 1:11, Gal. 2:20). Does His righteousness in us exclude the fourth commandment? Of course not.

Greasy Kid Stuff?

Christians misunderstand grace. Greasy grace is kid stuff! Years ago a hair cream ad claimed that "a little dab'll do ya." When it comes to greasy grace, a little dab'll kill ya! Grace is not license to disobey God. The "Second Testament" condemns those who turn grace into license. Those who say the law is done away are – probably unwittingly – doing just that!

Most are unaware that there are 25 different graces in the Bible. One of them is the grace to obey God's law. We can't do it ourselves. Legalists have proved it! It is Jesus' righteousness in us that enables us to obey.

Obey what? Some vague "lovey-dovey"idea? We have seen numerous Second Testament passages that repeatedly say we are to obey the laws of God. And they are not some laws that are different from the moral law expounded in the Hebrew Scriptures.

What we have is the same basic law, only expanded to show what God expects of a Christian filled with the Holy Spirit. The Holy Spirit writes the law on the *heart* of a Christian. Now that's grace!

Except for a few of the leaders and prophets in the First Testament, the only place the law was written was on stone. The problem was this: the law was on stone and the people's hearts were "made of stone." Their hard, Spirit-void hearts would not allow God's good law to be written on them.

Why is the law labeled the "bad guy?" It was the people!

God's Grace

In Titus 2:11-12, we see only two of the 25 graces in the Bible. But these two are enough to show that grace involves obedience to God's law. God tells us to deny ungodliness.

What is ungodliness? Sin, of course. Breaking His holy law. Jesus redeems us from "every lawless deed" (Titus 2:14). So *grace* teaches us to ***obey God's law!***

But not by legalism! It is not our human adherence to the law that makes us holy. It is the holy God inside us who makes us holy. But the standard of holiness does not change because grace enters the scene. The standard of holiness is ***the law!***

Many disagree. Most who do agree with this teaching on holiness believe for some strange reason that it excludes one of the Ten Commandments. In their view "law" is a good word. "Sabbath" is the bad one.

When Paul used the phrase "under the law," he was talking to hardheaded, small-minded legalists who wanted to *earn* salvation by law keeping. The law – not the blood of Jesus – was their pathway to the Kingdom of God. They sought to be justified – made right with God – by their human, fleshly efforts to keep the holy law of God.

That's impossible! Only the blood of Jesus gives us forgiveness of our sins and salvation. But we must not only accept His sacrifice; we must let Him live in us. Romans 5:10 says we are reconciled to God by His blood, but "we *shall* be saved by His *life*."

Holiness by Grace

How can we keep the holy law of a holy God unless He *makes* us holy? By grace He put Jesus in us through the Holy Spirit. We are called saints – holy ones. Why? Because the Holy One lives in us. Our spirits are perfectly holy. It takes time for the soul – the mind, emotions and will – to catch on to the miraculous change in us.

That process is called sanctification. In the realm of the spirit, it's a done deal. In the soul realm, it's a process. It's the process of being sanctified, which simply means to be or become holy.

How can a Christian be wholly sanctified if he or she is not keeping God's holy day holy? Of all people, the saints or holy ones are supposed to be respecting what God says is holy.

The book of Hebrews, which clearly refers to the holy Sabbath in chapter 4, talks a lot about holiness: "Pursue peace with all people, and ***holiness*** (also translated *sanctification*), without which no one will see [Jesus]" (Heb. 12:14, NKJV).

Holiness obviously involves getting rid of sin. And since sin is the transgression of the *law*, one thing should be perfectly clear: God wants us to *keep His law perfectly*. Our target? Perfect holiness. Nothing less. We didn't write it: "Therefore you are to be perfect … (Mat. 5:48). And what defines perfection – God's holy character? It may have become a bad word in many Christian circles, but the answer is: *God's law!*

While keeping the law may sometimes involve legalism, legalism does not equal obedience to the law. I know what a legalist is, because I once was one. Coming into grace does *not* mean coming out of law. It means coming out of *legalism.* Legalism is the name of a group of demons. God's law is love (Rom. 13:10; I John 5:3).

In general terms, legalism is keeping the law by human effort and for all the wrong reasons. *Righteousness*, on the other hand – the New Covenant, Spirit-empowered kind of righteousness – has a different flavor and motivation. Its source is not human strength. It is – and this is not an oxymoron – ***law keeping by* grace!**

"See to it that no one comes short of the *grace* of God; that no root of bitterness springing up causes trouble, and by it many be defiled" (Heb. 12:15). What is bitterness? It is sin.

Is this a lawless grace? No! This verse says we *fall short* of the *grace* of God when we sin – when we ***break God's law!***

Some few see this as plain as day – unless, of course, you include in the discussion the *Sabbath* day. Somehow that's different.

Five is the biblical number of grace. The number 25 is 5 times 5, the perfection of grace. Without the Sabbath, we cannot attain to that grace of perfection. Our Father is the Giver of every perfect gift, and He only invites us into His intimacy on His day of love and grace.

We hope the 25 chapters in this book will bring you all of God's Sabbath graces. They are followed by a summary of this truth in the Appendix, "The Sabbath in a Nutshell."

It is so simple when God opens your mind to this understanding. Yet many sincere Christians have been blinded, like I was at one time, from seeing this truth. I was, and some of you are now, closed in a nutshell of weak excuses. Although we will not call them "nutty" in a demeaning way, they are without a doubt hard to crack. While they may not sound "nutty" to those who sincerely believe them, I believe when the nutshell of deception is cracked you will see how unfounded they are.

Because we know you are sincere people who, for the most part, want to obey the truth when you see it, these questions deserve an answer. I realize my words have been strong, perhaps too strong for some of you. If I have missed the mark in any way in endeavoring to correct in love rather than in mean-spirited condemnation, please forgive me. I am also in a learning process and have much to learn in presenting the firm truths God has mercifully given me. I believe, however, that once God has helped you study this material, you will be as convinced as I am of these truths.

God has blessed me by cracking my nutshell. I believe that when you peer out of your nutshell, you will also begin to hate the lies of Satan. He has used these excuses to keep us from the day that will bless us and destroy him. If you read the next chapter with an open mind, guided by the Holy Spirit and God's Word, I believe God can crack the hard nutshell of excuses. He did it for me. Twice. Once at the age of 16 and once again after allowing myself to be deceived after many years of keeping God's Sabbath.

When God enables us to crack the nutshell and thus crack the code that has hidden the Bible from our understanding, we will be able to do more than explain to ourselves the Sabbath in the proverbial nutshell or in succinct format. Keeping the day of Love will open up the Book of Love to us.

Paul's words will come alive to us: "…so that Christ may dwell in your hearts through faith. And I pray that you, being rooted and established in love, may have power, together with all the saints, to grasp how wide and long and high and deep is the love of Christ, and to know this love that surpasses knowledge—that you may be filled to the measure of all the fullness of God" (Eph. 3:17-19, NIV).

Receive all of His graces. Receive Him on His Sabbath day.

"Jewish"? So Are You!

"Those Sabbaths and feast days were for Israel," goes the argument. "The Old Testament may say that they were to be kept forever, but not by us Gentiles!"

These people don't believe Jesus meant what He said when He declared the Sabbath was made for man, not merely for the Jew (Mark 2:27-28). Fact is, Jesus gave it to Adam as a blessing for all mankind, and He never revokes a blessing (Rom. 11:29).

Besides refusing to believe the Bible, Gentile Christians go even further by denying their identity. In the very epistle that is supposed to do away with "all those Jewish days," God calls New Covenant believers the "Israel of God" (Gal. 6:16). Paul's letter even says Gentile believers are "Abraham's descendants," declaring that there is "neither Jew nor Greek...for you are all one in Christ Jesus" (Gal. 3:28-29).

God expects true believers to put their spirit man first, to recognize on a daily basis that they are sitting in the heavenlies with Jesus (Eph. 2:6; Col. 3:1; Phil. 3:20-21). Gentiles in the flesh are not to think in the flesh but in the spirit (Gal. 5:16). God expects them to accept their true spiritual identity. The name Israel means "believers," yet most believers today deny their identity as Israel. Whether or not they are physically Israelite is immaterial. If they would dwell with Jesus in heaven in their spirit man, putting the spirit above the flesh, they would automatically put the accent on their true identity.

How can they see their spiritual identity as Israelites if they hate everything Jewish? Demeaning God's commanded days as Jewish undermines the true identity of these physically Gentile Christians.

Most Christians have never thought their belief system through to its obvious conclusion. God commanded the Sabbath, holy days, and new moons "forever," to be "a perpetual statute throughout your (Israel's or the believers') generations" (Lev. 23:41), "required forever in Israel" (II Chron. 2:4).

Do you realize what this means? It means that Jews who become Christians are still required by God to keep these commandments and statutes. That is exactly what 99% of the church did for a number of decades, since only about 1% of the early church was physically Gentile. In fact, in the early church, 100% of the church, Jew and Gentile, kept the Sabbath, holy days, and new moons.

But what is the ultimate implication? It's a matter of unity versus division. God has never changed. He said He is One (Deut. 6:4). Jesus, the Father and the Holy Spirit are One, and Jesus' last prayer with His disciples was a fervent request of His Father that the believers of all time be one, perfectly united with Him and His Father (John 17:21). Paul emphasized that the need to be of "one faith, " attaining "to the unity of the faith" (Eph. 4:5,13), and he exhorted the church at Corinth "that you all agree and that there be no divisions among you, but that you be made complete in the same mind and in the same judgment" (I Cor. 1:10). Paul commanded the same church to celebrate the Feast of Unleavened Bread (I Cor. 5:8)!

How's that for a switch? Today most churches are united in one area: they keep Sunday and the traditional feast days found nowhere in the Bible, but they neglect to keep the days Paul kept and commanded. You can't call that the "unity of the faith." It is a unity in disobedience, albeit for the most part in ignorance.

How, pray tell, can we reconcile a God who never changes (Heb. 13:8) and wants His people to be one, perfect in unity, commanding converted Jews to keep the Sabbath days and telling the Gentile believers they should keep Sunday? Our God is not an old "fuddy-duddy," distracted and forgetful. He is definitely not a double-minded fool!

Jesus came to break down the barrier between Jew and Gentile. Imagine one local church pastor telling his congregation of Jewish and Gentile believers: "You Jews must keep the Sabbath, but you Gentiles should worship on Sunday." So you have one group that meets on Saturday and the other on Sunday. Is that unity? Is that what God intended? How could He command converted Jews to keep His Sabbath days "forever" and yet encourage the Gentile believers to be in total disunity with those Jewish believers?

The church began with power because they were all together in one accord in one place! And it was on the Feast of First Fruits commanded in Leviticus 23 to be kept forever. Yes, it was observed on a Sunday, but not because it was Sunday. It was one of God's annual holy days, made holy like the weekly Sabbath.

Did Jesus teach these disciples incorrectly? Did they somehow miss His new law that said we could keep pagan days and call them Christian? Of course not. Jesus kept the Sabbath, and John tells us to live as He did (I John 2:6). John "walked the walk." He kept the Sabbath days and, as history confirms, taught his disciple Polycarp to do the same.

So who's out of step with Jesus? Who is missing the unity of the true faith "once delivered" to the saints (Jude 3, KJV)? The 120 disciples who came together as one to keep one of God's holy days were "contend[ing] earnestly for the faith which was once for all handed down to the saints." They kept the faith "once delivered," and God delivered. Power came down in fulfillment of a prophecy for *Israel*, showing clearly again that Israel was no longer only a physical entity but a spiritual nation called the church of God (Joel 2:27-28; Acts 2:17). The blessings of physical Israel would now be poured out in abundance upon spiritual Israel, and one of those blessings was the Sabbath.

God always intended for Gentiles to follow Israel's example in keeping His commandments and statutes (Deut. 4:6-8). The Gentiles among the "mixed multitude" that came out of Egypt with Israel were encouraged to keep the Passover exactly like the true-blood Israelites (Ex. 12:48-49). In a prophecy for these last days, we see that God praises the "foreigner who has joined himself to [Jesus]" for keeping the Sabbath and for holding fast to the Sabbath covenant by refusing to profane it (Isa. 56:1-6). In verse 2 God calls Sabbath breaking evil -- a sin. Does God believe Israelite believers should not sin but Gentile Christians can sin every week without consequence?

In comparing Gentile believers to the branches of the olive tree that was Israel, Paul says they "became partaker with them [the physical Israelites] of the rich root of the olive tree" (Rom. 11:17). What a beautiful way to describe the powerful and anointed Hebrew roots of the New Covenant church! Those roots are indeed rich and full of Holy Spirit oil. What a shame that Gentile believers pay little more than lip service to those Jewish roots!

While many demean and undermine God's holy Sabbaths as Jewish, as if Jewish was a bad word, the truth is quite the opposite. If you are a physical Gentile who has accepted Jesus, you are -- in a spiritual sense -- a Jew! Numerous passages make that clear (Rom. 2:28-29; Eph. 2:12-13,19). What can the church achieve without the foundation of Hebrew roots (Ps. 11:3)? The first or Sabbath covenant is the root that opens the door to all ten covenants of God.

The word picture painted by the letters of the Hebrew word *Shabbat* is: "return to the covenant or cross." Return also means to repent. It is high time the church repented of breaking the first covenant God made with man. Returning to its Hebrew roots will cause the tree that is spiritual Israel to flourish.

If you are one who has demeaned God's holy days as Jewish, you are in for a surprise. Yes, the roots of the Christian church are Jewish, and *so are you*!

Sabbath *Selah's*
Has the Earth Passed Away -- and Winter Been Cancelled?

For truly I say to you, until heaven and earth pass away, not the smallest letter or stroke shall pass from the Law until all is accomplished (Mat. 5:18).

But pray that your flight will not be in the winter, or on a Sabbath (Mat. 24:20).

Last time I checked, heaven and earth had not passed away. All has definitely not been accomplished yet. Jesus came to be a sacrifice for us, so animal sacrifices are no longer necessary. The Holy Spirit came down to sanctify us, so believers no longer need to go through a tiresome ritual of washings (Heb. 9:8-15). Since the Sabbath is only ultimately fulfilled in our eternal rest with Jesus, it is decidedly not done away. Furthermore, Jesus' prophecy and warning to believers regarding fleeing in winter or on the Sabbath is indisputably situated in an end-time context (Mat. 24:20-22). If we believe the Sabbath is done away today, we must also believe winter is done away! Here in Canada we know better. Selah.

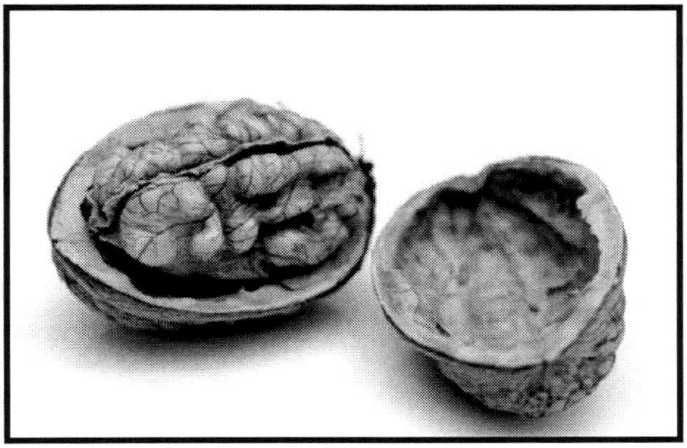

CHAPTER ELEVEN

Answers to "Nutty" Excuses in a Nutshell

Today as I was walking I encountered a mother and her three-year-old child. The little boy was fascinated by tracks he saw in the snow. "Look, Mommy," he said, "Look at these camel tracks in the snow!" The mother looked at me and said, "Oh, I'm sure there are lots of camels around today."

I think we would question any adult who would seriously say they saw camel tracks in the snow today. It is far-fetched. Yet some of the excuses people give for not keeping the Sabbath are just as concocted.

Sometimes the excuses are innocent, like my young son's excuse for having difficulty as I tried to teach him to swim at the local pool. I had told him how I had learned from the age of three. "But Daddy," he said, "you must have learned in different water!"

Other excuses are not so innocent. You may have heard the actual list of excuses for accidents compiled by the insurance companies. I remember one of them that stood out: "I was driving my car along minding my own business when out of nowhere a tree jumped out and hit my car!"

Some of the excuses for not keeping the Sabbath seem just as strange. The under*lying* thread (with the emphasis on "lying") for most of the following excuses is human reasoning. Whether logical or illogical, God says we are to live by what His Word says – not by what our minds conjure up, what men say about the Bible, what tradition has given us, or what demons have inspired. Here is a list of some common objections to keeping the Sabbath, although I'm sure vivid human imaginations could come up with many others – equally as unfounded.

We will consider the main excuses here, considering the ones that require more complete explanations in the later chapters. But first, a personal confession.

True Confessions: I Swallowed the Lies Too

Ever read the Bible and have a sentence or a word jump out of the Book and hit you in the face? Last night before going to bed I opened the Bible and it opened to Nehemiah 9. Staring at me were two verses I had encircled in my most righteous red pencil. Let's look at them: "Then You came down on Mount Sinai, And spoke with them from heaven; You gave them just ordinances and true laws, Good statutes and commandments. So You made known to them Your holy sabbath, And laid down for them commandments, statutes and law, Through Your servant Moses" (Neh. 9:13-14).

In the next chapter we prove from the Bible that the One who ***spoke*** from Sinai was not the Father. It was "the ***Word*** (John 1:1-18) who spoke. It was Jesus. He is the Word. These were *Jesus'* laws given *through* Moses – not Moses' laws. And notice that all the laws He gave at Sinai were called ***good***. And what was the only law these Levites who were speaking here mentioned? They mentioned the first biblical covenant and the centerpiece of the Ten Commandments – the ***Sabbath***. And surprise, surprise to the Christian world -- the Sabbath is called ***good***. Why do they call it bad – Jewish, legalistic, a burden?

The Sabbath is good. God said it, but do we believe it? In Nehemiah's time the people were all excited about the Sabbath and the feasts. They had just rediscovered the book of the law that Ezra read to them on Trumpets. They had joyously kept the whole Feast of Tabernacles. Ezra read every day during this feast to them from the book of the law. Two days after Tabernacles they kept a fast in which they confessed their sins and rededicated themselves to God – and they worshipped. The Levites stood before the people and recounted the history of Israel and how great God had been for His people. They spoke of their rebellion, how they cast God's law behind their backs, how God had to deliver them into the hand of their oppressors.

I couldn't help but think of God's mercy to me as I turned my back to Him, initially in unforgiveness and then progressively compromising on all kinds of things in my life. I would like to be able to say that I have believed in the importance of the Sabbath and kept it faithfully since I discovered it forty years ago. But I would be lying. For a short time I swallowed the lies.

Adversity, fear and deception came upon me and I began to lie to myself. It was a comfortable lie. It was Galatians and a faulty teaching about the understanding of the New Covenant, how we were free now, no longer slaves like Hagar referring to Mt. Sinai, but free people like Isaac, children of the promise. It was a clever argument, and I swallowed it.

Believing that the church had deceived me about the Sabbath, I became disgruntled with their teachings, even though many of them had been correct. I felt betrayed. The legalism to which this church had been in bondage now colored my view of the Sabbath. What God called good I began to call evil, or at least I began to feel that Sabbath keeping wasn't necessary. "It's not a sin to keep it," I thought and spoke.

Turning My Back on Father Love

What a deceptive twist! Satan had duped me into abandoning the day of Love. How could these words have come out of my mouth? Not a sin to keep the Sabbath? What a switcheroo from the slithering serpent! I had proved to myself in 1967 that the Sabbath was indeed one of the Ten Commandments, and that *not* keeping it was sin. As a person who formerly kept the Sabbath and ceased doing so, I became one of the hardest people to convince that the Sabbath was still a requirement of God as are all the other commandments of Love. The conviction and repentance that ensued had to be a work of the Holy Spirit.

I had abandoned the day of Love, the day into which Jesus poured Himself by blessing it, the day my Father Love invited me to sit on His lap in intimacy and "love on me." Thereafter I had a hard time believing that My Father in heaven loved me. I would not accept His love. Why? Turning my back on His day of love meant turning my back on His love for me. Not realizing it at the time, I had turned my back on my Father Love.

This pastor repented and, as the Hebrew word picture in *Shabbat* indicates, returned to the cross or covenant, the very first covenant of Love. While I first saw it as a day of New Covenant celebration, I begin to see how important it was to obey the fourth commandment, since God had given me the knowledge of the Sabbath day. That phrase Jesus spoke in John 14:15 about proving my love for Him began to resound in my heart.

I realized that blending in with the churches that for the most part sincerely believe the teachings of the First Testament are not necessary today was not obeying Jesus. Out of fear of rejection, I was trying to please all the wrong people.

Similarly to many of you pastors who read this, I was more concerned about what ***people*** thought than about what God thought. I chose a lie. I chose death – not life. Sunday is the day of death, the day of the god of death, Satan. The Sabbath is the day of Jesus, the Giver of Life. Life and love and freedom abound in the day that the Christian world calls slavery. The Sabbath is the day of freedom!

But it is only the truth that can set us free -- free from the falseness that locks the Book of love and freedom so that it remains a coded Book for us. So here they are, some odds and ends, odd arguments, and excuses ended by truth:

1. *"The Sabbath is Jewish – it's for the Jews. We're Gentiles and we're Christians. Our day is Sunday."* Was Adam a Jew? No. The term Jew comes from Judah, a son of Jacob. Jesus gave the Sabbath to Adam, blessing it and making it holy (Gen. 2:3). He made it for all mankind, to be kept by Gentiles (Mark 2:27-28) – not just the Jew. Jesus will require all mankind to keep it in the Millennium (Isa. 66:23). Isaiah 56 is an end-time prophecy, and God clearly says in this chapter that non-Israelites should keep the Sabbath. All Israel's laws were to be an example for the other nations to follow (Deut. 4:6-8), and those Gentiles who became a part of Israel kept the Sabbath as Israel did. Anyone in the camp, Israelite or foreigner, caught working on the Sabbath was to be stoned (Num. 15:32-36). Were Jewish and Gentile Christians to keep a different day, we would be mocking the God who calls us to be one in faith and doctrine (Eph. 4:4-13). No command to keep Sunday is given in the New Testament and no precedent for keeping that day is set. No verse should be twisted to contradict one of the Ten Commandments of God.
2. *"It's impossible to keep! To properly keep it, I would have to turn off my electricity and not even heat up a dish since no fires were allowed."* Like any verse, Exodus 35:3 must be understood in its context. The chapter speaks of the building of the tabernacle. So the people would not build fires for making elements of the tabernacle, God forbade the lighting of fires. The command had to do with work (35: 2), and the work at hand was the building of the tabernacle. He was specifically targeting fires for forging metals. The Holy Spirit guides us in understanding the Bible, but God has also endowed us with common sense, a commodity hermeneutics often throws out the window. Would it not be okay to light a fire to keep warm on a cold winter day? How can the Sabbath be a day of feasting and celebration if you're so legalistic you can't even turn on your stove? God never intended the Sabbath to be a burden. Just as He doesn't want us to spend all day cooking and neglect Him, neither does He want us to be so picky we can't spend a minimum amount of time preparing enjoyable meals. Most of the time-consuming preparations can be done on the preparation day before the Sabbath. God granted more leeway for food preparation on the annual holy days, since they were to be days of special feasting and celebration (Ex. 12:16).
3. "*Why get so bent out of shape by such a little thing? The Sabbath is only a*

detail. It's no big deal which day you keep." If you don't think God honors what He has made holy and expects us to honor it, look at the case of Uzzah (II Sam. 6:6-7). Remember, this was Jesus who dealt with Israel. He had given specific instruction for no human hand to touch the holy ark of God. Good human intentions are not enough. If they cause you to defile what God calls holy, they bring severe consequences. For His spiritual people under the New Covenant, Jesus doesn't dwell on holy objects anymore. He does, however, still hold high in importance His holy time. He also calls us holy as temples of God (I Cor. 3:16-17.) He says, "If any man destroys the temple of God, God will destroy him, for the temple of God is holy, and that is what you are." Sounds like God is still jealous about what is holy – even under the New Covenant. Though it may sound harsh to you, if you know about the Sabbath and continually refuse to keep it holy, God will destroy you. Because we are under the New Covenant administration of the law and not the administration of physical death (II Cor. 3:7-8), the penalty will not be immediate. You will miss out on Sabbath blessings, however, and if you knowingly continue to defile what God deems holy, you will eventually suffer spiritual death, a fate far greater than physical death.

4. *"Sunday-keeping follows the biblical command to give our first fruits to God. I give the first of my week to Him, and He then promises to bless me."* Wait a minute! You're trying to rewrite the Bible! God says in the fourth commandment to rest on the seventh day as He did. Trying to mix in the principle of first fruits is a mixed basket of truth and lies. That's dishonest. Twisting the Word of God reveals a lack of teaching and stability, leading to destruction (II Pet. 3:16).
5. *"Keeping the Sabbath isn't required for salvation, so I'm not keeping it."* Many good Christians who did not understand the importance of keeping the Sabbath have died in their ignorance. Jesus is their merciful Judge. But that doesn't give you an excuse to refuse to examine the evidence for the Sabbath. Jesus is the righteous Judge, and you may be surprised how strictly He judges you who are alive and know about the Sabbath. That doesn't mean you're hellbound if you die today, but it may mean a lesser reward or being resurrected as a physical being after the Millennium to receive the fullness of your salvation. While it is true in principle that Sabbath keeping is required for perfection rather than for salvation, the day is coming, "and behold, now is" for some of you who know the truth, when the Sabbath will be required for salvation. That doesn't mean you earn it -- the blood of Jesus paid for it. But in order to endure to the end to be ultimately saved and gain eternal life, you may literally have to lose your life because of the Sabbath (Mat. 24:13; Rev. 6:9; 12:17; 14:12-13). Why not accept the Sabbath bless-

ing and "escape all these things" (Luke 21:36)?

6. *"If we have to keep the Sabbath, then we have to be circumcised too! Jesus kept the Sabbath and was circumcised because He was a Jew."* Paul disagrees. He said, "Circumcision is nothing, and uncircumcision is nothing, but what matters is the keeping of the commandments of God" (I Cor. 7:19). That includes the fourth! Did Jesus refrain from lusting after women because He was a Jew? Did He refuse to hate and murder because He was a Jew? Physical circumcision has been replaced by the spiritual kind (Rom. 2:29). The Sabbath, although it does picture many things, including the millennial rest, was not replaced by anything. The seventh day of the week is still the seventh day of the week. Jesus is indeed our Sabbath, our Rest, but that does not do away with His commandment to rest on the seventh day. The Sabbath is a moral law. It may be a physical rest, but it is also a spiritual rejuvenation. Circumcision of the flesh is purely physical. It is no longer necessary, except for health reasons. Its importance under the Old Covenant is replaced by its spiritual importance under the New. We are circumcised into Jesus, cutting off the foreskin of the old ways of sin (Col. 2:11). Jesus was indeed circumcised and did all the "Old Testament stuff" Jews did. He was "born under the law" and had to obey all the points of the law He gave Israel, even those He would not require of New Covenant Christians, so He could redeem all Israelites who had failed to keep those laws perfectly in this life. We don't need to wear tassels to remind us that we are God's priests and must obey His laws. The Holy Spirit and our identity in Jesus as kings and priests accomplishes this without a physical reminder. Yet Jesus wore those tassels. He had to obey and then pay for by His death every law Israel broke. While keeping any First Testament ritual is not sin (Acts 18:18), washings and sacrifices have simply been rendered unnecessary because of the coming of the Mediator of a better covenant (Heb. 9:8-14). Jesus' blood and the Holy Spirit whom He sent wash us clean. Food and drink offerings, blood sacrifices of animals and various washings were imposed upon a physical people to prophesy what Jesus would do for them. None of these have anything to do with the Sabbath. Jesus is the One who made the Sabbath for Adam as a blessing and declares it was for all mankind. He kept it because He was a man and because He was the sacrificial Son of God and thus had to be perfect in keeping all the commandments He Himself had given. If He had not kept it, He would have sinned and could not be our Savior.

7. *"I agree that the Sabbath is God's day. But hey, we gotta go with the flow. The way the world is set up today goes against it. People almost always have Sundays off, not Saturdays. You can't buck the system. It's impos-*

sible to have churches start keeping Saturday instead of Sunday. We can't go against the world's system." If you could only hear yourself! God said not to love the world (I John 2:15) and that to do so would be adultery and make you His enemy (James 4:4). Will you be among those who bed down with the Babylonish, Sunday-keeping system that will soon dominate this world? If it were impossible to obey God, He would not require that obedience. We can do all things through Christ (Phil. 4:13). Whether on an individual or a church wide scale, obedience may be difficult and inconvenient, but it is never impossible. Is church tradition more important to you than what God says? If you are a church leader, is your reputation and financial security more important than the Word of God? Jesus is your Provider. He is only limited by your disobedience. Whose praises do you seek – men's or God's?

8. *"It doesn't really matter."* Yes, it does. Sabbath breaking is sin! You're saying that sin doesn't matter. That's serious. Jesus told the Pharisees they were guilty because they knew what they were doing was wrong (John 9:41). The same principle applies to those today who become aware of the Sabbath and know it should be kept (James 4:17).
9. *"Everybody keeps Sunday. Everybody can't be wrong!"* Oh, yeah? Everybody thought the world was flat! Satan has deceived the whole world (Rev. 12:9). So the majority, when it comes to spiritual matters, is basically always wrong.
10. *"The many Christian slaves in the early church could not have kept the Sabbath since they had to be subject to their masters or die."* Christian Jews were free to observe the Sabbath in the same way as any other Jewish slaves, of whom there were many in the Roman Empire. It is important not to think of slavery in Roman times in the same terms as slavery in the United States prior to 1865. The right of Jews, even slaves, to observe the Sabbath, was widely recognized[1], even though many Romans didn't like the fact, since their wealth and leisure were based on having others work for them.
11. *"A number of early church leaders condemn Sabbath keeping and defend Sunday worship in their writings. Surely they couldn't be wrong".* Oh, really? Were they infallible? Paul warned that wrong doctrines would enter and that "among yourselves" people would rise up to deceive and take followers after them (Acts 20:28-30). When John wrote, antichrists had already arisen. One branch of the Gnostics taught that the writings of the First Testament were not to be taken seriously. Already men arose to turn

---

1 Strand's *The Sabbath in Scripture and History*, on page 151, states: "Even slaves would work only five days so that 'on the Sabbath-day and the Lord's day' they could 'go to church for instruction in piety.'"

the grace of God into license to disobey, and that included the Sabbath. One leader, Diotrephes, even put faithful people out of the visible church (III John 9-10). Why be so naïve as to think that all early church leaders were following the truth once delivered to the saints?

12. *"There's nothing that makes one day more special than another. They're all alike to God. I keep every day as holy unto God."* The implication is that you are holier than those who keep the Sabbath, since they keep only one day holy. The difference is that they are doing exactly what God said to do, not following misguided human reasoning. We are holy and we do indeed present ourselves to God to be employed for holy purposes every day of the week. Holy people and holy days are two different things. Because we are holy and we dedicate ourselves to God all the time does not mean that every day is holy, the misunderstanding of Romans 14 (explained later) notwithstanding. God says only one day is holy. Psalm 132:13-15 shows that Jerusalem will no longer be a temporary place of God's visitation. In the seventh millennial "day" of 1000 years, God will make Zion His resting place, His habitation. Zion symbolizes the church. He may make visitations throughout the week to His people collectively. It is only on the Sabbath day, however, that He comes to dwell with us. He inhabits the Sabbath day, His presence making it holy. Unless we rest with Him and inhabit that day with Him, we will not inhabit Jerusalem with Him in the Millennium and beyond. If we follow the same reasoning with the tithe God calls holy (Lev. 27:30), we could say, "All my money is holy and I use it for holy purposes, so I don't have to give You ten per cent, God." We are to keep our hands and feet off what God calls holy, period.
13. *"The Sabbath commandment is not a moral but a physical law and therefore we need not obey it. Only the commandments that have to do with love are important in the Christian era."* It is men who quibble about moral versus physical laws. God doesn't. He says He shows His loving kindness to those who keep His commandments (Ex. 20:6), period – all of them (Deut. 5:29; James 2:10). I John 5:3 says love is the keeping of the commandments, confirmed by Exodus 20:6. Is the Sabbath physical? So is your neighbor's wife, his property, and his life. God never distinguishes between "physical" and "spiritual" sins. He intended the commandments to be kept by all peoples. He called them good laws, as did Paul (Rom. 7:14). God wanted the entire world to follow Israel's good laws (Deut. 4:6-8). He specifically includes the Sabbath in the "good" category (Neh. 9:13-14). We are morally bound to obey God because He created us, which the Sabbath commemorates. Is communing with God, fellowshipping with Him for a whole day not a moral endeavor? How can you act morally the rest of the week if you

don't receive His Word in weekly corporate worship? Critics cannot dispute that fact. They agree. So why lie? Truth is, they only dispute the day. Why would the day God rested, the seventh day of the week, change? He didn't rest on Sunday. If detractors were frank, they would admit the problem is not the morality of the fourth commandment, but the fact that it does not fit into man's logic. If your father told you as a child to stop all TV watching and rest on Saturday one week and did not immediately tell you why, would you say it was moral to disobey His command? Understanding often comes *after* obedience. Excuses only delay the blessings and the understanding. If the Sabbath were a ceremonial law with no moral value, why would God place it in His "Big Ten"? Stop lying to yourself -- and to God.

14. *"The Sabbath was part of the Old Covenant and was therefore done away when the New Covenant was established."* Jesus gave the Sabbath to Adam and blessed it long before the establishment of the Old Covenant. If the Sabbath were done away, then all the Ten Commandments were done away. All the Ten Commandments are the basis of the New Covenant (Heb. 8:10, Jer. 31:31-33). In Exodus 20 Jesus gave Moses the Ten Commandments, the basis of the Old Covenant, and only in Exodus 24:6-8 did Moses ratify and seal it with blood. In the same manner, the great Lawgiver Jesus spent three and a half years expanding on the very same law that became the basis of the New Covenant. At the end of His ministry Jesus shed His blood to ratify and seal the New Covenant. Yet some err and say that all Jesus said and did before His death was Old Covenant. Those who say the law was done away when Jesus died are saying that the Ten Commandments were done away when Moses sealed it with the blood that prefigured the blood of Jesus. Untrue! Sealing the New Covenant and Testament in His blood in no way did away with the terms of the covenant. Jesus' blood certainly didn't do away with the legacy of promises He left us in His will or testament – the New Testament in His blood. Jesus' blood did not do away with the law. It washed away *sin* – defined as the *breaking* of the law (I John 3:4).
15. *The Sabbath is legalistic and we should avoid legalism.* Legalism and law are two different things. You can keep any of God's laws legalistically, which usually has the connotation of being picky and proud of it – with a self-righteous, Pharisaical, hypocritical attitude. God would strongly disapprove of anyone who would keep any of His laws with such a mindset. Jesus condemned the Pharisees more than anyone. He chastised them for their stinking attitude and the picky way they kept the Sabbath, but He never condemned them for keeping it. Legalism is a spirit. He tries to get people to keep the law the human way, with human rules and picky regulations added to the law. Furthermore, the basis of legalism is doing things in

your own strength, not allowing God's grace through the power of the Holy Spirit to work through you. God's grace and His love make obedience to any law easy (I John 5:3, Mat. 11:30). Trusting in the flesh brings a curse (Jer. 17:5).

The accusation that the Sabbath is inherently legalistic is an utterly false and flimsy excuse. Do you tend to believe someone when they give you four or five reasons why they didn't do what you asked them to do? You usually discern the truth: they didn't want to do what you asked them to do. The more reasons they give, the more you wonder, "What is the real reason?" All these excuses seem so fishy. They are. The people who give them are not swimming fully in God's stream. They are not going in His flow. Like Satan, they are using the Word of God selectively to get out of obeying Jesus.

Theologians try to complicate the simplicity of Christ with all these excuses. As Jesse Duplantis says, "It takes a theologian to help you misunderstand something so simple."

It's Simple: Crack the Nutshell of Excuses and Crack the Code

But the simple truth remains, the truth that cracks our nutshell of excuses and thus cracks the code, the Bible code, solving the puzzle that is the Word of God. Here it is: "***Remember the Sabbath day to keep it holy. Six days you shall labor and do all your work, But the seventh day is a sabbath of the [Eternal] your God. In it you shall not do any work…***"

This seventh day truth is the simplicity of Jesus Paul did not want us to reject (II Cor. 11:3). Which do you choose? The simplicity of Jesus Christ – or the complicated, convoluted, corrupt lies of Satan? Choose truth. It will set you free.

One more excuse or set of excuses deserves at least a whole chapter. People have a false idea about the commandments of Jesus. They believe He reduced the law to one, or maybe two commandments. All you need to do is love. Or simply love God and love others. They say, "I'll obey the commandments of ***Jesus***, but I don't have to obey the Jewish Sabbath." They will also say, "We don't need to keep the Sabbath. That's Old Testament."

Because these concepts are so ingrained in Christian thinking, we have chosen to cover them in more than one chapter. We don't ask you to believe anything that is not taught by God's Word. We will give you Bible proof that the above ideas are false. Check us out. Open your bible and prove all things. Break the hard-to-crack shell of feeble excuses. Break the code and break free.

The Uproar that Wasn't

"The Sabbath commandment is repeated nowhere in the New Testament, so we don't have to keep it." While this is one of the favorite arguments *against* the Sabbath, it is actually a powerful argument *in favor* of the Sabbath.

Why? The simple truth is that the very reason the Sabbath commandment was not repeated in the New Testament is that the people of that time and the Bible writers took the Sabbath ***for granted***. The idea that one of the Ten Commandments would have been changed or done away was so unthinkable that it was unnecessary to repeat it. Indeed, not every commandment was repeated verbatim in the New Testament.

For example, when Jesus addressed the rich young ruler He gave a short list of the Ten Commandments, only naming the last six (Mark 10:19). Does that mean that Jesus had done away with the first four, which explained how to love God? Does that mean that under the New Covenant we don't have to love God?

Religious Jews of that day made a show of loving God, especially when it came to their strict Sabbath observance. This young ruler needed to show love for his fellow man, proving his love for God by giving to others. So that is what Jesus emphasized by testing this rich man.

None of the first four commandments were repeated verbatim in the Greek Scriptures, and even veiled references to the first three are hard to find. You will find much more information and instruction about the Sabbath than about any of the first three commandments.

Such an inter-relationship exists between the first four and last six commandments that they are inseparable. John declares that you cannot love God if you don't love your brother (I John 4:20-21). And it works both ways (I John 5:2).

God is Love. Love is the same yesterday, today, and forever. Love never fails. All of the aforementioned applies also to God's law, for it also is love (Rom. 13:10). The Sabbath can only change if God changes, but He doesn't (Mal 3:6).

Have you ever wondered why you don't read about any change from Sabbath to Sunday in Acts? The greatest evidence that the Sabbath was not changed to Sunday in the early church is this: that change would have caused such colossal controversy that the book of Acts would have recorded it. Acts 15 speaks of the controversy over circumcision, but nothing is said about a Sabbath change to Sunday.

A change in the Sabbath would have caused an uproar.

No uproar. Rather, the silence roars.

Circumcision was an important physical covenant between God and His people, but it was physical. Moreover, God made this covenant with Abraham, long after the Sabbath had been given to man. The Sabbath was "made for man" (Mark 2:27), beginning with Adam.

Unlike the Sabbath covenant, circumcision was not a covenant made with all mankind. It was a health law that made Israel special to God. While its benefits have been recently proved to be a deterrent to AIDS and other diseases, it has nothing to do with salvation. This is why circumcision and other purely physical rituals of the Law of Moses were not imposed on Gentiles in the dispute of Acts 15. James even says that the Gentiles could easily hear what the council did impose on them by listening to those who preached the Law of Moses in the synagogues every *Sabbath*, as did Paul (Acts 13:42-44).

What *is* significant is that it was the issue of circumcision that caused a great kerfuffle in Acts. Not the Sabbath! While the rolling away of the foreskin was a covenant with powerful spiritual parallels, in no way is it on the level of importance of one of the Ten Commandments.

To the surprise of most today, it was not Sabbath keeping, but Sabbath *breaking*, that was heretical. Historians confirm that the early church in the Jerusalem area kept the Sabbath and the holy days of Leviticus 23. It is true that most of the church was composed of Jews who had become Christians. They did not, however, keep the feasts God called "*My* appointed times" (Lev. 23:2) because they were Jews. They were doing as Jesus did and commanded (Mat. 28:20).

One thing is sure: if all those Jews were forced to give up the Sabbath and the holy days when they became Christian, the uproar would have reached to high heaven and you would have heard about it! Had there been tabloids on the streets of Jerusalem at the time, venders would have shouted, "Christians change our Sabbath to Sunday! Read all about it!" Had Jewish TV host Larry King gone back in time, he would have had all the Christian leaders on a panel to question them about this monumental change.

Sabbath observance wasn't heresy in the early church. The problem arose when the heretics who began keeping Sunday, initially in addition to the Sabbath, became more numerous than the true believers. In time the churches in the West centered in Rome gained power and persecuted the steadfast Sabbath keepers in the Judean birthplace of Christianity.

This book cites historical documents proving that the apostle John's successors kept the Sabbath and the holy days.

If you think Sunday observance was part of "the faith once delivered" to the saints, think again. The real heretics became so strong in the physical, organized church that they called those who held fast to the true faith heretics.

But does might make right? Will you have the courage to obey God rather than men? Those who oppose the Sabbath today greatly outnumber those who keep it. Will you follow the crowd who follow the big names? Or will you show Jesus you love Him by obeying Him? Your obedience may cause an uproar around you, but it will cause shouts of joy in heaven.

Sabbath *Selahs*
A Strange Brew

Cowardly religiosity has concocted a strange brew of excuses not to keep the Sabbath, and the following one is a dandy:
"You can make the Bible say anything you want. Others get Sunday worship from the Bible, so why should I believe you?"

You can make the Bible say anything you want -- unless you are honest. We should learn from the story below:
A man and his wife were having an argument about who should brew the coffee each morning. The wife said, "You should do it, because you get up first, and then we don't have to wait as long to get our coffee."
The husband said, "You are in charge of the cooking around here and you should do it, because that is your job, and I can just wait for my coffee." Wife replies, "No, you should do it, and besides it is in the Bible that the man should do the coffee."
Husband replies, " I can't believe that, show me." So she fetches her bible, opens the New Testament and shows him at the top of several pages, that it indeed says "He...brews."
Who brews? In this case, Satan brews. The above excuse is a witch's brew prepared by demons. It takes courage to prove all things according to the Word (I Thes. 5:21). The righteous do just that.

Now these [the people in Berea] were more noble-minded than those in Thessalonica, for they received the word with great eagerness, examining the Scriptures daily to see whether these things were so...But when the Jews of Thessalonica found out that the word of God had been proclaimed by Paul in Berea also, they came there as well, agitating and stirring up the crowds (Acts 17:11,13).

If you don't read the Bible along with this book and pray for understanding, the devil can come along with his witches' brew to steal the Word sown in your heart. Don't buy his brew.

"When anyone hears the word of the kingdom and does not understand it, the evil one comes and snatches away what has been sown in his heart...And the one on whom seed was sown on the good soil, this is the man who hears the word and understands it; who indeed bears fruit... (Mat. 13:19,23). *Selah.*

CHAPTER TWELVE

The Sabbath is a Commandment of Jesus!

While on my recent honeymoon in my native Carolina, I had the blessing of conducting an informal Bible study with some family and friends. The subject of the Sabbath came up. A young man I had known growing up had related to his sister a few years earlier what I told him about the Sabbath. At the time she pooh-poohed the idea, as most Christians would.

This night was different. Four words I said to her in private stopped her in her mental tracks: "Jesus is the Word."

"Yeah!" she said, open-mouthed. "Yeah, Jesus *is* the Word." She knew the New Testament well. She knew John 1. She could almost quote these words by heart: "In the beginning was the Word, and the Word was with God, and the Word was God. He was in the beginning with God. All things came into being through Him, and apart form Him nothing came into being that has come into being. In Him was life, and the life was the Light of men. The Light shines in the darkness, and the darkness did not comprehend it."

She knew these verses spoke of Jesus. She knew He was the Word. But the full concept and its relationship to the fourth commandment had never connected. That night it did.

I told her, "Jesus was the Word, the *Logos* in Greek, who spoke in the 'Old Testament.' He was the Spokesman for the Godhead Trinity. It was ***Jesus*** who spoke the fourth commandment at Sinai and wrote it with His finger on stone." It finally clicked. In an instant the nutshell of stubborn excuses began to crack. It may have been only a beginning, but God had allowed me to plant a seed in her heart.

Verses We Skip Over Explain A Lot

Isn't it funny – no, sad – how we mentally skip over verses in the Bible that we don't understand and that don't register with us?

Like John 6:44-46: "No one can come to Me unless the Father who sent Me draws him [saving souls is not our responsibility; it is the Father's job and He draws people to Jesus when He pleases]; and I will raise him up on the last day. It is written in the prophets, 'AND THEY SHALL ALL BE TAUGHT OF GOD [everyone who has ever lived and died will have an opportunity to know Jesus; all means all].' Everyone who has heard and learned from the Father, comes to Me. *Not that anyone has seen the Father*, except the One who is from God; He [Jesus] has seen the Father."

Several verses say the same thing in different words. John 1:18 says, "No one has seen God [obviously the Father here] at any time; the only begotten God [Jesus refers to Himself here; He is God, much greater than a lowly lord, who was five to seven levels below even a king] who is in the bosom of the Father, He has explained Him."

John 5:37 adds to this: "And the Father who sent Me, He has testified of Me. You have neither heard His voice at any time [that includes the time between Adam and Jesus] nor seen His form." Yet the God of the Hebrew Scriptures who spoke to men spoke to Moses "face to face" (Ex. 33:11) and Moses even saw His form when He appeared in a glorious state (Ex.33:20-23).

The One called the Eternal (Yahweh should never be translated "Lord") appeared to Abraham (Gen. 18:1-14). God, accompanied by two angels, even ate a meal with the patriarch.

So where did we get this idea that the Father was "the God of the Old Testament?" Why do we see the Father as a rather harsh God in the First Testament and Jesus coming with a gentler, more compromising, graceful truth in the Second Testament? Who gave the Father the bad rap? Why, Satan, of course. And if we had met Jesus in the day into which He poured Himself, we would understand this. We would know that He was the Word who spoke to men in the First Testament.

The same Word who said, "Let us make man in our image…" (Gen. 1:26) and "Let there be light ["Light, be!" in Hebrew]" (Gen. 1:3) is the same Yahweh or Eternal One [not Lord!] who thundered out at Sinai the Ten Commandments. That member of the Godhead is none other than the Word who became flesh (John 1:14), the One who was born of a virgin and whose name was given by an angel in Luke 1:31.

Who is this "God of the Old Testament"? It's simple. His name is Jesus!

The Hebrews may have called him Yahweh or more likely Yehovah – or even Yah, as in Hallelu…yah. He is nevertheless the One who became Jesus.

Do we need more proof?

The Scriptures Prove It

Why did Jesus come to reveal the Father if Abba Father God had been known by people in the Hebrew Scriptures? Why did Jesus make statements like He did in John 14:7? "If you had known Me, You would have known My Father also; *from now on* [not before] you know Him, and have seen Him [by seeing Jesus]."

Look at the important prayer Jesus prayed in John 17:25-26: "O righteous Father, although the world has *not known You*, yet I have known You; and these have known that You sent Me; and I have made Your name known to them, and will make it known…"

You have possibly memorized at some point one of the most quoted parts of the Bible, Psalm 23. "The [Eternal] is my shepherd, I shall not want." Yet how many Christians know who that Shepherd is?

Some of you may be ahead of me here. You may realize that references do exist in the Hebrew Scriptures regarding the Father. You're right. Daniel refers to the Ancient of Days and differentiates between Him and the "Son of Man" (Dan. 7:13). Some of Jesus' intimates in the First Testament were indeed aware of the existence of the Father. But they didn't really know Him.

Notice Psalm 110:1, which says, "The [Eternal or Yehovah, obviously the Father here; all the members of the Trinity are eternal and thus can be called "the Eternal"] says to *my* [*Adonai* or Divine Master]: 'Sit at My right hand…." (See I Cor. 15:25). David distinguishes the Father, whom He calls here Yahweh, from *His* Master, the One He knew intimately, the Word who became Jesus.

So was the Father David's Shepherd? No. Then who was? John tells us: "The thief comes only to steal and kill and destroy [things that are important to God's people, like the Sabbath]; I came that they may have life [Jesus was the Way, the Truth and the Life; He poured His life into the Sabbath day, and those who want the fullness of that life must meet with Him on this day of revival], and have it abundantly. I am the Good *Shepherd…*" (John 10:10-11).

Can we as Jesus' sheep hear His voice of truth here? No mystery. The One who became Jesus, the One who was David's Shepherd, is also our Shepherd. Did you ever make that connection? The implication is clear: the Shepherd of the "Old Testament" is the same as the Shepherd of the New. He's Jesus!

Why are we surprised? Jesus is the Word. He is the One who speaks in both Testaments. He says His sheep hear His voice. Will you hear and heed His voice of truth today?

Rock of Offense -- or Rock of Defense?

Several Hebrew prophecies, when compared with their fulfillment in the New Testament, show clearly that Jesus was the "Eternal" (YHVH or Yahweh) of the First Testament.

How prophetic these verses are indeed: "The stone which the builders rejected Has become the chief corner stone" (Ps. 118:22). Jesus Himself quoted this very verse in Matthew 21:42. Peter quoted it as well in I Peter 2:7-8. Peter also quotes Isaiah 8:14. But let's begin with verse 13, where Isaiah refers to this Stumbling Block as "the [Eternal – LORD in all capital letters, while always a bad translation, always translates Yehovah] of hosts."

Yes, how prophetic, or should we say pathetic? It was not only the Jews who stumbled over Jesus, the "rock to stumble over" (Isa. 8:14), the "ROCK OF OFFENSE" (I Pet. 2:8). Christians have also stumbled over Him.

Will we stumble at Jesus as Divine Master of the Sabbath? Will He be a Rock of Offense for us -- or a Rock of Defense? As we are still in Him on His Sabbath, dwelling in the secret place of the Most High, He promises to fulfill His role as our Defender in the fullness of the term. When we reject His time of intimacy He offers with Him on His day, we reject Him. He becomes an Offense for us rather than a Defense.

Many have because of deception stumbled over the real Jesus in His Sabbath. They don't even know who He is! They don't know for the most part that He was the God of what they often disparagingly refer to as "the Old Testament."

More than a Commandment – A Perpetual Covenant

No wonder! Jesus Himself gave the Sabbath as "a *perpetual* covenant" (Ex. 31:16) to Israel, a name that simply means "the believers or overcomers." This was the name Jesus gave to Jacob when he persevered with God in order to receive the full blessing of the believer (Gen. 32:24-30). Here again we see that Jacob referred to the One he wrestled with "face to face" as "God" (32:30).

While you are not responsible for this knowledge until the Holy Spirit convicts you of it, the truth about believers in the last days may surprise you. Jesus will not call them His own if they with full knowledge and conviction reject the perpetual covenant He made with believers – those who, like Jacob, want all of God, not only the parts of Him that agree with their tradition.

End-time believers will not be able to know the real Jesus without keeping the first covenant God made with man, the covenant he renewed in Exodus 16 before Sinai. He reemphasized the importance of this covenant in Exodus 19:5, also before He made the Old Covenant with Israel on the mountain.

This Sabbath covenant is a covenant completely separate from the Old Covenant. You find it over ten chapters after the Sinai covenant, the one that was replaced by the New Covenant. Without respecting this covenant, without keeping this sign or mark of a true, Jacob-turned-Israel wrestler with God, wanting-all-of-Jesus believer, you can't fully know who Jesus is!

Strong words, but true. We have shown evidence from the Bible, from both Testaments, that the majority of Christians today don't know who Jesus is. How can we say we fully know Him if we don't even know He was the God of the "Old Testament"?

Because of this lack of knowledge (Hos. 4:6) that came because church leadership rejected the knowledge, the church has rejected the Sabbath covenant. If it were only one of the Ten Commandments, it would be serious enough. The situation is compounded because the Sabbath is more than a commandment. It is a covenant, a perpetual, never-ending one for the true grit believer.

Don't Blame it On Moses – Jesus Spoke This Covenant!

Health expert and author Jordan Rubin made an excellent comment in an interview. He said, "The 'law of Moses' is not the law of Moses. It is the law of God." Good for you, Dr. Rubin! It was God – Jesus – who gave good laws to Israel. While it is true that some, meaning the sacrifices and rituals (Heb. 9:8-15), were no longer necessary when Jesus gave His life for us, they were all good. God doesn't do bad stuff. He doesn't give bad laws. He doesn't make bad covenants. It's bad people who break good covenants.

The Sabbath is both a law and a covenant. Satan knows, even if Christians don't, that the Sabbath is probably more important than any of the Ten Commandments. Why? It is a covenant that is a sign of God's true believers, those who go the extra mile. Never will the extra mile be so important as in these last days. Only those who endure and persevere to the end will be ultimately saved (Mat. 24:13).

But the Sabbath is more than a sign that will distinguish God's elect from those who take the sign or Mark of the Beast. It is more than a gateway to intimacy with God. It is...well, we'll let Jesus tell you, since it is He and not the Father who speaks to Moses in Exodus 31:12-13.

In these verses the Eternal, Yahweh, the Word, the Spokesman, Jesus is speaking to Moses, telling him to speak to "the sons of Israel." In Galatians, the epistle that supposedly does away with the Sabbath, believers today are referred to as "the Israel of God," and remember, this covenant is perpetual, and was made with *mankind* (Mark 2:27-28; Gen. 2: 1-3) before it was ever made with a Hebrew. He tells them: you believers "shall surely [no ifs and maybes here] observe My Sabbaths [Christians say these days are Jewish; Jesus says they are *His* –and He never changes (Heb. 13:8)]; for this is a sign [or mark of identification] between Me and you throughout your generations, that you may know that I am the [Eternal, Jesus] who sanctifies you [sets you apart as My people, makes you holy, as one of Jesus' names, *Makkadesh* signifies]..."

"Do Not Refuse Him Who is Speaking [Jesus!]"

Jesus sounds quite serious here. He (not some supposed harsh Father God) declares: "Everyone who profanes it shall surely be put to death; for whoever does any work on it, that person shall be cut off from among his people [He or she will not be considered a believer and will die]" (Ex. 31:14).

If the Sabbath was this important to Jesus for His Old Covenant believers, how serious do you think He is about it today? The only difference is the people. The Old Covenant believers were under the "ministry of death" (II Cor. 3:7). Jesus, yes, the real Jesus, had them stoned if they broke the Sabbath covenant (Num. 15:36).

Moses may have uttered the words, but it was Jesus speaking. A warning for New Covenant believers who think the Sabbath is done away is in order here: "See to it that you do not refuse Him [Jesus] who is speaking. For if those did not escape when they refused him who warned them on earth, much less will we escape who turn away from Him who warns from heaven" (Heb. 12:25). If you read the context, you will see that New Covenant believers, while Jesus has given them a looser rope and no longer punishes immediately, will be held more accountable – and eternally so.

So every reader should take this book seriously. It is not a doctrinal treatise. It is a matter of life and death – and that could be both physical and eternal. We can be thankful that while Jesus is a consuming fire (Heb. 12:29), He is also a merciful judge (Heb. 4:14-15). Sabbath breakers will not necessarily be condemned eternally. In these last days, however, the stakes are higher.

We need to listen to Jesus. We need to take Him seriously. He is saying in Exodus 31 that He has made a covenant with the believers, "a sign between Me and the sons of Israel [and that includes the "Israel of God" today] ***forever***" (Ex. 31:17).

What is it about the word "forever" that we don't understand? Forever is forever. Yes, even in the conceptual Hebrew. And Jesus, who is "the same yesterday and today and ***forever***" (Heb. 13:8) is the One who said "forever' in speaking of this covenant.

If Jesus Instituted Sunday, He Would Have to Die!

Hebrew covenants were serious business. If you as the head of your family, men, made a blood covenant with someone, you kept it. If you didn't, the other fellow came and killed you and all your family. That's right. A blood covenant was a life and death matter. You fail. You die.

If the forever-the-same Jesus were to change the Sabbath to Sunday, He would have to die! Since that is impossible, Jesus *can't* change it. He would lying and He would literally have to cease being God, along with the Father and the Holy Spirit.

While this may sound overly simplified to the eminent theologians who write commentaries and explain Jesus away, it is nevertheless true: if you keep Sunday, you are calling for the death of God!

Whoa. "Now, just a minute!" you say? That sounds bad, doesn't it? Even heretical. But it's not. What is heretical is trying to change the Sabbath to Sunday – with no biblical basis whatever.

God is not dead. Jesus is alive. He means what He says. He is Life itself. And if we want to live forever, we would do well to listen to the Word Himself.

He is the First and the Last – and we may not last if we don't listen to Him. Jesus gives an ominous warning to those who take away from His Words and attributes words to Him that are not His (Rev. 22:18-19). We should take those words seriously. They are the third and fourth last verses of the Bible, spoken shortly after the words, "I am the Alpha and the Omega, the first and the last, the beginning and the end" (Rev. 22:13). Yes, He has been there as the Word speaking out the truth from the beginning to the end of the Bible.

Moreover, to put another nail in the coffin of Christian misconceptions, we quote the Eternal One who spoke in the First Testament: "I am He, I am the first, I am also the last" (Isa. 48:12). He is the Speaker in both Testaments. He calls Himself the First and the Last, the Beginning and the End. If we don't believe what He said in the beginning, we may see our end.

The Bible calls Jesus our Rock. Even the "New Testament" says it: "… and all drank the same spiritual drink, for they were drinking from a spiritual rock which followed them; and the rock was *Christ*" (I Cor. 10:4).

Will we drink from the Rock? Or will what the Word Himself is saying to us today make Him a "Rock of offense," a "stone of stumbling" for us?

Will you escape "all these things that are about to take place" (Luke 21:36), and be saved from Satan's and God's wrath (I Thes. 1:10; 5:9)? Will you be saved alive in these days of sorrow and tribulation? In order to escape, you will need to know the real Jesus, the Word who spoke out all commandments and covenants of God, in both Testaments.

He is the Divine Master of the Sabbath day and our Savior – the only One who can save us from the turbulent times ahead. At this point it shouldn't surprise us to hear the One who speaks throughout the Bible declare in the "gospel according to Isaiah" 43:11,25 that He is indeed our Savior.

The Sabbath Covenant: Forever and Today

Jesus continues to speak of His covenant and offers you an opportunity to confess having broken it, whether knowingly or in ignorance. In Isaiah 56:1-7 Yeshua (Jesus' Hebrew name) speaks of salvation in these last days:

Thus says [Jesus – we hope we have proved by now that Yahweh is Jesus], "Preserve justice and do righteousness, For My salvation [yeshua] is about to come [This could only be an end-time prophecy, culminating in the millennial rule of Jesus on earth] And My righteousness to be revealed. How blessed is the man who does this [Jesus confirms that those who become convicted about the Sabbath in these last days and begin to keep it will be blessed, not cursed and "under the law" as some say], And the son of man who takes hold of it; Who keeps from profaning the Sabbath [Oh, so the Sabbath is still in effect at the time just before Jesus brings His salvation to the whole earth], And keeps his hand [Comparing Revelation 13:16 and Exodus 13:9, we see the hand or will or action is involved in implementing what is in the forehead or our decision-making processes, whether to keep God's days or the days enforced by the Beast] from doing any ***evil*** [This is extremely important, signifying that Sabbath breaking is called evil in the last days. Whether we know about it or not, it is sin to break the Sabbath. It always has been since it was instituted in Genesis, and it always will be (Isa. 66:23)]. Let not the foreigner who has joined himself to [Jesus] say, "[Jesus] will surely separate me from His people [Being cut off from the company of believers is therefore still a result of Sabbath breaking in these last days]." Nor let the eunuch [who were Gentiles] say, "Behold, I am a dry tree." For thus says [Jesus], "To the eunuchs who keep My Sabbaths [The Sabbath is for Gentiles too], And choose what pleases Me [Oh, so Sabbath keeping still pleases Jesus in this end time. And conversely, Sunday keeping does ***not*** please Jesus. Some seem to think Jesus is the same yesterday and forever, but not today. According to them He has suspended His Sabbath for 2000 years], And hold fast ***My covenant***, [This is referring to the Sabbath covenant, instituted in Genesis, reaffirmed twice pre-Sinai and once again just after the Old Covenant ratification. While, like tithing, it is open to all mankind to be a blessing for those who rest on that day, it carries added significance as a covenant sign for the believer. While the Sabbath is mentioned elsewhere in strong covenant language, these verses use the word "covenant" and thus confirm that it was the first covenant made with man. And Adam, while being the first man, was also a believer.] To them I will give in My house and within My walls a memorial, And a name better than that of sons and daughters; I will give them an everlasting name which will not be cut off [Sounds like the Sabbath covenant holds great blessings for the present and future]. Also the *foreigners* who join themselves to [Jesus], To minister to Him, and to love the name of [Jesus – the two major end-time tests will be the Sabbath day and using and loving the name of Jesus rather than calling on "the Lord"], To be His servants, every one who keeps from profaning the Sabbath And holds fast ***My covenant*** [We see again Gentiles keeping the Sabbath covenant in these last days and being blessed abundantly for their obedience].

Jesus does not take the Sabbath covenant lightly. Neither should we. He wants us to reap the end-time blessings in meeting with Him on His day.

A Command from the King – Not A Voting Matter

Whether the Sabbath is Saturday or Sunday is not up for discussion. As I write these words today, I had the blessing of hearing Myles Munroe speak on TV. He has a unique way of explaining the Kingdom concept. It is simple.

We have been blessed to understand the Kingdom concept for some forty years. Both Munroe and Dutch Sheets are beginning to expound and amplify this understanding. God spoke these words to Dutch Sheets: "I ***am*** government."

A kingdom is made up of king, a territory or domain (king-dom), citizens, and laws. We cannot disobey one of the main laws of the Kingdom of God, the very one that prophesies God's government over the whole earth, and call ourselves good citizens.

In the Kingdom of God, we don't vote. We read and listen to the decrees of the King and we choose to obey or disobey. It is that simple.

In a lighthearted photo on the annual Sabbath that pictures the coming of the King of kings (featured in the projected sequels), author Robert Scott dons a crown. The weekly Sabbath also celebrates our dominion over the earth with Jesus.

Dominion Day

Myles Monroe has a special teaching anointing that expands on principles we have been blessed to understand for many years. He grasps deeply what few do: the Kingdom concept. The Ten Commandments are the basic framework of the law of love that governs the Kingdom of God. It is not a democracy. The King's word is law. If the church did vote on the fourth commandment, which in one way it has, it would vote not to keep it. What arrogance! You don't tell the King that His law needs changing! Only Satan would lead the church to rebel against the immutable law of love of the King who *is* Love. Though we may not yet realize it, when we trample on God's day, we "set our minds on earthly things" and we are not being obedient citizens of the Kingdom.

The God Family is also a Kingdom, an ever-expanding family of rulers. Jesus came to be the King of this Kingdom. He divested Himself of the trappings of the Godhead to become the first man to die and be born into the Kingdom of God. He did this to show us the example. While the Father is ultimately the Head of the Family Kingdom, God the Father delegated His Son to have all the direct dealings with man on this earth. Jesus then sent the Holy Spirit to be the Governor of the Kingdom Family called to Jesus on earth in this age. The Governor is also our Teacher who focuses our eyes on Jesus. Jesus will finally at the very end submit all headship to the Father, who comes down to a New Earth to rule (Rev. 21:3; I Cor. 15:24-27).

In the interim period, Jesus is the Head of His Church and the King of the Kingdom. The Kingdom of God is not a democracy. It is not a religion. Religion is a system, while a kingdom is a government, an absolute monarchy. The King's Word is an unchangeable decree. As we have seen, He is the embodiment of the Word, the Spokesman for the Kingdom. He rules. Whether the Sabbath is Saturday or Sunday is not up for discussion. King Jesus has spoken.

He has given laws, commandments, and instructions (*torah* in Hebrew). They are not up for committee or church board approval. Most church boards at this writing would not agree with His Sabbath commandment. Some would argue that in our modern world keeping Saturday is not feasible, and it's not a big deal. But Jesus doesn't ask for your church board's opinion. He is the same forever, and when He speaks, His Words are enacted as law. He is Lawgiver, Executor, and Judge.

The Father has committed to Jesus all authority to speak out the laws of the Kingdom of Love. No disagreements exist in the Godhead. They are in perfect unity. Jesus always speaks the Father's will.

While Jesus gave some temporary ordinances in the Hebrew Scriptures, He made it clear that only the rituals that foreshadowed what He and the Holy Spirit would come to do later would be rendered unnecessary. Not forbidden, only unnecessary. Any law keeping done to justify oneself before God is in itself a breaking of the law, putting oneself as a god above Jesus, who died to save us and justify us. It is a breaking of the first commandment. Legalism is idolatry.

The focus of Jesus' message was not His Person but the Kingdom He came to announce. He prophesied that the end would not come until His people preached in power to the world the gospel of the Kingdom (Mat. 24:14). The church cannot effectively publish that message unless and until we begin to keep the day that celebrates and explains the Kingdom, the Sabbath day.

Not only is the church commissioned to bring the heart of the children to their fathers (including sitting on their heavenly Father's knee in intimacy on the Sabbath day), but we are also to announce the future Sabbath rest in the Millennium (Heb. 4:9-11; Mal. 4:6). How can we announce that rest if we do not rest in Jesus on the day that pictures the time when the world will rest from sin?

Jesus is our Sabbath. This does not mean the Sabbath day is done away. Au contraire! We rest in Him on His Sabbath day. We cannot fully know and love the real Jesus unless we are keeping His day of rest. Since Jesus is our Sabbath and commands us to rest on His day, when we knowingly reject the Sabbath we are rejecting Jesus!

Jesus is the King of the Kingdom we announce. We must know the King in order to preach His Kingdom. The fourth of the Ten Commandments is the crossover point of the

Decalogue, making the transition between the laws that show love toward the King and those that show love to the other members and future members of the Kingdom.

The Sabbath commandment is also the seal of the covenant. In ancient times a king would put in the middle of his law His seal of identity. The only commandment that reveals the identity of the King of the Kingdom is the fourth. He identifies Himself as Creator of all things. No other commandment reveals the identity of the King.

We are ambassadors of the Kingdom and the King. An ambassador not upholding all the laws of the government he represents is unthinkable. Yet the vast majority of those today claiming to represent God's Kingdom do not even keep the only commandment by which King Jesus identifies Himself. The Governor of the earth, the Holy Spirit, is surely not happy with this state of affairs. He is grieved when we disobey the Kingdom laws (Acts 5:32; Eph. 4:30).

In the culture of the Bible, if a covenant partner broke the covenant, he had to die. Saying that the Sabbath law is done away is saying that God must die, since He would have changed His mind and broken the covenant. Would a citizen of a kingdom be allowed citizenship if he called for the death of the king? Certainly not! We will not be allowed citizenship in God's Kingdom if we knowingly break the Sabbath. Idolaters and thieves are not welcome in the Kingdom (I Cor. 6:9-10). When we knowingly put another day before God's day and steal the time He set aside to be with us, the Kingdom doors cannot open to us.

It is time that the church representing God's Kingdom on earth began to preach the gospel of the Kingdom. It is time the citizens of the Kingdom began to keep the day that prophesies the coming of the Kingdom -- the day that releases Kingdom power and authority.

Prove You Love Jesus: Keep His Sabbath

We hope the truth has begun to crack the nutshell of falseness that has surrounded you. My friend in South Carolina began to understand what it means to say that Jesus is the Word. Do you?

What this means should change the whole way you look at God and the Bible. This book is not our opinion. It is based on the Word of God. That Word is law -- Kingdom law. It is not religion, which is a system of rules and regulations in a legalistic format. Legalism is a demon. The Kingdom has nothing demonic in it. While the Kingdom laws are specific, they are always based on love. They are not subject to our private interpretation.

Our strong pronouncements based on the Law of the King may not be politically correct, but we are not called to be a part of this political and social system. The way we say the truth may not sit well with some, but we know those God is calling to understand these truths will forgive the package and accept the present -- the Sabbath blessing.

We have proved from the Word of God who it was that spoke as God in the Hebrew Scriptures. We could have given much more evidence, but space did not permit.

Jesus was and is the Word. So if you have truly heard the Word of God in this chapter, you can no longer cling to your favorite excuses to avoid the Sabbath truth. Some will continue to say, defying the Word of truth, "Well, Jesus didn't say in the New Testament to keep Saturday. That's Jewish. He just said to love God and love your neighbor. That's it. I'm not legalistic. I don't keep those old Jewish laws. I don't want to put myself under the law again."

That's your opinion. Neither our opinion nor Satan's opinion counts. The King has spoken. His Word has become law. It is unchangeable, like Him.

When Jesus said to prove your love by keeping His commandments, He was not only talking about the commandments He gave through the gospel writers.

The words that came thundering from the mountaintop at Sinai were not the Father's words. They were not the devil's words. They were not the words of Moses. They were not the words of a Jew for Jews. And they were definitely not the Ten Suggestions. They were not the Ten Proposals for our church board to approve, disapprove, alter or amend. They are law. All ten. Not nine. Ten.

The One who blasted them out from the top of Sinai and wrote them with His own finger *twice* was none other than the One who became ***Jesus Christ***!

In John 14:15, Jesus was referring to every single commandment He gave from Genesis to Revelation. And by the way, they number much more than ten. To be exact, Jesus gave 613 commandments of love in "Part I of Jesus' Words of Love"

("Old Testament") and 613 more in "Part II of His Words of Love" ("New Testament"). To obey them is not legalism. It's love.

If you think this is a burden, you are contradicting the words of the King. He said through His closest apostle, whose disciple Polycarp kept the Sabbath and the holy days: "By this we know that we love the children of God, when we love God and observe His commandments. ***For this is the love of God, that we keep His commandments; and His commandments are not burdensome***" (I John 5:2-3).

"Oh," you say, "but it can't be done – not in our society the way it is set up today. I'd lose my job!"

John answers you in the next verse: "For whatever is born of God overcomes the world; and this is the victory that has overcome the world – our faith."

Jesus Himself said that if we seek His Kingdom and His righteousness first, all our needs are met as ambassadors of God's Kingdom (Mat. 6:33-34). The King pays our bills.

Remember the Red Sea. What Moses and Israel faced was more dramatic than asking your boss for Saturdays off or trusting Jesus for perhaps a new and better job. When did the sea open for God's people? When Moses obeyed Jesus. Jesus told him to tell the people to go forward. He told Moses to lift up his rod, and Moses obeyed. And voila! Jesus opened the sea. I saw *The Ten Commandments* as a child the year the film débuted. But what really happened was better than Cecil B. DeMille could ever portray it (Ex. 14:15-16,21).

As a pastor for 35 years, I've seen the Red Sea open hundreds of times for believers who discovered the Sabbath and decided to obey. Obedience opens seas, and doors.

The voice of God in that famous movie sent chills down my young spine. I listened. Will you listen to the voice that actually spoke the Ten Commandments? Will you show Jesus you love Him by obeying Him?

Will you obey ***all*** of Jesus' words of love, or only those with which you agree – only those you read in the "New Testament?"

Remember What?

The Sabbath is the only commandment God specifically said to remember. What does Jesus want us to remember about the Sabbath?

1. The Sabbath covenant was made to be eternal as long as God would live.
2. The Sabbath covenant is confirmed in the breaking of the Bread of Life in communion. The body of Jesus broken in two reminds us of the double blessing of manna given on Friday for that day and the Sabbath. Jesus is our Provider, Sustainer, Reviver, and Preserver of our lives. No worms infected the manna of the faithful. Jesus preserves our physical bodies and will provide a new body for us at the resurrection.
3. God Himself rested on the Sabbath.
4. Only the righteous will seek to obey and keep this covenant.
5. The position of this commandment in the Decalogue (in the middle) shows the need for the cross. If we cannot accept the cross, we cannot accept the covenant.
6. This day is a time of intimacy with God.
7. This is a resting time to receive love from God, not only to praise Him.
8. This is a day to learn of and walk in the excellencies of God. We can excel in any domain in which God excels.
9. This is a time that calls for the end of Satan's rule and the establishment of the Kingdom of God on earth.
10. God multiplies provision on this day. We claim in the Sabbath the right to have our seed multiplied by the Creator God of increase.
11. This is a time to admire God and praise Him corporately.
12. This is also a time for admiring God's creation.
13. The Sabbath is the time for the release of all the blessings of God.
14. This day is a time of refreshing.
15. The Sabbath is a time of revival. We can call forth renewal and new life.
16. This day is a time of reformation. We can call for the past to be reformed.
17. This is a time of confidence. We call forth boldness as we walk in the spirit rather than the flesh.
18. This day is a key to understanding the Word of God. Everything in the Bible is related to the Sabbath.
19. This is the day of resurrection power.
20. This is a day to wear freshly washed garments, representing the resurrection of Jesus and our new life in Him. In Exodus 19 Jesus commanded the believers to wash their garments before receiving the law of the government of God.
21. This is a time of releasing or loosing every binding Satan has put upon us.
22. This is a day of memorial, commemorating the Creator and our redemption from sin.
23. This is a time of reflecting on God's Word and seeking understanding from the Holy Spirit.
24. This is a time to covet closeness with God. As Jacob wrestled with Jesus and held on tight to Him, so we hold tightly to Jesus and His Sabbath covenant to receive His blessings.
25. This is a day to heal and to do good, to be a witness of Jesus' light. We speak life and healing into everything.

Sabbath *Selah's*
Uh-oh, Uzzah! Uzzah "Wuzza" and then He "Wuzzn't"

Jesus had amply warned Israel not to touch that which was holy. As an example for all time to all who would touch what God says is holy, Uzzah fell dead when he touched the holy ark of God (II Sam. 6:1-8). While Jesus acted with more severe and immediate judgment for His physical people under the Old Covenant and gives us more rope today, His principles do not change. He expects us to respect those things He makes holy. Because Jesus has poured Himself into the Sabbath day as He put part of His very presence in the ark, when we trample underfoot His day, we are stepping on Jesus! To disrespect the holy Sabbath is to disrespect the Holy One who made it holy. Jesus made an example of the man gathering wood on the Sabbath, directing the people to stone him to death (Num. 15:35). Sabbath breaking is serious and leads eventually to death (Rom. 6:23). But Jesus offers to those who choose to keep it now abundant life. Selah.

CHAPTER THIRTEEN

Jesus Loved "All that Old Testament stuff"

To hear some Christians talk about "all that Old Testament stuff," you would think the devil wrote it! No, but it is certainly Satan who inspires believers to dismiss important Bible teachings with "That's Old Testament."

These kinds of comments are doctrines of demons. They are part of a diabolical plan to undermine, underestimate, minimize, disparage, slander, put down, negate, malign, attack, and destroy the Word of God. This is such a blockage to accepting the Sabbath that we have dedicated two chapters to this important subject.

What men have called the "Old Testament" may be older than the gospels, but it is not out of date. Nowhere in the Bible does God call this part of His Word old. Men have labeled it old. This is Satan's way of making it sound like it is no longer to be considered, read, and obeyed.

The "Old Testament" makes up about three-fourths, 75% of the Word of God. Yet in Christendom it is sadly relegated as unimportant, outdated, outmoded, old hat, and backward. Millions of "New Testaments" are printed and some Christians are content to read that 25% of the Word only. Even if they have the complete Word of God, they rarely delve into what they often consider "that boring stuff."

The put down of this part of God's Word is not always blatant. Slurs abound. One lady moderator on a religious TV program said something like this in reading a verse from the Hebrew Scriptures: "I know this sounds kind of Old Testamenty, but..." While she meant well, her comment reflects the attitude of many Christians. They seem embarrassed about this first part of the Bible – even embarrassed for God. They feel they need to excuse God for writing such harsh, vindictive, and boring text.

Many soul-saving crusaders, defying what God says in almost 700 Bible verses, including from the Greek Scriptures, go on soul-winning campaigns and try to save people whether the Father has drawn them or not (John 6:44; 15:16; Acts 13:48). They frequently give the new converts a small "New Testament." It's as if they are scared to hit them with the whole Word of God, afraid these new ones might be offended at the Hebrew part of the Bible. After all, they themselves have a hard time swallowing it.

I don't think God is happy about us apologizing for Him. Jesus surely isn't. Those words are His words, whether people like to admit it or not. He will expect us to apologize for apologizing.

Did you know that without "that Old Testament stuff," it is impossible to prove that Jesus is your Savior? Did you know that without that first 75% of God's Word, you can claim only 10% of the promises of God? That's right. 90% of our covenant promises are in that first part of the Bible, as well as all the ten covenants God makes with man except one.

Have you ever tried to fight with one-fourth of a sword? The Word of God is our sword of spiritual warfare against Satan (Heb. 4:12). Do you think we're going to do much damage to the enemy with such a pitiful sword? Jesus defeated Satan in the desert with the Sword of the Spirit – the Word. It was *all* "that Old Testament stuff."

How many of you over 40 or 50 like to be called old? One day a young man saw me dancing at a praise and worship concert. He told me how young I looked, that I seemed like I was in my twenties. The very same day I bought a pack of bus tickets and the store clerk asked me if I was a senior. Few people like to be called old, especially not an old fuddy-duddy. But that's the way we make the Hebrew Scriptures sound when we call them old.

Men added the terms "Old Testament" and "New Testament" between those two parts of the Bible that were written at different times. But God did not invent those terms. We could just as well call the two testaments the Hebrew Scriptures and the Apostolic Writings. You can probably see how much of a challenge it is for me as an author to use different terms for these parts of the Bible. It's awkward. It's hard to make it clear without coming up with accurate but long descriptions of the two Testaments.

Both Testaments speak of the Old and New Covenants or agreements. To be fair, they both also speak of a testament, a will ratified by blood. The Old Covenant was ratified and sealed by animal blood that prefigured the blood Jesus would shed later to seal the New Covenant, which is also a new testament or will.

While Paul does speak of Moses reading to the people the Old Covenant, as it should be properly translated, (II Cor. 3:14), he is not referring to what men call the "Old Testament."

Different Administrations – Same Message of Love

Paul calls the Old Covenant period "the ministry of condemnation" (II Cor. 3:9) because Jesus had not come to die and be raised again. No eternal life was available. Jesus only offered people a blessed life on earth if they obeyed, and those who had the Holy Spirit would come to life when Jesus descended to the place of the dead. They would ascend with Jesus when He ascended to heaven (Eph. 4:8).

Jesus had his servants administer death for those who disobeyed under the Old Covenant. While rightly severe for evildoers, even Paul calls this system "glorious." The law never changed. Jesus only expanded it during His ministry (Mat. 5:17-19). It was the administration that changed because of different people and their limitations, but it was the same Jesus who administered both systems.

Jesus, for instance, ordered Old Covenant believers to be executed for knowingly breaking the Sabbath. And of course, they all knew about the Sabbath. While He is merciful to the ignorant today, when they do come to the Sabbath knowledge, He says they will lose out on eternal life if they refuse Him in His day (Heb. 3 and 4 and 13:18-29; Ex. 31:15). Jesus hasn't changed. His punishment for Old Covenant Israel was a temporary death followed by a later resurrection. Today the punishment is a permanent, eternal one.

The Jesus who exacted the penalty of disobedience upon Uzzah for touching the sacred ark of the testimony is the same Jesus who struck Ananias and his wife dead for lying to the Holy Spirit. Jesus has always had radical punishment for radical disobedience. And if Jesus considered touching a holy thing expressly forbidden to be touched a radical gesture deserving radical punishment, what do you suppose He thinks about Christians trampling on His holy time of fellowship with them (Isa. 58:13-14)?

The Jesus who was called in the First Testament a consuming fire is still a consuming fire in the second (Deut. 4:24; Heb. 12:29).

"The First Words of Jesus" Must Be Honored

Jesus is not outdated or outmoded, and He hasn't changed. Nor have His words in Part I of the Bible. While God inspired the text and had it written many long years ago, its principles are up to date.

God's words are never called old. And if we can use the word "Testament' for convenience and for clarity's sake, both Testaments agree on this point. In fact, it's hard to read the Second Testament without the first. The first is heavily quoted in the second. The Hebrew Scriptures are the foundation on which the Greek Scriptures were based. Peter quoted this powerful verse: "The grass withers, the flower fades, But the word of our God stands forever" (Isa. 40:8; I Pet. 1:24-25).

Jesus said: "Heaven and earth will pass away, but My words will not pass away" (Mat. 24:35). We proved in the last chapter that it was Jesus who spoke in the Hebrew Scriptures. This understanding brings that neglected 75% of the Word to life. Remember that John 1 says Jesus *is* the Word.

To be technically correct, the "Old Testament" should be called, **"The First Words of Jesus (Who *is* Love)"** and the "New Testament" should be named, **"The Last Words of Jesus (Love)."** No red letters exist in the original text. All of the words of the Book called the Bible are the words of Jesus. While His words as a human during His ministry do carry considerable weight, they are no truer than the words He spoke in Part I of the Bible. Progressive revelation adds more truth to what Jesus gave earlier, yet all the words He speaks are true.

It's all good. It's all true. It is the complete Word of God and it's all connected. You can't understand Part I without Part II and you can't understand Part II without Part I.

Part I explains who Jesus is, His character. Part II explains who we are in Him. Part I explains the prophecies of Jesus to come in the flesh and at His return in glory. It also allows us to understand the plan of God. Part II adds to Part I all the empowerment of the Holy Spirit, all the graces of God to carry out all the instructions and moral laws of Part I. Most importantly, it adds the blood of Jesus – His death and resurrection – without which we could not live Part I. The Holy Spirit enables us to love God and neighbor.

Like Hand in Glove – A Perfect Fit in Love

Some men have teased their mates with this declaration: "We have a great complementary relationship: I have many excellent qualities and my wife has lots of faults."

Amazingly, that is how many view the relationship between Part I and II. Part I has lots of faults, but Part II redeems it with all kinds of great qualities. Untrue. Part II is incomplete without Part I. They are complementary and both important, in the same way that mates add to one another. They have the same message said in different ways.

That message is eloquently stated in Part I: "You shall love the [Eternal] your God with all your heart and with all your soul and with all your might…you shall love your neighbor as yourself…"(Deut. 6:5; Lev. 19:18). In both parts the message is love. Part II simply makes it possible to love (Deut. 5:29; Rom. 13:10). The symmetry of love is astounding: 613 commandments of love in Part I and exactly the same in Part II.

That's a shocker – for the greasy grace gang. We've discussed it elsewhere in this book, but it needs accenting in this context.

The resistance and disdain of "that Old Testament stuff" is encapsulated in a phrase you often hear: "Come on, now. Don't tell me about this Sabbath stuff. I'm into grace, man. Don't burden me now with a bunch of do's and don't's." But if you look honestly at the Bible, including Part II, you must admit that the Bible is full of do's and don't's. But it's not about do's and don't's. It's about our attitude toward the do's and don't's. It's about a heart transformation. It's about what both parts espouse: love.

When you're in love with Jesus, you don't look on any commandment as a burden or restriction. You look at each law as a protection – a boundary given by the God who *is* Love. You obey because you're in love. It's not "I gotta…." It's "I wanna …" "It doesn't matter how many commandments you have for me, Jesus. I'll do 'em all 'cause I love You!" On your honeymoon did you take your new wife out to a lovely restaurant because that's what husbands are supposed to do and you felt obligated? I don't think so.

I rented the best Bed and Breakfast in Asheville, N.C., with the romantic package complete with champagne, chocolate, and flowers for my wife because I was and am in love with her. No specific law in the Bible tells me I had to do that. But if there were such a commandment, I would willingly submit to My Divine Master and Supreme Commander Jesus. I would obey. In this case, it would be easy. Some laws require more self-denial.

The Hour is Coming, and Now Is, for a Gut Check and a Spell Check

The Sabbath is usually, at least at the beginning, one of those commandments. It's a test. You have to go against the flow of the world like a salmon fighting to go upstream against the current. But it's worth it. The temporary pain brings a permanent joy.

The point is this: it's not the law that is the issue. It's our attitude toward the law. The law is simply love – love spelled out. Not love left for *us* to spell out. The church has misspelled love by changing the Sabbath to Sunday.

I was in many spelling bees in my youth. I know what one letter can mean. One letter was the difference between winning the county bee and coming in second. One letter. The Sabbath is one commandment in ten. But it is far, far, far from being the "least of these commandments" (Mat. 5:19) that Jesus warned us not to annul.

As an author now, I am extremely thankful for the handy-dandy computer spell-checker. While I didn't need it for the word "spell-checker" that I just spelled correctly, sometimes I need it. Some commandments are easy to discern and obey. It comes almost naturally because we're in love with Jesus. Others, like the Sabbath, have been so twisted by deceived theologians and pastors, with an encouraging historical push from constantly compromising Constantine, that it gets complicated.

We need help. Especially from the Helper and Teacher, the Holy Spirit. And He has anointed me to give you some help, at the price of resistance from the spirit of religiosity. While it will not be easy for most of you to make this end-time paradigm shift without some amount of initial sweat and tears and some persecution, it can be done.

We must first, however, allow the Holy Spirit and the Word to make a paradigm shift in our thinking. We can't swallow the lie that obeying the law is legalism. While obeying the law of gravity is automatic and obeying God's law of love is not, both laws are inexorable. They exert a penalty whether you know about them or not.

The church has been falling from the top of the edifice represented by Jesus and the apostles, falling headlong for seventeen or eighteen stories (centuries) and has almost reached the point of tragic impact. The consequences of Sabbath breaking are about to greet us in devastating fashion, as tragic and destructive as a seventeen-story fall to a cement sidewalk can be. Things may seem A-OK for sixteen stories, but the end is almost in sight, and it isn't pretty.

Before blood and guts fill the end-time street of sorrows and tribulation below, it's time for a gut check – and a spell check. It's time we got a witness in our gut from the Holy Spirit based on the Word – a Sabbath gut check. It's also time for a spell check from our Spell-Checker par excellence, Jesus.

His opinion, His Word – yea, His inexorable law of love – is more important than the opinion of any man or woman of God. It matters little how famous they are, how many people read their books or watch them on TV. They have made a grave spelling error. They have missed one of the most important laws and covenants of God. Consequently, the fullness of the prophesied, end-time glory cannot be released until we push the computer control key and with one mouse click correct our spelling.

It will require a gut check. And it will take guts.

The Sabbath is not spelled "S-u-n-d-a-y." Any reputable Bible scholar, even one who keeps Sunday, will confirm this truth. They know when the Sabbath is. But they have their strange but universally accepted reasoning to explain it away in favor of Sunday or any day of the week. Their explanations don't hold water, definitely not the waters of the Holy Spirit. The Holy Spirit cannot disagree with the Word, so if you think "the Lord" is telling you that we are giving you a false teaching, you better check which "Lord" is talking to you.

Baal was called "Lord" – and his day was and is Sunday. Quagmire, we know by years of deliverance experience, is a demon who calls himself "Lord." He pushes people from one ditch to another, an apt picture of the church today. He wants you to stay in the Sunday sewer so you won't be blessed by the powerful anointing of the Holy Spirit that is reserved for the day Jesus blessed and calls holy.

The major healing ministries have understood by experience that the most healings occur on Friday night after sunset to Saturday sunset. They hold their healing services then because it works. We pray they will soon make the connection. They may rethink their "Jewish Sabbath, under-the-law" paradigm and opt for God's day. It pays.

Personal Experience in Sabbath Freedom

I know. I began to observe the Sabbath in 1967-68. Forty years is biblically the test and trial of man. It has indeed been a test, trial and error with more error than trial. I started to keep it full of youthful and Holy Spirit enthusiasm, and it was a veritable joy. When I allowed unforgiveness to enter my heart, I cut myself off from the Holy Spirit. The joy of Jesus was transformed into a legalistic Sabbath observance, full of man-made do's and don'ts because I was walking in the flesh.

My family and I went through twelve tragic years where I was not the same person who was previously my children's daddy. But in 1998, God was good to me. He had heard my plaintive cry, I believe, before I was even born. He knew what I would go through because of my unforgiveness and dead works, and He had the redemptive solution.

I asked for a human being to help me. And one day that divine appointment occurred. I had cursed myself and others had cursed me. I didn't even know what a curse was at the time. But God is so good He led me in a crowded room to focus on the face of a man who has become by the grace of God an authority on the misunderstood subject of curses. He was prophesied and ordained as an apostle for the release of God's people – to be an instrument to set us free, all glory going to God.

Freedom is a process -- and still is for me. God is truly a merciful God, or I wouldn't be writing these words.

My Sabbath observance began to change radically in 1998, the year God instantaneously healed me of two incurable illnesses that had turned my life and family upside down. Now God was putting me right side up. I begin to taste some of the gifts of the Holy Spirit, granting me a freedom I had never known and enabling me to experience the true freedom of the Sabbath day.

Guidelines from the Word and Holy Spirit Are Not Legalism

Sabbath freedom is not an oxymoron. I begin to wonder why James called the Ten Commandments the "law of liberty" (James 2:12). My freedom was enhanced because when Jesus healed me in 1998, he also removed spiritual, demonic blockages that opened me up to change. I began to reexamine my legalistic approach to the Sabbath.

While God gives general guidelines, especially as we look at the way Jesus kept the Sabbath, it is a personal area of our lives. My friend showed me that it was a day of celebration. My friend would relax with a special Sabbath snack and watch an uplifting movie on Friday night. That would have been a legalistic no-no to me before.

As a golfer, I remember asking my friend about golfing on the Sabbath. He said, "The Sabbath is a day of family celebration. If you put the priority on being at Jesus' appointed time for Sabbath services and celebrate with the Family of God, there's no problem with going for a golf game with the family." Since I had no family with me at the time, I didn't do it. But the liberating thought was refreshing: God is not a picky legalist. I was still thinking, "Yeah, but with our service schedule, I could only get in nine holes." I had to change my legalistic mindset, but I could see the freedom in the Sabbath I had never seen before. Mind you, everyone is different.

That's where the *principle* of the chapter people like to twist comes in. Romans 14 is not talking about the fourth commandment, which is not up for discussion as to *whether* we keep it. It's talking about whether you eat meat or just veggies or about when during the month or week you decide to fast. But the principle, and only the principle, does apply to the Sabbath. We don't condemn others for the way they keep the Sabbath.

It's a day of rest – a rest from our normal routine. So, barring emergencies and true exceptions as guided by the Holy Spirit, it's not the day to do your house cleaning, your wash, or your shopping. It's not the typical Sunday way, where you go to church for an hour or maybe less and you spend the rest of the day doing your thing. It's special. It's holy. It's nothing like the other days. It's time to rest and celebrate – enjoy creation, enjoy life, enjoy your family, and the Family of God, enjoy seeing people healed and set free.

Go With the Flow and You'll Be a Dead Fish

Because I'm writing about the Sabbath, some of you may judge me as a legalist. But if you've never kept the Sabbath in the freedom of the Holy Spirit, the freedom in which Jesus kept it, how can you judge? Try it. You'll like it. You will also see that this "Baalish" banter that calls the Sabbath Jewish and a burden is a bunch of… uh…Baal. It's a lie from Satan that you may have swallowed. Why? Reasons vary: "My pastor said that's being under the law." Or: "How come you're telling me this is what we're supposed to do when I don't see anybody else who's anybody in the church doing it."

Go with the flow if you like. But mark our word: you will soon flow into the deep, treacherous waters of Great Tribulation. That's not a fear tactic. It's simply the truth. We pray that you will be able to avoid taking the Mark of the Beast, which is more than some computer chip in hand or forehead. It's Sunday, Baal worship and will soon become Beast worship, based on a belief in your head and action of your will as pictured by the hand.

Go against the flow and you may be spared the wrath of Satan in "the hour of testing" (Rev. 3:10). Be a Sabbath keeping "salmon" that goes against the prevailing current. Go upstream with Jesus. Don't swallow the stupid lie that says, "That's Old Testament. That's history." If you do accept that lie, *you* may be history.

Sabbath *Selah's*
What Does Oil Have to Do with All?

You shall therefore keep *every* commandment which I am commanding you today, so that you may be *strong* and go in and possess the land...(Deut. 11:8).

...the Holy Spirit, whom God has given to those who *obey* Him (Acts 5:32).

The Spirit of the [Eternal] will rest on Him...The spirit of counsel and strength, The spirit of knowledge and the [reverence, love, respectful obedience] of the [Eternal] (Isa. 11:2-3).

Some Texans pronounce the word "oil" almost like the word "all." A connection does exist. Keeping all *the commandments of God makes us stronger, increasing the presence of the anointing* oil *of the Holy Spirit. Keeping all the commandments erects a wall of protection around us and makes us strong. Without the Sabbath commandment, a breach exists in that wall or circle of love. We are called to repair that breach (Isa. 58:12-14). Possessing the land pictures the Kingdom and the time when Jesus calls us up to be with Him. Without all the oil, we cannot be ready (Mat. 25:1-13).*

"Then all those virgins rose and trimmed their lamps. The foolish said to the prudent, 'Give us some of your oil, for our lamps are going out." "But the prudent answered, 'No, there will not be enough for us and you too; go instead to the dealers [persecutors] and buy some for yourselves.' (Mat. 25:7-9). *Selah.*

CHAPTER FOURTEEN

The Bible is All Ture: If You Pick and Choose, You Lose

While God gives us full freedom, even to reject Him completely, He does not mince His words in the Bible. He sets before us life and death as choices (Deut. 30:19). Satan has given us his day of death through a pagan emperor who wanted to pollute Christianity with pagan sun worship on Sun-day. Jesus, the Way, the Truth, and the Life, offers us Himself, the Way, the Truth, and the Life, in His Sabbath day.

Jesus says, "Choose life" (Deut. 30:19). Choose *all* of Life. Choose *all* My words of life. Don't pick and choose which words of Mine you accept and which You reject.

I once gave a sermon on this subject in which I introduced the topic by reading three pages of Scripture – only the words without chapter and verse. I asked the audience before I read them what they all had in common. No one guessed. They were powerful passages, some quite well known. Many were unique and stated principles only revealed in those verses.

The surprising answer was that they were all part of "that Old Testament stuff." Oh, but it was good. All were powerful words of love – words of Jesus.

The two parts of the Bible were like a loving couple – made for each other. You can't have one without the other. They fit together like hand in glove – a perfect fit in love.

But not everyone likes the fit. Some take only the parts of Part I of the Bible that fit their fancy. Some don't even like all of Part II. They throw out the gospels and take only the epistles. Some swear only by Paul. And some want it all. How about you? Do you want all of God, all of Love? Do you want all of the Words of

Love Jesus offers you? Or do you want to pick and choose the amount of Love you receive?

It is said of one of the first American presidents that he took his Bible and literally cut out with scissors the parts he didn't like. Most Christians do the same today – without the scissors. But if you decide to pick and choose, you lose. You lose out on the blessing of living by every Word of God as Jesus did and told us to do.

"It Is Written" – All of the Word Must Abide in Us

In his titanic battle with the devil in the desert, Jesus kept saying, "It is written…" Where was it written? Those who are totally new and who receive only a little New Testament must wonder. They must ask themselves, "Am I missing something?" Yes, they are.

Jesus quoted His own Word when He said, "Man shall not live on bread alone, but on *every word* that proceeds out of the mouth of God" (Mat. 4:4). Satan had no answer. He lies, but He knows the truth. He knows the Word and trembles before it. He didn't come back with, "That's Old Testament." At that time, of course, that's all that existed. It was then, and it still is the Word of God. In fact, Jesus was the God, the Word that spoke it (Deut. 8:3).

How can you obey Jesus and live by every Word of His if you only take seriously one-fourth of His Word of Love?

What percentage of Your prayers are answered? Maybe, just maybe, the percentage of your prayers could depend on the percentage of the Bible you take seriously? Is that possible?

It's more than possible. It's a truth Jesus spoke: "If you abide in Me, and My words abide in you, ask whatever you [desire[1]], and it will be done for you" (John 15:7).

Most people do more wishing than praying, even Christians. Satan will hear their "prayer" and give them what they wish for – with great backlash they didn't expect. Even Christians who do pray to the Father God don't get many answers because they do not fulfill the conditions for answered prayer. One important condition is found in the words of Jesus cited above and recorded by the Sabbath keeper and apostle of Love who believed all the Words of Love.

Jesus said we could expect answers to our prayers. Prayer doesn't have to be a desperate last resort. Sadly, for many Sunday worshippers who have been pushed

1 "Wish" is a bad word from witchcraft, asking Satan rather than God for something. It is an inaccurate translation originated by King James translators who delved into sorcery. None of them were true Christians.

by Lord Quagmire from ditch to ditch, prayer is often an exercise in wishful thinking.

They've actually failed to meet two conditions in this verse. "Abide in Me," commands Jesus. But they don't take seriously the words of the Divine Master, the Supreme Commander of Love. They take seriously the days of the Lord, the days of Baal, even though they know they have pagan origins. But they don't take Jesus seriously when He says He is Divine Master of the Sabbath.

They surely can't abide truly and fully in Him when they fail to meet with Him on the day where He shows up in a special way – a way He doesn't show up on regular days.

Not a Regular Day

When I got a diary for Christmas at the age of eight, I wrote in my new journal only several times. It seemed that my eight-year-old life was uneventful. Every day seemed the same. So after a few days I simply wrote a big R on my diary page for that day. That signified for me: "regular day." I am thankful God has anointed me since to be a more prolific writer. And even if I am not as gifted as some authors whose prose is awe-inspiring, what God has given me to write is far from regular or unimportant.

The day He has appointed me to write about is not a regular day, no matter what men of the cloth have told you. Listen instead to what Jesus taught about His special day. It hasn't registered with the champions of religiosity that it was none other than ***Jesus*** who thundered out the Ten Words (Hebrew *dabar* or "word") -- some extremely emphatic statements by the One who later came to die for you and me. Jesus said, "Remember the Sabbath day, to keep it holy. Six days you shall labor [that includes Sunday] and do all your work but ***the*** [not any day, not any day of the week ***we*** choose, but the day He later kept as our example, the same day the Jewish people have kept without a change since Jesus kept it among them then] ***seventh day*** is a sabbath of the [Eternal] your God [who was the One speaking, the Word Himself, Jesus]" [Ex. 20:8-9].

God's Access Point to His People

If we are not keeping Jesus' *dabar* or words here – the *dabar* or *logos* of the Logos Himself -- then we are not abiding fully in Him. He abides in the Sabbath day.

While Jesus said He would never leave us because He lives inside us, He has poured Himself into a space of time in order to meet in a special way with His people. On that day and on no other in the same way, He gives of Himself and abides or dwells with His people. The Sabbath, along with the cross it represents, is ***God's access point to His people***. If we are not abiding in Him on His day, we cannot have full access nor expect to have 100% answered prayer.

Jesus adds another condition, a word many Christians don't like. But "condition" is a covenant word. Jesus set conditions. He demands total surrender to Him. The Sabbath is the great, end-time test of total surrender.

Here is the second condition to assurance of answered prayer: "...and My words abide in you." Some Christians have red-letter Bibles with the words of Jesus in the gospels marked in red. In one sense, the whole Bible should be marked in red. All the words are the words of Jesus, even the words in that "Old Testament."

They are all written in red in the blood of the One who died for us so that He, the Word, might live in us. How can we say that His words abide in us if we only take seriously and meditate upon one-fourth of His Word of Love?

All God's Words Must Be Taken Seriously

Part II is abundantly clear in declaring that Part I is to be taken seriously. Listen to what Paul told Timothy: "...from childhood you have known the sacred writings [Like the Sabbath, the Hebrew Scriptures are called holy] which are able to give you the wisdom that leads to salvation ["That Old Testament stuff" can actually lead you to salvation, Yeshua in Hebrew, the very name of Jesus, as witnessed in "the gospel according to Isaiah"] through faith which is in Christ Jesus. All Scripture is inspired and profitable, says Paul, "so that the man of God may be adequate..."(II Tim. 3:15-17).

What a powerful testimony from the lips of Paul of the importance of the Hebrew Scriptures! They can bring you to salvation in Jesus. They are profitable despite the bad press Christians give them today. You can't be adequate without them.

When Paul wrote this only a few Second Testament scrolls were being circulated. The only codified Scripture was what some call the "Old Testament." Paul never thought of it as old. Nor should we. The entire Word of God is timeless, God-breathed, infallible in its original form, and useful to us – not merely the last 25%.

Jesus has severe warnings for those who reject His Word – any part of it. He decries what the wicked do when He says, "And you cast My words behind you [The Amplified Bible adds, "discarding them"]"(Ps. 50:17).

Jesus commanded Joshua to meditate on and practice *all* of the *torah* or words of instruction that He had given to Moses (Joshua 1:7-8). How can we go into our Promised Land without reading and living all of God's instruction in His Word? The Promised Land rest looked forward to the rest of the Kingdom of God. If we don't enter into Jesus' weekly Sabbath rest, we block our path to the Kingdom rest (Heb. 4:8-9).

Honoring every word of Jesus, who is Life, can actually save your physical life and "keep you from the hour of testing...to come upon the whole world" (Rev. 3:10). To whom does Jesus promise this protection in these last days? To those who "have *kept My **word*** and have not denied My name [His name is not "Lord"]" (Rev. 3:8). If we demean and discard 75% of Jesus' Word as we snarl, "That's Old Testament," we won't qualify. In this end time, only those who value and use the entire Word and the name of Jesus will "escape *all* these things" (Luke 21:36).

Paul continues to uphold all the words of Jesus: "Let the word of Christ richly dwell within you [25% doesn't sound too rich to me], with all wisdom teaching and admonishing one another in *psalms...*" (Col. 3:16). Where are the Psalms? In the "Old Testament." Many Christians and New Testament distributors add Psalms and Proverbs to the New Testaments they hand out. It's almost like they're saying, "God, we approve of these two books in Your outdated and boring Old Testament, so we're doing a good public relations job for You, avoiding embarrassment for You when these new people start reading Your Word." God isn't embarrassed. But we should be if we dishonor His Word.

Remember that when the apostles spoke of the law, they were using the Hebrew term *torah,* which carries the larger meaning of instruction or teaching. When James was upholding all the law of God, including the fourth commandment, He was also validating all the Hebrew Scripture (James 2:8-10; 4:11). In fact, the meaning of *torah,* when you take the letters separately, means "*that which comes from the man on the cross*." All Scripture comes from the Word, Jesus.

We have already examined Matthew 5:17-19 regarding the Sabbath commandment. Jesus said He did not come to destroy the law, but people interpret His words here to say that He did just that. The Phillips translation makes it clear: "You must not think that I have come to abolish the Law or the Prophets [a shorthand reference to the three-part Hebrew Scriptures – law, prophets and writings]; I have not come to abolish them but to ***complete*** them" (Mat. 5:17). Well said. Jesus came to fill up (fulfill) or complete the revelation, instruction, law or Word of God. He came to add to it, not do away with it.

Hebrews 1:1-2 confirms this. Jesus only continues the revelation given by Hebrew prophets. It's simple math: addition, not subtraction.

Sacrifices are no longer necessary, but the words written about the sacrifices are rich in meaning for us. They all point to Jesus. The tabernacle is long gone, but the description of it in the Hebrew Scriptures describes Jesus in detail.

Jesus preached about His Messiahship from the Hebrew Scriptures. He openly spoke of and upheld the tripartite organization of the Scripture, the Law, the Prophets, and the Psalms or Writings (Luke 24:44-45). "Then He opened their minds to understand the Scriptures." Jesus led people to Jesus from the "Old Testament."

The Bible is a Complete and Perfect Book

Seven is God's number of completion and perfection. He speaks of seven days in the recreation of the earth and says that He "completed His work" by resting on the seventh day (Gen. 2:2). In the same manner He will perfect and complete His plan for man in seven one thousand year "days" (II Pet. 3:8). The last of those days is the millennial Sabbath day, signifying the Kingdom of God on earth.

The seven annual Sabbaths and the seven annual feasts culminate in the seventh month. A brief skim in a concordance will demonstrate the frequency and significance of the number seven in the Bible.

When Peter asked Jesus how many times we had to forgive our brother, Jesus gave the ultimate perfect and complete number (490 or 70 times 7) to show Peter that our forgiveness should be complete and perfect. The number 49 is 7 times 7 and also represents perfection and completion.

It is no coincidence that God inspired not 66 books, but originally 49 scrolls, to make the complete Bible – 22 Hebrew scrolls corresponding to the 22 letters of the Hebrew "aleph-bet" and 27 Greek scrolls. Moses, Ezra, Peter and John did the major selection of the canon or inspired group of Scriptural scrolls.

Three major sections and seven minor sections compose the Hebrew canon, while seven sections also comprise the Greek canon. All the scrolls were finalized during seven periods of canonization. Seven major sections comprise the complete Bible as well. The inspired order differs from the order arranged by later translators. Interestingly, canonizers put the seven General Epistles (James, Peter, and John) before Paul's epistles, giving readers a foundation to understand the more difficult verses penned by Paul.

It is obvious that God planned the Book of Revelation to come last. The contrasts show a beginning-to-end thread that is unmistakable. In Genesis we see a Tree of Life, a garden, the first heavens and earth, and in Revelation we see the same, except the heavens and earth become new. We see Jesus in both books as the Alpha and the Omega, the Beginning and the End, the Beginning in Genesis and the End in Revelation.

John was responsible for sealing the last books and the entire canon of the Bible. When he sealed the entire Bible with the forty-ninth scroll, He had strong words for anyone who adds to or takes away from the perfect and complete 49 scrolls (Rev. 22:18-19). That warning should ring loudly in the ears of those who would reject the First Testament.

When you reject any part of the Word of God, you are rejecting all of it. Paul said, "For I did not shrink from declaring to you the whole purpose [or counsel] of God" (Acts 20:27).

Day of Completion

When an artist puts his finishing touches on his creation, it is that last brush stroke that changes everything. Without it, his work would be incomplete. While God had finished the physical creation, what He created on the seventh day was His finishing touch that actually represented a new creation -- a spiritual one as well as a space of time. It was a space of time that was dear to Him and would be dear to the heart of every believer who deeply desired to be near His heart.

For six days of re-creation, through the words of Jesus, the God Family spoke order into a renewed creation that had been previously marred by Satan. A beautiful garden emerged that met man's every need -- except one. That need was what set him apart from the rest of the creation. Man was created to be like God, a spirit being made up of spirit, soul, and body. Without God's character being molded into the tripartite entity that was man, the creation was incomplete. Indeed, the very reason God created man could not be fulfilled without the creation of the Sabbath. It would be the day of the week that God would meet with man, to fellowship with him and form a new spiritual creation in him.

Just as Jesus had redeemed the chaos Satan had caused by remaking and refinishing the earth, so He made the Sabbath as the day for celebrating the completion of God's physical creation as well as the day by which God's human creation would be completed spiritually to become exactly like God.

It's like "finishing school." English children of means often attend a finishing school to perfect them in all areas. The Sabbath is God's finishing school. Without it, you cannot be complete -- whether in knowledge, understanding, wisdom, or in the character of God. Jesus Himself grew in wisdom and spiritual stature by faithfully keeping the Sabbath (Luke 4:16). He even taught on the Sabbath (4:31). Jesus has not changed, continuing to teach His people on the Sabbath through the Holy Spirit. He preached the Kingdom of God on the Sabbath (4:43-44), and He continues to reveal the secrets of the Kingdom on the day that prophesies the Kingdom of God on earth.

How can His Kings and Priests prepare to rule in the Kingdom here on earth now and later if they do not meet with the King and the teaching Priest, Jesus, on His day?

The Sabbath is the day of final completion, as the number seven implies. We cannot be the complete spiritual creation without this day of intimacy with Jesus. It is a test. It is the time into which Jesus poured Himself so we could come into our full identity, into His righteousness, excellence, and glory. When we refuse to keep the Sabbath, we are entwined in the world and its ways, swept up in the system of this cosmos. We cannot rest in Jesus. We cannot know Him in the way He wants us to know Him. We limit ourselves and Jesus' working in our lives.

As with the new moon celebrations, to be discussed in the sequel to this book, it is somewhat like trying to have a marriage without sexual intimacy. We cannot know our mates without the consummation of the marriage and regular sexual intimacy. The Sabbath is the only day that our Bridegroom makes Himself available to us for the intimate contact we need to know Him fully.

Jesus is called the Author and Finisher of our faith. The Sabbath is His main vehicle for accomplishing this purpose. It is the day of the defeat of the one who tries to finish us in the negative sense. It is the day of victory of the One who brings us to perfection.

"That's Old Testament" – A Sorry Excuse for Rejecting Jesus

My colleague and I once spoke on a long distance phone call to the leader of a large church. We were answering questions about healing. We cited Psalm 103:3: "Who pardons all your iniquities, Who heals all your diseases…" He didn't believe, based on his experience, that we could be sure God promises to heal today. His response to this verse was, "That's Old Testament." I hope he has more confidence in God forgiving his sins than in healing his diseases.

To such leaders and pastors Jesus, in defense of His Word, would likely say: "That's My Word you are undermining. If you undermine My Word, you undermine Me. If you reject My Word, you reject Me!"

Once confession is made, God is prompt to forgive. But He is calling those who reject His Word to repent.

Satan has undermined the Hebrew Scriptures because he knows the anointing that accompanies the words. He knows the powerful verses it contains that Christians would use against him.

His teaching has been: "Accept my doctrine of greasy grace and let that Old Testament slide. Jesus came to give you grace, not condemnation like that harsh Father in the Old Testament."

Such false teachings have robbed Christians of a veritable gold mine of knowledge and understanding. Each Hebrew word has at least four meanings. In the prophecies, for instance, a verse has a first and final fulfillment, a meaning for the church in these last days and a personal meaning for each reader.

How Much Life and Light Do You Want?

Jesus said, "…the words that I have spoken to you are spirit and are life" (John 6:63). All the words Jesus ever spoke have life, whether in Part I or Part II of His Word. If you want only 25% of the life Jesus promised, read only the "New Testament." If you want to vibrate with the fullness of the Life of God, read it all, study it all, speak it all – obey it all. Blessings will pour down like rain.

Many powerful words and principles are contained in the Hebrew Scriptures that are not found in Part II. Without Part I, you can't declare that no weapon formed against you shall prosper (Isa. 54:17). You have little basis to claim your children's salvation (Isa. 49:25). What about the restoration of what Satan has stolen from you (Joel 2:25; Prov. 6:31)? What about all the promises of the Psalms and the wisdom of the Proverbs?

What about the Ten Commandments? The principles are all repeated, but the exact and full wording in order of these landmark laws of love is only found in Part I.

John sealed the entire book with the Book of Revelation, but you can't understand Revelation without Daniel, Zechariah, Ezekiel, and many other books, including, believe it or not, the book of Job, the most prophetic book in the Scripture and the subject of another of the books we plan to publish.

You can't fully understand the gospels without reading "the gospel according to Isaiah." Jesus preached Jesus from Isaiah.

If you only had access to Volume 4 of a four-volume series of books on "How to Build a Fallout Shelter," and you knew a bomb was going to be detonated tomorrow, do you think you might be interested in finding promptly the first three volumes so you could finish your shelter? You're going to need a shelter under the shadow of the Most High (Psalm 91) to escape what is to come (Luke 21:36). Do you want 25% of a shelter, wide open to attack? Or do you want full protection? By the way, you can't fully abide under the shadow of the Most High unless you are abiding with Him in His Sabbath day.

How can you know who you are in Jesus if you don't know who He is? You can't fully know who He is without the First Testament.

If you picked up this book and only read the last fourth of it, do you think you would get a full picture? What about a Stephen King novel?

Would you -- could you -- buy a house without a foundation? Part II of the Bible is built on Part I (Eph. 2:20). If you found that less than 1% of your house foundation was not necessary, would you destroy your foundation and build your house on sand? The sacrifices and rituals that are rendered unnecessary in Jesus compose only a small part of Part I, yet many Christians throw it all away because of those temporary ordinances.

David said God's Word was a lamp to his feet and a light to his path (Ps. 119:105). Do you want a little flashlight or a laser beam? To fight your spiritual battles in prayer, do you want a fly swatter or a mighty sword?

We have seen how God prophesied the New Covenant in the First Testament, saying He would write His law on men's hearts. Law or *torah* includes the broad meaning of all of God's teachings. So New Covenant believers have missed it. The goal of the New Covenant is to have the "Old Testament" written on their hearts.

Is the "Old Testament" done away? No way! But *we* may be eventually done away if we do away with 75% of Jesus' Word.

Isaiah prophesied the completion of Part I by the addition of Part II. Jesus made the law "great and glorious," or as one translation says, magnified it (Isa.

42:21). That's a far cry from being abolished. "Bind up the testimony, seal the law among my disciples" (Isa. 8:16). Jesus' disciples, notably Peter and John, put the final seal of completion on the *torah* and made binding its testimony.

Jesus said that Part I testified about Him (John 5:39). Seeing how Jesus was prophesied in detail in Part I is another lengthy subject, but it should fill us with faith and hope. Paul said it well: "For whatever was written in earlier times was written for our instruction, so that through perseverance and the encouragement of the Scriptures [Part I] we might have hope" (Rom. 15:4).

Jesus loved and upheld all His words and covenants that He spoke in Part I of the Bible – including His words about the Sabbath and His Sabbath covenant.

If we are to be fully pleasing to our Father, we need to cherish all the words His Son spoke. We must not malign or discard "The First Words of Jesus" ("Old Testament"). On the contrary, we need to do what Jesus did. We need to embrace, uphold, cherish, read, study, meditate upon, speak, and obey all of God's Word and covenants, not only the "New Testament" and the New Covenant (the ninth of ten biblical covenants).

Jesus words to the Pharisees in John 5:46-47 should ring in the ears of the guardians of today's religious system: "'For if you believed Moses, you would believe Me, for he wrote about Me. But if you do not believe his writings, how will you believe My words?'"

The words of Jesus in the Second Testament cannot be understood without reading and grasping the words Jesus Himself gave to Moses in the *Torah*, an important part of the Hebrew Scriptures, the part that contains the Sabbath commandment.

Paul agreed with Jesus on this key matter. ***Unless we are partakers of the rich, Jewish roots of Christianity by reading and believing Moses' words, we cannot begin to understand the words of Jesus in the gospels*** (Rom. 11:17). That is both "Pauline theology" and gospel truth! It also explains why many Christians today simply do not believe Jesus meant what He said.

As Jesus said in the Sermon on the Mount, all who uphold, teach and obey all the commandments and instructions of love contained in the whole and complete Word of God will be called great in the Kingdom of heaven.

Sabbath *Selah's*
The Stone Was Rolled Away -- not the Law!

Then they [Jesus' feminine followers] returned and prepared spices and perfumes. And on the Sabbath they rested according to the commandment... And they found the stone rolled away from the tomb...(Luke 23:56; 24:2).

When the day of Pentecost had come, they were all together in one place (Acts 2:1).

According to popular theology, the Sabbath was done away with Jesus' crucifixion and resurrection. Yet His most faithful followers were still keeping the fourth commandment after His crucifixion. Furthermore, they were united fifty days later keeping one of the annual *Sabbaths, the Feast of First Fruits or Pentecost, which means "count fifty." It is the only annual Sabbath that always falls on a Sunday, but they were not keeping it as Sunday but as an annual holy day (Lev. 23:15-21). Selah.*

CHAPTER FIFTEEN

"the stone was rolled away..."

That's what we read in Mark 16:4 (KJV). Five words that mark one of the greatest events in history.

A last stone must still be rolled away so we can see the real Jesus and know whether or not He was resurrected on a Sunday. This premise of a first day resurrection is the most frequent justification for Sunday worship. It has no foundation.

As I write, Hollywood hype is trying to resurrect an insignificant archeological find from 1980. This spurious resurrection is trying to cast doubt on Jesus' resurrection. Competent archeologists have refuted this gratuitous, "Titanic" attempt to say that Jesus' bones have been found.

But surprisingly, the greatest attempt to put a cloud over the resurrection comes from within the church. This effort to discredit Jesus does not focus on the resurrection itself, but on the exact timing of the resurrection.

Jesus' resurrection is a given. The apostles would not have died for a Jesus who married Mary Magdalene, had a child with her, and died a normal death. Interestingly, Jesus did not base the proof of His Messiahship on His resurrection, which He took for granted. The only sign He gave as proof He was the Messiah was the faithfulness of His prediction of the exact timing of this event.

What may surprise you and even offend you until you see the truth is the ultimate meaning of Easter Sunday observance and the subsequent Sunday-keeping that resulted.

Do you realize that almost the entirety of the Christian world rejects the only proof Jesus gave that He is our Savior?

Our Father is merciful. He foreknew the titanic deception that Satan would cause to reign in the church. After such a seduction that has lasted so long and has been taken for granted, your reaction may be disbelief. Yet the statement that follows in the next paragraph will be proved in this chapter. Please give us an opportunity to present the proof.

When Christians keep Sunday as a commemoration of Jesus' resurrection, they are, unwittingly for the most part, saying that Jesus is not their Savior! He is not the Savior of the world. Every Sunday they are, by their actions, rejecting the only sign or proof He gave that He was not just any Jesus, for Jesus was a common name of His day. He was and is Jesus the Christ, the Messiah, the Anointed One of His Father Love who came to die so we might be united with our Father.

When we deny the only sign He gave that He was the Anointed One who came to give His life for us, we are denying Him. When we willfully and knowingly refuse to meet with Him on His day, we are denying Jesus!

The stone was rolled away 2000 years ago. But another stone remains. That stone blocks believers from meeting with the real Jesus on His day and truly understanding who He is.

A Matter of Mathematics

Two simple mathematical operations prove the claims of this book. The first is so elementary that great scholars have overlooked it, or perhaps denied it because of its simplicity.

Jesus gave a simple, clear command to work six days and rest on the seventh (Ex. 20:8-9). All you need is a calendar, a dictionary, and simple math.

But it's more a question of belief than arithmetic. We don't seem to truly believe Jesus means what His says.

Our inability to believe in this only sign Jesus gave must mean we are indeed part of the "evil and adulterous generation" who would not believe Jesus. The only sign He gave to unbelievers is the one that is rejected by almost all believers today. What irony!

Speaking of this generation that wants proof and refuses to believe, Jesus said: "…no sign will be given to it but the sign of Jonah the prophet; for just as JONAH WAS **THREE DAYS AND THREE NIGHTS** IN THE BELLY OF THE SEA MONSTER, so will the Son of Man be three days and three nights in the heart of the earth" (Mat. 12:39-40).

The Christian world believes Jesus was buried late Friday afternoon and was resurrected early Sunday morning. Let's do some simple math: Friday night makes one night; Saturday during the day makes one day; Saturday night makes one more night. That makes one day and two nights. That falls short of three days and three nights by 2 days and 1 night. We have only half of the total number of days. In hours, we have 36 at the most, when 72 hours are required for Jesus to be truthful and to be our Savior.

The main problem is less arithmetic than idolatry. We have chosen to worship tradition over Jesus. That's much more tragic than bad math.

The Origins of Deception

Where did this deception originate? In the year A.D.147 Hermes, Pope Pius' brother "received instruction from an angel, who commanded that all men should keep the [Passover] on the Lord's day [Sunday]."[1] We will see later what Paul thought of angelic pronouncements that contradict the Word (Gal. 1:8-9). This angel was obviously a fallen one who had no light (Isa. 8:20).

This must have been the conception of the idea of keeping Easter in place of Passover and the Days of Unleavened Bread. Hermes was also coincidentally the name of a Greek god (demon) who gave fast translations of texts that twisted the meaning. We owe a lot to this god, a lot we should not want. His name formed the basis of the practice of hermeneutics, a scholarly and demonic aid to biblical understanding that has replaced the Teacher, the Holy Spirit.

This letter from Hermes helped Pius' successor, Anicetus, fight with John's disciple, Polycarp. The issue was whether Passover should be transferred to a Sunday. It's the same battle that rages today – a fight between Rome and the truth. Rome won. Satan thus cleverly sneaked Babylonian Mysteries into the organized Christian religion, at least in Rome. The staunch Sabbath keepers in Judea continued to believe and follow Jesus and His truth. Unlike the bishops of Rome, they believed what He said.

Had church fathers continued in believing and practicing Jesus' words as did Polycarp and later Polycrates, they would never have been deceived about the timing of Jesus' resurrection. Anyone who believes Jesus meant what He said when He commanded us to keep His feasts in Leviticus 23 would be able to grasp this truth.

Annual Sabbath on Thursday Solves the Mystery

The whole mistake of missing Jesus' sign of Messiahship is based on ignorance of

1 Joseph Bingham, *Antiquities of the Christian Church,* p. 1149.

God's Sabbaths and annual Sabbaths. Ask any Jew what a "high day" is and he'll tell you it's an annual Sabbath day, a day of high celebration. It's high time we understood these days, and we will in the sequel.

The crux of the problem is assuming that Jesus was taken down from the cross and buried before the weekly Saturday Sabbath on the day of preparation, Friday. But that's not what John 19:31 says: "Then the Jews, because it was the day of preparation, so that the bodies would not remain on the cross on the Sabbath (for that Sabbath was a *high day*)..." John adds, "Therefore because of the Jewish day of preparation, since the tomb was nearby, they laid Jesus there" (19:42).

This was no ordinary Sabbath, nor was this an ordinary day of preparation: "Now it was the day of preparation for the Passover..."(19:14). Other translations make clear what is obvious to someone who has kept the feasts (Lev. 23:5-8). It was the day of preparation called the Passover, a day of preparation for Passover week or the Days of Unleavened Bread, the day to prepare for the first holy day or high day of that seven-day feast.

More than a problem of readin', writin', and 'rithmetic, this seems to be mainly a reading problem. More than that, it's one of those problems of understanding that work both ways. We don't understand that Sunday is not the day of the resurrection because we don't keep the Sabbath and the high days. Conversely, we don't keep the Sabbath and the high days because we believe Sunday is the day of the resurrection and we've kept it because it's our church and/or family tradition. Satan's merry-go-round can make us rather dizzy. And it's hard to get off.

If Jesus did rise early Sunday morning, which we can prove was not the case, they would have had to bury him early Thursday morning to arrive at the 72 hours required by Matthew 12:40.

We know, however, that He was buried before sunset, before the beginning of the Sabbath, which begins at sunset. Luke records this, and because the verses he writes are key to determining the timing of the resurrection, we will quote them: "And he took it [Jesus' body] down and wrapped it in a linen cloth, and laid Him in a tomb cut into the rock, where no one had ever lain. It was the preparation day, and the Sabbath was about to begin [which Sabbath?]. Now the women [some of His most faithful followers] who had come with Him out of Galilee followed, and saw the tomb and how His body was laid. Then they returned and prepared spices and perfumes. And on the Sabbath [which Sabbath?] they rested according to the commandment [This had to be the weekly Sabbath in view of the reference to the commandment, meaning the fourth. They are still keeping the Sabbath, yet some erroneously claim Colossians 2:14 says the law of commandments was nailed to the cross of Jesus]. But on the first day of the week, at early dawn, they came to the tomb bringing the spices which they had prepared. And they found the stone rolled away from the tomb..." (Luke 23:53-24:2).

The Only Proof Jesus Gave that He Is Our Savior!

We're on the verge of seeing another stone rolled away, a stone that is blocking our understanding. We as the body of Christ must understand the all-important timing of the resurrection. ***Without grasping this we cannot confirm that Jesus is our Savior.***

First notice the timing of the burial, a key factor since once we know when the burial occurred, we have a simple math problem to calculate. We add 72 hours to the time of burial. Jesus was buried as the Sabbath was about to begin (Luke 23:44-46,54). It had not begun, so He was buried just before sunset on the day before the Sabbath. Which Sabbath?

When did the women return and prepare the spices? No timing is given in this verse. That's where Mark 16:1-2 comes in: "When the Sabbath was over, Mary Magdalene, and Mary the mother of James, and Salome, *bought* spices, so that they might come and anoint Him. Very early on the first day of the week, they came to the tomb when the sun had risen."

Reading both passages in Mark and Luke, the only possible conclusion comes clear. Here we have women who see Jesus' body laid in the tomb just before sunset ushers in the annual Sabbath. They would not be able to buy spices and have time for the elaborate preparation of these ointments for burial purposes that night or the next, since it was a Sabbath and all shops were closed. They could only make these purchases and do these preparations on the day after the Sabbath, which Mark 16:1 confirms. But Luke 23:56 says they prepared the spices *before* the Sabbath. God is not a liar and does not contradict Himself. They certainly did not buy their spices before and after the same Sabbath.

The answer? This was a special week with two Sabbaths because of the spring feast. The weekly Sabbath was on Saturday, the preceding day, Friday, being a workday in which the women could purchase and prepare the spices and they kept another Sabbath, a high day, that preceded that Friday workday. That high day would have been Thursday, Wednesday being the preparation day or Passover. We know Jesus was put in the tomb on the day before the high day, which we now know was Thursday. We can see therefore that the Passover had to be on Wednesday in the year of Jesus' crucifixion.

All of this fits in perfectly with Daniel 9:24-27. Messiah was to be cut off in the midst of the prophetic week of seven years but also in the midst of a literal week. As the German word for Wednesday shows, Wednesday is the exact middle of the week. Because most Bible prophecy teachers do not keep the Sabbath, they have not fully understood these prophecies. While these verses have other historical applications, the focus is Jesus. Even the famous Bible code indicates the name

Yeshua or Jesus throughout this passage.

While too long to elaborate on here, the dates for the issue of the decree to rebuild Jerusalem bring us to the time of Jesus with pinpoint accuracy. The aspects of this prophecy are manifold and amazing.

It's Not All Greek to Me – It's Hebrew

Critics like to say that in Greek the phrase "three days and three nights" can mean parts of that period. What they fail to realize is that Jesus makes reference to a passage and an event in the Hebrew Scriptures. In Hebrew, which is most likely the language in which Jesus spoke these words and the language of the book of Jonah, no such compromise is possible. It had to be 72 hours, no more and no less, which satisfies all the other references about three days that are given in a more general way.

In fact, Jonah even compares his position in the fish's stomach to "Sheol"(Jonah 2:2), the place of the dead or the grave. That's exactly where Jesus went. His body was in the grave while He descended soul and spirit into the different levels of sheol (Eph. 4:9; I Pet. 3:18-20).

Moreover, Jesus did know the definition of a day. He spoke of "twelve hours in a day" in contrasting day with night (John 11:9-10).

The common passages quoted to try to prove Jesus rose on Sunday morning not only go against the biblical chronology, but they also say nothing about Him being resurrected on Sunday morning. They say that He was *already* risen Sunday morning. He was already risen "while it was still dark" (John 20:1). The angels said, at "early dawn," "He is not here, but He *has* risen…" (Luke 24:1,6).

There you have it: simple grammar and simple math. Too simple for scholars. Too true for theologians.

The Bible doesn't fill in all the details. We don't know for sure what Jesus did between Saturday afternoon just before sunset until early Sunday morning. He probably communed with His Father, especially since He had been greatly affected by His Father turning His face from Him because of the sin He had to bear on the cross.

Jesus was not raised on Sunday. Not only does no command exist to keep Sunday in honor of the resurrection, but the biblical evidence also demolishes the claim. A cruel hammer that drove nails into Jesus confirmed the crucifixion. The hammer of God's Word has driven nails into the Sunday resurrection theory and confirmed the stone was rolled away for Jesus' Sabbath resurrection.

We hope the stone has been rolled away in more ways than one. We need to get rid of the rock that blocks our understanding and see the stone rolled away. We should ask God to help us grasp the truth about the resurrection and the timing of it that proves Jesus was not a fake and a fraud. He was and is the Messiah, and He wants us to know the real Jesus. Do you?

While seemingly innocent, steeples have a sinister and even perversely sexual origin that identifies them with Nimrod (Gen. 6:9), a powerful and rebellious sexual deviate who called himself Baal or "lord of heaven." Most people have no idea what the steeple entails in its phallic symbolism, and our churches today continue to emphasize the title "Lord" rather than the mighty name of Jesus. While this "lord worship" has been replaced by the name of Jesus in some churches, the lock it puts on Bible understanding has only been partially broken. For those who have eyes to see, this book busts that lock.

Sabbath *Selahs*
The Giant Gut Check

You…have kept My word, and have not *denied My* ***name*** (Rev. 3:8).

…you will call me Ishi And will no longer call me Baali. For I will remove the names of the Baals from her mouth… (Hos. 2:16-17).

The two giant gut checks in the last days will be the Sabbath and the name of Jesus. While we have delayed the controversial chapter on "Lord Worship -- the Ways, Days and Names of Baal," it is important to emphasize the name of Jesus, the only name "given among men by which we must be saved" (Acts 4:12). Isaiah predicted that God would speak to His people about rest, especially Sabbath rest, but they would not listen to the Word spoken or written in a foreign tongue (28:11-12). One reason is a mistranslation made famous by King James: "LORD" comes from the Hebrew Yehovah *or* Yahweh, *meaning the Eternal and* Adonai *(My Master) when referring to God obviously means "My Divine Master." The* Yahweh *who spoke to Israel was born as Jesus, whose Hebrew name* Yeshua *or* Yehoshua *is packed with meaning. The name Jesus in any language opens a door to anointing, power, and intimacy. Regrettably, in the church today we hear more about "the Lord" than about Jesus. The English rank of nobility denoted as "Lord" was five to seven levels below the king. Is that where we want to put Jesus? What is worse and more controversial but true is that saying "the Lord" for Jesus instead of Jesus or Lord Jesus as a title of respect has a decidedly idolatrous connection, not to mention a demonic one. For those who want to know the surprising truth, we will show in the sequel how our modern Christian holidays have roots in Canaanite Baal worship. We will see that when we have used the term "Lord" by itself and have prayed to "the Lord" instead of the Father in the name of Jesus, we have unwittingly connected our Savior (and sometimes the Father and the Holy Spirit) to Baal, a god worshipped as a well-endowed whoremonger. The sexual connotation of "Lord" notwithstanding, English lords were forced to submit their soldiers for the king's armies and enforce the king's laws. So if we say that Jesus is Lord of the earth, our church or our life, understanding that Satan rules as king and god over the earth at this time (II Cor. 4:4), what is the obvious conclusion so few have seen? It is alarming.* ***We are saying that Satan is god and king of our life and Jesus, whom many of us call Lord, is under Satan.*** *Maybe it's time for a gut check. Selah.*

Stop! Rest! Think of what Jesus has done for you.
The Sabbath is the day for rest and prayerful intimacy with our God of love.

CHAPTER SIXTEEN

The "Sabbath Rest" of Hebrews 4:9

Many believe Paul wrote the book of Hebrews. Whether he did or didn't write it, the book stands as the inspired Word of God. And it contains an amazing verse about the Sabbath.

We shall look at the context, but let's first read this surprising verse. "So there remains a **Sabbath rest** for the people of God." Both the NIV and the NASB, the two translations with the least number of errors, translate the Greek word *sabbatismos* as *Sabbath rest*. The KJV margin is even bolder, rendering it "a keeping of the Sabbath."

What is intriguing is that throughout Hebrews 3 and 4 the word *rest* is the translation of the Greek word *katapausin*. Only in 4:9 is there a direct Sabbath connection to this rest. This word is not known in classic Greek. The writer of Hebrews apparently coined it. It underlines the multiplicity of meanings of Greek words used in the Bible. Greek words usually have at least four meanings.

Those who feel the word *rest* in these chapters refers only to our rest of grace in Jesus are incorrect. We shall see that the meaning is fourfold. That rest refers to our rest from our own works, living under the restful grace in Christ, to be sure.

But that's only part of the picture. It also refers to the entry into the Promised Land, where God gave Israel progressively greater peace from their enemies, a peaceful rest that prefigured yet another rest. That rest is the millennial rest of the Kingdom of God on earth, which is later extended to be an eternal rest with God. But there is more.

Let's begin by examining Hebrews 3. Verse 12 begins to warn against unbelief. Unbelief in Greek is inextricably tied to the idea of disobedience, and that connection is clear here. The author refers to Israel's provocative disobedience in the wilderness for forty years (3:16-17). He quotes from Psalm 95, a psalm often sung on the Sabbath day by the Israelites.

Sabbath Breaking a Part of Israel's Wilderness Disobedience

The psalm refers to the rebellion regarding complaints about water. Hebrews 3:17, however, refers to the forty years in general, and uses the word *sin*, which is often defined as the transgression of the law (I John 3:4). Which law did they break that especially provoked God? It was one that involved something especially holy to Him.

In Exodus 16, before Jesus gave the Ten Commandments, He tested their faith and obedience by commanding them not to go out to gather manna on the Sabbath day. Some did anyway, so He asked them in verse 28, "How long do you refuse to keep My commandments and My [laws]?" Sabbath before Sinai? No doubt about it.

What did these rebels fail to do? They failed to enter into ***God's rest – the seventh-day Sabbath rest***. An important part of the unbelief or disobedience that is a theme of these chapters is Israel's defiance of the Sabbath in the desert.

Why, pray tell, did God call Israel's breaking of the seventh-day Sabbath disobedience and not call it disobedience under the New Covenant?

Do you think it is extraneous to mention disobedience to the fourth commandment in this context? Is the Creator's seventh-day rest from His creation not an important part of the context of these two chapters? We shall see.

Up until chapter 4, verse 1, only one meaning of the word *rest* has appeared. In the context of Israel, this rest only refers to the Promised Land of Canaan. It clearly prefigures, however, the 1000-year reign of Christ on the earth.

As you have read earlier in this book, the millennial reign of Christ is a fulfillment of the seventh-day Sabbath. Joshua, a Hebrew name almost identical to Jesus, was a type of Christ, leading God's chosen ones into a land of peace and abundance foreshadowing the Millennium. So the Sabbath is involved in a certain way even in chapter 3.

Hebrews 4:1 obviously refers to the rest of the believers in the grace of Jesus. It may also refer to some of them not being counted worthy – because of disobedience or unbelief -- to experience the millennial rest ruling with Jesus and the subsequent eternal rest with God. We group them together since the one is an extension of the other.

Verse 3 refers to our present rest in grace in Jesus. It is at the end of this verse, however, that the Holy Spirit inspires the author to begin to introduce a discussion of the works of God's creation in Genesis.

Written to Sabbath Keepers

As we read these verses, we should ask ourselves one question -- an important one that may not have occurred to us: Does it sound like the author of Hebrews is writing to Sunday-keepers?

Remember, Paul said in the church we are neither Jew nor Greek – but one in Jesus. We are to be doing the same thing – keeping the same days.

Even under the Old Covenant, Gentiles who lived among Israel were to keep the same days as Israel. "One law" existed for both Israelites and Gentiles (Ex. 12:48-49).

Does it seem logical to you that Christians of Gentile and Jewish origin should keep different days? How can we be united – one in Christ – if we keep different days? The Sabbath is not a personal option. It is one of the Ten Commandments!

As we will see, the author is talking to people who were not only familiar with the Sabbath. They were keeping it! The writer would not have said it the way he did if they were not presently entering into the seventh-day Sabbath rest.

Verse 4 is remarkable: "For He has said somewhere concerning the seventh day: 'AND GOD RESTED ON ***THE SEVENTH DAY*** FROM ALL HIS WORKS.'" Notice that these words are not qualified -- no disclaimer is given.

The Holy Spirit had a superb opportunity to set the record straight about the day of worship. He could have said, "Now God rested on the seventh day back then, but of course, we rest on the first day – or any day will do."

Don't you think that if such a ***monumental*** change had been made under the New Covenant, that the Holy Spirit would have told us so? Do you think God would have done away with one of ***His top ten*** moral laws and not made it clear that it was no longer to be kept?

Some may think this argument is overdone, since this is only an historical statement of fact – or even worse, the basis of a cute analogy.

But read on: "... and again in this passage [Psalm 95], 'They shall not enter my rest'" (4:5). Do you think the author is using the word *rest* and "seventh day" in the same breath without thinking as well about the seventh-day rest? Remember, the Bible and history show the early church never abandoned the Sabbath.

One thing is sure: the author here does ***not*** sound like a ***Sunday-keeper.*** Why would he use the example of the seventh-day Sabbath and not be keeping it? Does "holy hermeneutics" forbid us from asking such a question?

We read Sunday worship into the Bible. But it's ***not there!*** Millions hear the Sabbath preached every Sunday as they listen to passages cited in sermons that mention it all too often. But they don't hear it.

A clever spiritual adversary has blinded us to the acceptance of this seventh day that spells the end of his rule. He knows all too well that the millennial Sabbath means curtains for him! So he wants to pull the curtain over our eyes. He wants to pull the wool over the eyes of God's precious wooly followers. He does not want God's sheep to lie down in the restful pastures of the ***Sabbath-day rest.***

What a coup Satan has pulled! It's the same sabotage he wrought in the Garden of Eden. We have seen how jealous he became when He saw mankind in a deeply intimate relationship and fellowship with God. He tries to bring confusion into Hebrews, but here's the clincher.

The Clincher

Hebrews 4:9 is the key. "So there ***remains*** a ***Sabbath rest*** for the people of God." The New Testament by Henry Alford translates *sabbatismos*, as the KJV margin, "a keeping of sabbath…" Goodspeed says "a promised Sabbath of rest of God's people."

All this is not to say that this word is only referring to the keeping of the seventh-day Sabbath. But to claim that the author does not allude to the literal seventh-day rest here is to deny the obvious. It was certainly obvious to the Sabbath keepers who received the letter. It is not obvious, of course, to a modern-day body of Christ that has been deceived on this point.

After all, how many Christians at this writing keep the seventh-day Sabbath? Probably less than 1%! You will probably be branded a cultist if you dare keep the Sabbath. Admittedly, there are cultish legalists who keep it and feel those who don't aren't Christian.

These legalists may or may not be born-again Christians. Whether they are is for God to judge. Too often Christians assume that those they consider to be in "cults" cannot be Christian and cannot have truth that they don't have. Both conclusions are not necessarily true. Cults often have truths that attract followers --- truths that have been overlooked by the mainstream.

We can judge the actions of people even though we must not condemn them, leaving it to Jesus to evaluate their inner spiritual state. We can safely say, however, that it is wrong for a Sabbath-keeper to judge others in the body of Christ as not belonging to that body because of unwittingly breaking the fourth commandment. It is equally wrong, however, for Christians to brand Sabbath keepers as non-Christian cult members.

Sabbath keepers identify with Hebrews 4:9. Sunday-keepers have a hard time seeing it. And it is all too easy to try to explain away the obvious reference to the Sabbath day here. For the doubters, verse 10 is probably the most powerfully convincing verse.

Hear it: "For the one who has entered His rest has himself also rested from his works, ***as God did from His.***"

Those who deal in spiritual mumbo-jumbo will likely find a way to explain this verse away. But let him who has an ear, hear what the Holy Spirit – not hermeneutics – is saying.

How and when did God rest from His works? Was His rest a rest in grace so that God would do His works in Him? No. He *is* God. He doesn't rest in His own grace. We rest in His grace. How do we rest the way ***God*** rested? How and when do we rest "as ***God*** rested"?

Jesus rested on the ***seventh day!***

We may be able to rest in the grace of God. We may be able to have a millennial rest and later a Kingdom rest for eternity. But that is not resting "as ***God*** rested."

God rested on the ***seventh day*** of creation week! If we are going to rest as ***God*** did, we will be resting from our labors on the ***seventh day of the week.*** That is the ***only*** way we can rest as God rested.

"Jewish Christian" is not An Oxymoron!

The Sabbath was a law of God before the Old Covenant was made. He gave it to Adam, remember? He made it for ***man***.

He commanded Israel to keep it as part of the Old Covenant. Gentiles who became a part of Israel, however, kept it too. God's desire was that Israel be a light to the nations (Deut. 4:5-8). He wanted the nations to see how blessed Israel was, how wonderful their laws were, and how awesome was their God. He wanted the nations to have all the blessings of Israel, including the blessing of the ***Sabbath***.

Jews and even Jewish Christians today who believe the Sabbath is not for Gentiles are wrong. The Sabbath joy is not for "goys," they say. That's not kosher. That's hogwash! The Sabbath is for ***mankind.*** Why would God keep Gentiles from sharing in one of His greatest blessings – the weekly ***Sabbath rest***? He didn't. He doesn't. And He won't – even in the Millennium (Isa. 66:23).

The idea that the Gentile Christians in the early church did not keep the Sabbath is completely unfounded. Admittedly, Hebrews was written mainly to Jewish Christians, but they were Jewish *Christians*. Furthermore, this letter was written to us today, Jewish and Gentile *Christians*.

Christians are supposed to do what Jesus did and teach what Jesus taught. He taught the Sabbath. He kept the Sabbath.

More important than being a Jew, Jesus was the first Christian, the example for all future believers to follow. He was Jesus the Christ – the Anointed One. The anointing oil set Jesus apart as holy. He was the Holy One who kept holy the day He made holy. He expects – yea, commands – His holy ones to keep His day holy.

He set us the example, that we might follow His steps. Paul said "Follow me, as I follow Christ (I Cor. 11:1). Paul clearly kept the Sabbath. Paul's decision to keep a Nazarite vow in Acts 18 to show the Jews he was not against their law was exceptional. It was not required under the New Covenant, being a part of the ritual law, but it was not forbidden either.

The Sabbath was not a ritual, sacrificial law. It did not involve the shedding of animal blood, which was fulfilled in Christ's sacrifice. Christ shed His sacrificial blood because we broke the law! We broke the moral law summed up in the Ten Commandments, a law that is neither unnecessary nor optional.

The Sabbath is a moral law that shows how to love and worship God. It is just as moral as the law against idols, images, and taking God's name in vain. Would Paul or any Christian want to disobey a law whose violation caused Jesus to die for us?

"Becoming like a Jew to save the Jews" does not refer to obeying one of the Ten Commandments to please the Jew. Obeying the fourth commandment pleases *God*.

How could Paul say that the law was "holy, and the commandment holy and just and good (Rom. 7:12)" if he didn't keep it? Paul was of one mind and one spirit with James, and James said, "Break one, and you break 'em all." Paul kept them all.

You Don't Have to Cut Your Body to be Saved, But Don't Cut Out the Sabbath!

Paul made an important distinction between the ritual and moral law. He said in I Cor. 7:19, "Circumcision is nothing and uncircumcision is nothing, but ***keeping the commandments of God*** is what matters." Does that sound like a guy who threw away the law in the name of grace? He did not uphold the physical rituals, the sacrificial system, or the physical laws of holiness. But he did uphold and establish, teach and obey by the grace of God the spiritual, moral laws of holiness.

How could he ignore the commandment that brings us into the anointed presence of the Holy One on His holy day? How could he disobey the only one of the ten points of the law of holiness that uses the word *holy*?

He did not believe that any day would do. While *we* are to be holy to God every day, only one day will do as a day of commanded corporate worship. Just any old anointing oil or incense didn't "do" for Israel. God said it had to be the specially made holy oil. No other oil would do.

When two men offered incense on the altar that was not the exact formula of the holy incense, God was incensed! He struck them dead on the spot (Lev. 10:1-3).

Now, under the New Covenant, our obedience is even stricter, as Jesus taught on the Sermon on the Mount. While the administration of the law is different, on occasion God does bring swift punishment on those who flaunt His laws (Acts 5:1-11).

Because God made us with free will, He has not stopped Sunday observance. But Jesus is coming back soon to a church without spot or wrinkle, a holy bride walking in obedience to His holy law.

While God is patient, enough is enough. After 1700 years of deception, the bride must be prepared for Jesus.

While few Christians are ready for the even stronger Sabbath teaching coming in the sequel, many will benefit by beginning to keep the Sabbath holy. Such obedience breaks the Bible code and opens up awesome understanding of God's Word. Prophecy comes alive. Questions you've always asked about God get answered (Ps. 111:10).

The goal of this book is to whet your appetite for stronger meat. You may be surprised at the appetizers in the next chapter. The Sabbath and the cross are not enemies as some think. They are intimate friends.

"Where Do They Get That?"

Much of the revelation in this book is probably new to most. Some may ask, "Where in the world did you come up with all that?"

Although it has been overlooked for centuries, understanding the truth that the Sabbath is the seventh day and must be kept is a simple truth. It's as easy as 1-2-3. Actually, it's 1-2-3-4, the fourth of the Ten Commandments.

It is obedience to that simple truth that brings greater understanding. "A good understanding have all those who *do* His commandments (Ps. 111:10)." The initial receiving of the Holy Spirit is based on obedience (Acts 5:32). The same principle applies for receiving more of the Holy Spirit's guidance. As we obey the laws of love, the Holy Spirit "searches all things, even the depths of God (I Cor. 2:10)."

The keeping of the Sabbath and holy days opens up rich depths of understanding most Christians have never tapped.

Although we may not always be able to cite chapter and verse to prove every facet of the diamond-like Word of God, we have put these truths to the test and have seen the fruits. Unlike traditions that clearly contradict the Word, such as the pagan Sunday touted as God's day, these profound insights do not go against the Word. The Holy Spirit is merely leading us into all truth (John 16:13). In fact, every year we keep the holy days, God reveals something new and exciting about those days.

To those who have been fed at the trough of tradition, these truths may seem far-fetched and untrue. But when you begin to obey the simple Sabbath commandment, you will be able to prove these truths.

Rather than drifting far afield in speculation, you will discover hidden treasures of wisdom that will give you depth of understanding and at the same time lift you up to "ride on the heights of the earth" (Isa. 58:14). That's the glorious promise of obedience to the fourth commandment. Try it. You'll like it!

Santa's hollow "Ho! Ho! Ho!" needs to be replaced by the "Ho" of Isaiah 55. "Ho! Everyone who thirsts, come to the waters; And you who have no money come, buy and eat...Why do you spend money for what is not bread [not according to the Word and giving no life], And your wages for what does not satisfy? Listen carefully to Me [not to tradition], and eat what is good, And delight yourself in abundance (Isa. 55:1-2; compare with 58:13-14)."

Why tear yourself apart by eating at God's table as well as the table of demons?

Come feast at God's table. The knowledge of good and evil, the mixture of pagan and Christian fare (Deut. 12:29-32; Jeremiah 10) is a sorry soup that does not qualify as God's pure water of life. It's a feast polluted by unclean foods that soil the soul. God's people deserve better. They deserve the best, the richest of fare – God's spiritual manna given on the days He made holy.

God is good and He is Love. And so are *all* His commandments! They are love. They are good. "Taste and see that [Jesus] is good..." (Ps. 34:8). Taste *all* of His goodness, *all* of His love – *all* His commandments of love.

Don't settle for milky mush. Come and eat of the "lavish banquet" God prepares on the day that pictures the physical and spiritual richness of the Millennium (Isa. 25:6). You don't know what you're missing!

Sabbath Selah's
Turnover Time

Thus says the [Eternal]: Take heed to yourselves and for the sake of your lives bear no burden on the Sabbath day… (Jer. 17:21, AMP.).

This verse applies to more than physical burdens. Because the Sabbath is a day of joy picturing the Kingdom of God on earth, He does not want us to bring any burdens (cares, concerns, problems, regrets of the week) into this holy time. We are to lay these burdens down to Jesus on His cross as we approach sunset Friday.

Fast food chains serve apple and cherry turnovers. The Sabbath is turnover time in a different sense. It's the turnover to the great Caretaker Jesus of all our weekly burdens and oppressions from Satan. And since it's a day of celebration, you can have your apple turnover too!
How appropriate for this day of redemption. Jesus takes our lemons and makes lemonade. The meaning of the letter combinations of the word Shabbat *is the following:* shem bet *is the root* shoov. *It literally means "destroy the house," i.e. burn our bridges with Satan's kingdom and embrace Kingdom Day. We can have no* shalom *if we are torn between two kingdoms. The meaning is: "return" to the* tav, *the cross or covenant.* Shabbat *means to repent and come back to the cross of Jesus, for the Sabbath is indeed the day Jesus reminds us that He redeemed us by His blood from all the sins of our former life in spiritual Egypt (Deut. 5:15). TGIF (Thank God It's Friday)! We can lay down our burdens to Jesus on His cross on His day of redemption. "Redeem" is* gaal, *meaning "lift up God," picturing Jesus being lifted up on the cross. When we lift Him up in praise on His Sabbath day, He redeems us from our sins and burdens as we profit from "turnover time." Selah.*

CHAPTER SEVENTEEN

Redemption Day

Redemption is one of the most important concepts in the Bible. Few grasp it. They may know the word and vaguely understand its basic meaning: ransomed, purchased, bought back from Satan with the price of Jesus' blood, set free from sin, release and rescue. The reality of redemption, however, has not come alive in them.

While many good Christians who don't presently keep the Sabbath do have a good understanding of the subject, redemption cannot be fully grasped, internalized and manifested without the depth of understanding Sabbath keeping brings.

Here's why. One of the main reasons for the Sabbath is to teach and remind God's people of their redemption. "You shall remember that you were a slave in the land of Egypt [sin], and the [Eternal] your God brought you out of there by a mighty hand and by an outstretched arm; *therefore* the [Eternal] your God commanded you to observe the sabbath day (Deut. 5:15)."

Israel (the believers) had been slaves in the land of sin or Egypt under Pharaoh (Satan). Jesus bought them back from the captivity in which Satan had enslaved them (Deut.7:8), even though He allowed them to go back into captivity to other enemies when they abandoned the day of freedom, the Sabbath (Ezek. 20:23-24). The price of freedom? The blood and body of the lamb.

It was the blood that spared them certain death. The blood of Jesus is also the ransom price for us. Jesus redeems us or "buys us back" from Satan's grasp and the way of sin he inspires, including the resultant poverty, sickness and death. His blood has freed us from sin's slavery.

The Redemptive Process

This redemption and freedom is a process. Unfortunately, however, the lives of many Christians -- especially leaders who make scandalous headlines -- are characterized by the word "struggle." No victory – only struggle. These defeated ones are living soap opera lives, constantly struggling along in their own fleshly efforts to do what Jesus already did. They never realize the powerful redemption He has already bought for them.

Furthermore, they never surrender to Him and enter the Sabbath rest that prefigures both the rest in Jesus' righteousness and in eternal intimacy with Him – all pictured in the Sabbath day. They will never fully understand and complete the redemptive process without the *sabbatismos* (keeping of the Sabbath or Sabbath rest) of Hebrews 4:9.

Redemption has a legal side and a vital side, the difference between legalese and real release. Redemption must be more than stuffy legal language in a dusty document called the Bible. It must come alive in us! That's one of the reasons Jesus gave us His Sabbath.

This purpose of the Sabbath ties in with the initial purpose stated in Exodus 20:11 and 31:13, a memorial of creation to identify the one true Creator God and us as His people – sanctified, made holy, by Jesus' blood. God redeemed us for Himself, to be His holy people (I Chron. 17:21, Isa. 62:12). Part of our identity is that now we are the redeemed. That's what God called Israel at the Red Sea (Isa. 51:10-11). They realized they were no longer in the slave pits of Egypt, but they kept their slave identity and continued to submit to the spirit of control.

God wants us to begin to realize our new identity as the redeemed when we accept Jesus and His blood shed for us. Then we can come shortly thereafter to the waters of the Red Sea (baptism) and declare our willingness to bury the old ways for good. The process continues as we are spiritually baptized into Jesus, choosing life in Him and His ways above all else. Some go further. They surrender every aspect of their lives to Jesus and He then baptizes or fully immerses them in or into the Holy Spirit.

Jesus redeems our spirit, making it new by His blood and His life in us. The Holy Spirit performs the work of rendering our souls (heart, mind and will) holy like our spirit. The Father then completes the redemptive process – the redemption of the body. We go from divine health in our bodies now to the resurrection when we put on glorified physical bodies to rule with Jesus.

The Triune Godhead works with our triune, God-like make-up of spirit, soul, and body to make us like Him. He then completes this redemptive regeneration by one of His major tools of sanctification – the holy Sabbath day. It's the day for the building up of the holy ones. It is the day of redemption – the holy day that points us to our holy God every week and enables us to be instructed to become a holy trinity of spirit, soul, and body like Him.

This process can be understood in a different way as we see how God redeemed Israel. Jesus redeemed them by the blood of the lamb, brought them out of Egypt in order to bring them into the land of promise, called "rest" in Hebrews 3 and 4. Just as leaven or sin must be replaced by unleavened bread or Jesus' righteousness, Jesus brings us out of Egypt into the Promised Land of rest – the Sabbath or Millennial or eternal rest (Deut. 6:23-24). We cease from our works of the flesh, our worldly, "Egyptian" ways in order to come into the Sabbath rest in Jesus' righteousness. This weekly rest prepares us for the eternal rest – eternal righteousness in Jesus. We cease from our works and take on His works.

The Alpha and Omega Covenant: Do or Die

Our Redeemer is called the Alpha and Omega, the beginning and the end. He made the Sabbath at the very beginning to point to the cross and later to remind us of our redemption by the cross. Jesus is our Sabbath – our Rest. Just as He is the beginning and the end, so the Sabbath was made at the beginning to picture the end – the final eternal Sabbath rest in Him. That eternal, perfect rest of our spirit, souls, and bodies is the final step in the process of redemption.

You might call it spiritual R & R. But instead of rest and relaxation, it's redemption leading to rest. Jesus redeems us so we can enter His final rest. As with the Christian life here and now, rest in Jesus does not mean inactivity. It is the greatest result and productivity with the minimum effort. We simply choose Jesus, rest in Him, and let Him do the works through us.

The Sabbath is all about the cross of Jesus – His blood redeeming us from fleshly works and sin. The Holy Spirit has even shown us this principle in the Hebrew word for "because" (Gen. 2:3) He has given us a hint of the Sabbath/cross connection. The word is a conjunction, a crossover word. Remember, the Sabbath commandment is in the very middle of the Ten Commandments in the Hebrew text, the *cross*over point between love toward God and love toward man.

The word "because" in Genesis becomes more than a mere hint when we understand that both the Sabbath and the cross are the crossover points to eternity. The blood of Jesus ushers us into the Holy of Holies with the Father and into eternal life. The Sabbath pictures that eternal rest.

The infinity symbol (resembling a figure eight) actually originates from the covenants Jesus cut with our forefathers. It pictures the eternal infinity of the Alpha and Omega. Both Jesus and Abraham walked in a figure eight fashion through the pieces of the animal sacrificed. Both parties vowed death if they did not fulfill their part of the covenant. In Genesis 15 Jesus was promising Abraham the eternal Sabbath rest in the Promised Land if Abraham obeyed all His commands (including the Sabbath).

What Jesus was vowing as He walked the infinity sign through the sacrifices was nothing short of earthshaking. He was saying, "If I am not faithful to grant you and your children the eternal Sabbath rest as a result of your faith and obedience to all my laws, then I, my Father, and the Holy Spirit will cease to exist!" God promised to die forever if He did not come through. While such a death was impossible, Jesus did come to die as a human so He could redeem Abraham's children from death in order to live eternally in the Promised Land -- Earth (Mat. 5:5).

This amazingly powerful promise Jesus made applies to all of God's covenants with His people. It could not exclude the very first one -- the Sabbath covenant. He promised that He would give mankind rulership as kings and priests over the earth if they kept the Sabbath covenant. As we have seen, if God did away with the Sabbath and the Sabbath covenant, He would have to die forever!

If God changed the Sabbath to Sunday, He would have to die!

God would never do away with such an important covenant. Every major Bible concept is tied in to the Sabbath. Among the most significant is that of redemption.

The Passover is the most important, the most pivotal and the most joyous of all of God's feast days. Although the Sabbath encapsulates the entire plan of God from beginning to end, the central message is the same as the Passover: redemption by the blood of Jesus -- freedom from the slavery of Egyptian bondage to sin.

If God did away with the Sabbath, He might as well do away with the cross!

The Sabbath and Redemption

Our God of love has provided a way whereby we see the reality of our redemption come fully alive in us. That way is the Sabbath day. Every week He reminds us that we were formerly slaves but we have been redeemed – redeemed from every cruel yoke our former taskmaster tries to tell us is still around our necks (Ps. 78:42). Every Sabbath Jesus tells us, "Don't believe the liar! Remember I have already redeemed you – from all sin, sickness, debts, and burdens." It's the day for laying down all weekly burdens – and receiving the joy and peace of Jesus.

We are the redeemed, and every Sabbath we say it -- and sing it (Ps. 107:2). No dirges. No sad songs. Only sounds of joy over our redemption. We learn more of the truth that sets us free. We cease from our works in more ways than one, resting in Jesus' righteousness. The Sabbath teaches us every week to know and declare this powerful truth: ***"I am redeemed from all Satan tries to throw at me – because my Father loves me!"*** What a joy! What a blessing!

Now let's see how, in a practical and a prophetic way, the Sabbath brings redemption.

What better way to redeem and restore bodies wearied from a week of work than a day of true Sabbath rest! It not only pictures "times of refreshing" and the "restoration of all things" (Acts 3:19-21) in the future; it restores and refreshes here and now. It's the pause that refreshes -- the rest that restores.

David said of Jesus, "He restores my soul (Ps. 23:3)." We know we are renewed day by day (II Cor. 4:16), but God in His love and wisdom knew we wouldn't always receive that renewal. He knew things would pile up and we would need a weekly refreshing.

Our beloved African-American brothers use the term "soul food." One such brother who was also a football great, of whom I will speak later, ate Sabbath soul food. We all need it. Our minds need to be redeemed from the weekly onslaught of concerns (Rom. 12:2). Our emotions need to be settled by the love and comfort of the Father on His day of love. Our wills need the motivation and strengthening of resolve provided by Sabbath songs, teaching, and fellowship.

But let's not forget our spirits – the spirit man that is who we really are. Although our spirits have been perfectly redeemed by Jesus, they can still be edified (I Cor. 14:4, Jude 20; Eph. 3:16). This weekly spiritual exercise is profitable in every arena, building up our spirits for the challenge of another week (I Tim. 4:6-9).

Redemption is salvation. Jesus says, "...In repentance and rest you will be saved, In quietness and trust is your strength (Isa. 30:15)." Redemption and salvation are a process. The rest and quiet trust of the Sabbath makes us holier. "And the work of righteousness [including resting in Jesus' righteousness on the Sabbath] will be peace, And the service of righteousness, quietness and confidence *forever* (Isa. 32:17)." God's holy day prepares His people for the final stage of salvation – the eternal Sabbath rest.

The Sabbath Even Redeems the Time

In a prophetic verse for our generation, Paul exhorts us to redeem the time, especially as we enter these last evil days (Eph. 5:16). Jesus the Redeemer is the only One who can truly make up for lost time and opportunities.

The Sabbath time redemption principle is almost identical to the tithing law. When you give God the money and the time that belongs to Him, He promises to make the rest stretch miraculously. It's the "Sabbath stretch." You relax in Jesus, stretching out on your Sabbath easy chair, and you're making money and saving time as you stretch. Jesus will astound you to see what you can get done in six days.

The letter combination of *Gaal* (Redeemer) is *gimel* and *al* or *el*: lift up God. Jesus was lifted up on the cross to redeem us. And when we lift Him up in praise on the day of redemption, He redeems. It's the Sabbath version of "seek ye first the kingdom" (Mat. 6:33, KJV). Ask a tithe-payer or a Sabbath-keeper. It works!

It will work for the whole world. Satan has taken six thousand-year days to do his dirty work on mankind. What the devil took six days to mess up, Jesus will need only a day to clean up! The Redeemer will bring back the joy and peace Satan stole from mankind. As in Genesis, Jesus will speak His redemptive Word into a *tohu* and *bohu* mess and make a garden for kings to dress and keep. Jesus redeems the waste -- even the time waste. Every Sabbath we picture the 1000-year day when Jesus will redeem the time of mankind. And He'll keep time according to His holy days. Instead of Greenwich Mean Time, it'll be "Jesus Good Time!"

The glorious millennial Sabbath will soon dawn. Whereas men labored in their own fleshly works for six millennia, Isaiah declares: "The whole earth is at rest and is quiet; They break forth into shouts of joy (14:7)." This thorny, cursed briar patch of desert wasteland will soon blossom like the rose (Isa. 35:1-7).

The Redemptive Rest that Gives Perspective

Many Christians today never recover from their week: they're still trying to recover from their weekend. But the Sabbath redeems the week -- and something else we often lose in the weeklong whirlwind that can leave us weary and disoriented: our perspective.

The world around us seems to be spinning faster and faster. Our society is in rush mode. The whole world is in a maniacal mad rush -- and we never stop long enough to figure out what all the rushing is about. Oftentimes even we Christians get caught up in our week and find ourselves rushing about in a fleshly frenzy. We lose the perspective of resting in Jesus' grace and righteousness. We never stop at the stop signs. Our rolling stops are barely under the speed limits.

That's where the Sabbath comes in. "Thank God it's Friday" is more than a worldly saying. Our loving Father gives us a day to catch our breath and our bearings. We end the week resting in Jesus. It makes it much easier to walk restfully in the Spirit as we start the next week. (Perhaps we can begin to grasp why the typical Sunday-keeper has a harried life that can encourage walking in the flesh. Satan's day doesn't give you true rest in Jesus.)

A Day for Redeeming All Mankind

But this day is not only for *our* redemption. It's a day for speaking redemption in the name of Jesus over those who need freedom from Satan's oppression. God calls us to do good to all, not only to those of the household of faith. The Sabbath was a big giving day for Jesus. He healed. He delivered people from Satan's yokes. He prayed for others.

The Sabbath was made for man – a day for receiving blessings and giving them out to others. It's the day of love. And what greater love than to lay down our lives and our time – in this case God's time – to be the priestly administrators of the blood of Jesus to redeem the oppressed (Luke 13:16).

The priests in Israel offered more blood sacrifices on the Sabbath than any other day. God calls us priests. The Sabbath is the perfect day for us to apply the blood of Jesus to redeem others and set them free.

This day of redemption is not only for the here and now. It is a celebration of the time when the whole world will be redeemed. We celebrate our redemption and the world's salvation.

Adam gave the world away to Satan. Jesus bought the whole world back by His blood. But the return does not officially take place until the millennial Sabbath. The Divine Master of the Sabbath, whose presence will permeate that millennial day, will replace the cruel taskmaster who has enslaved the world for six millennial days. Pharaoh's crew went down rushing after Israel, fighting in the flesh to the last bubble of breath. We don't want that rush to judgment. That's why we stop on the Sabbath to catch our breath -- and celebrate the fact Satan's chariots are at the bottom of our Red Sea.

We not only celebrate the redemption of the world every Sabbath. We pray the ***living*** prayer, "Thy kingdom come," every time we keep the Sabbath. We also prophesy that day of universal redemption by our obedience. We hasten the day of His coming and show by our weekly obedience that we love His appearing. So Sabbath keepers have -- if everything else is in place -- a crown of righteousness laid up for them (II Tim. 4:8).

Moreover, because the Sabbath includes the glorious eternal rest, we prophesy the time when all people who have ever lived will be resurrected and given an opportunity to be redeemed from sin and death (Rom. 5:17-19). Those untold millions who many think are in hell forever with Satan will be redeemed from the grave (Rev. 20:5a). That's great news you've probably never heard. God has revealed it because we keep the day of redemption.

To put the capstone on God's awesome plan of redemption, the groaning of all creation (Rom. 8:19-22) culminates in an eternal Sabbath rest for the whole universe! All Satan's works will be burned up and replaced by the new heavens and new earth -- redeemed from all the effects of sin. That's the good news we celebrate every Sabbath day: the whole universe redeemed from the devil!

Jesus grants a special place in His kingdom to the overcomers (Rev. 3:21). But many Christians are floundering in the folly of sinful habits that enslave them. The reason is simple: they have not let the truth that Jesus has already redeemed them from all sin come alive in them. They have not understood it, nor have they become pregnant with that truth.

Sadly, they haven't declared it! God commands us to speak out our redemption "from the hand of the adversary…"(Ps. 107:2). When necessary, be specific. ***"I am redeemed from ________ by the blood of Jesus – because my Father loves me!*** (Deut. 7:8)" Victory comes through the realization and confession of redemption.

The perfect day for the redeemed, holy ones to declare their freedom from Satan is the day that celebrates our redemption – the holy Sabbath. Sabbath-keeper David said his lips and his soul shouted for joy because He was redeemed (Ps. 71:23).

As a pastor and praise and worship leader, I often declare our redemption in prayers and songs. Those words bring power to set people free. It is the holy day of redemption and freedom that helps us live up to the name God gave us: Freedom Church of God. Our freedom is not in the day itself but in the Redeemer who is Divine Master of the Sabbath day.

Redeemed from Lack

Exodus 16 recounts the fascinating story of the manna. But it's more than an interesting story. It not only reveals the Sabbath commandment as a test commandment (16:4), but it also reveals Jesus as our Provider and Provision.

Jesus, the Bread of Life, gave them manna for two days on Friday. They rested on the Sabbath and did not need to receive provision by fleshly works. They rested in Jesus, their Provider, and He gave them supernatural provision.

Both the Sabbath and tithing are keys to provision. When we seek first the Kingdom, God adds all the physical things we need.

We at Freedom Church of God have literally seen $1000 bills appear miraculously in the Bible on the Sabbath day for our provision. When you combine Sabbath keeping with an understanding of redemption, Jesus pours out the blessings. You may remember the incident during which Jesus told Peter to go fishing and take the first fish and open its mouth. Peter's mouth must have dropped open as well. Out he pulled the money they needed for tax.

The tax people surprised me once with a bill of several hundred dollars I wasn't expecting. I asked God for provision in my Bible. As my colleague preached on the Sabbath, I turned to the verses cited and found over a thirty-minute period $350, covering the tax money and tithe. Jesus is amazing!

You can be cynical if you like, but I saw it with my own eyes, and I put the money into my own wallet.

At first, being small, we had no bank account and kept the money in a metal can. The can was always full. We've spent over the years between two-and-a-half and five times what we received in tithes and offerings! The financial anointing has flowed like the widow's oil.

Even the Sabbath Redeemed!

The Sabbath is the day that pictures redemption, but Jesus must in a sense redeem even that day. His people have broken His covenant by rejecting the sign He gave originally that we were His people and He was our God the Creator.

You can still be married without a wedding ring, but the ring is a sign of covenant faithfulness. The true believers throughout the centuries who did not keep the Sabbath were still God's people. The end-time bride, however, must have the Sabbath sign.

Jesus desires with all His heart that in these last days His bride wear His wedding ring. In this end time when that sign is revealed to the church, the foolish virgins who reject the Sabbath sign will not be part of the bride Jesus will spare from the troublous times to come (Rev. 3:10).

By His blood Jesus will redeem His people from the sin of Sabbath breaking. That's what He has done throughout history.

Adam was the first to keep the Sabbath, but after years of the intimacy that Sabbath keeping brought, Adam sinned and lost both intimacy with Jesus and the Sabbath. As all mankind rejected the Sabbath through Adam, so in the millennial seventh day, "… from sabbath to sabbath, All mankind will come to bow down before Me, says [Jesus]" (Isa. 66:23). He will redeem Sabbath breaking by His blood and restore that holy day.

Jesus repeated the Sabbath command to Israel so they would remember that they were redeemed from Egypt's slavery. Alas, when we neglect the day of freedom, bondage can be the only result. Because Satan convinced them to forget what God said to remember, He sent them back into slavery (Ezek. 20:23-24). What a paradox!

It will happen again -- to modern Israel (We're referring mainly to the tribes who lost their identity because they lost the identifying sign of the Sabbath – not to the small nation of Israel descended from Judah). They will be taken captive principally to the land of the Assyrians, today a modern European nation with a warlike history (Isa. 10:5).

But wait! Remember, Jesus is the Redeemer. In His mercy He is going to rescue His physical people of Israel out of the beast power in Europe where they will be taken captive – once again because of Sabbath breaking. The ransomed or redeemed of Jesus will return by the Highway of Holiness to Jerusalem to worship Jesus and keep His holy days (Isa. 27:12-13; 35:8-10), later joined by all mankind (Zech. 14:16-19).

That's not all. Spiritual Israel – the church -- went into a kind of slavery when Satan got them to throw out the day of redemption and freedom. When the day that pictures the end of satanic oppression was out of the way, the devilish dictator began to enslave them with over 9000 doctrines of demons.

As you read these words you are hearing a call from God to repentance. He is now setting His heart to redeem His spiritual people from Sabbath breaking. Obedience to the Sabbath will open the door to new anointing, revelation, and many positive changes. Jesus is going to redeem the day Satan has stolen from the church for almost 2000 years. The Sabbath is coming back to a church near you! This is the "trailer" -- a preview of what is coming soon.

Maybe you'll only be one, two, or three to start. But the bride will begin to remember the day Satan has hoodwinked the church into forgetting. Religious bigots will cry "heresy!" But don't believe what any man says. Don't even believe what you read here. Look into God's Word for yourself. Study it. Prove it. It's always been there in God's Word waiting to be discovered. When you see it for yourself, do it! Sabbath blessings will flow. A whole new world will open up to you.

It's Your Choice!

In the judgment (and our judgment has already begun – I Pet. 4:17) it won't matter what the neighbors say. What Aunt Gertrude thinks won't matter. What blinded seminary theologians taught your pastor will be of no consequence. What *will* matter is what God says. Believe Him. Let God be true and every man a liar (Rom. 3:4). Jesus is our Advocate – the only Lawyer who can't lie.

He has blessed us with the privilege of presenting the case for the defense – the defense of a day that has been under attack for a long time. The persecuting (sic) attorneys will lie and twist and deceive and misrepresent the words of the defense. But God's Word stands. The humble and childlike will listen. The wise will obey.

Jesus' Sabbath pictures His redeeming blood shed to set us free. He redeemed us to be a people holy unto Himself, redeemed from Satan and sin (II Sam. 7:23; Ps. 74:2; 78:42; Isa. 43:1; 44:22). The blood of Jesus, His love, and His day of love set us apart as God's holy people.

Will you be a wise virgin? Will you put on the engagement ring and the wedding band Jesus bought for you with His blood? Will you let the Sabbath anointing oil flow in your life? Will you rest from your labors and rest in Jesus on His day of redemption?

Jesus is calling out to you: "Love Me! Obey Me! Come meet with me at My appointed time. Come sup with Me at My table. Come experience the depth and reality of My redemption. Don't choose tradition. Choose Me and My day, and the truth will set you free!"

Sabbath *Selah's*
Swallowing Fishy Tales: "Hook, Lie, and Sinking"

One of the most eloquent proofs the early church kept the Sabbath is silence. Had the mainly Jewish believers in Judea changed from Saturday to Sunday, the uproar from the surrounding Jews would have been deafening. Louder today is the big Sunday lie that naïve Christians have swallowed "hook, line, and sinker" -- or more accurately, "hook, lie, not thinking." Talk about revisionist history. Christian martyrdom would likely have occurred much sooner than A.D. 34 when Stephen perished. Jewish leaders would have left no stone unturned in their prompt persecution of fellow Jews who had become traitors to the Sabbath. Jewish zealots, certain they were doing God a service, would probably have thrown literal stones to kill the Messianic Sabbath breakers (Num. 15:32-36). The Jewish reaction and backlash would have been enormous and swift. The only real dispute was in Acts 15. The kerfuffle was over circumcision being required for salvation (15:1), and in the only peripheral mention of the Sabbath, its observance is tacitly upheld (15:20). Selah.

CHAPTER EIGHTEEN

From Sabbath to Sunday: An Overview of Church History

The Bible is the ultimate authority. What men say and do carries no weight apart from the Book. The prominence of the people makes no difference. Yet some try to prove we should keep Sunday because some important people did or do observe that day. So what?

We might ask the question: "In whose eyes are these people important?" God says if you discount even the least of the commandments, He calls you least in His Kingdom. As Myles Munroe has so effectively taught, the Kingdom of God is not a democracy. What King Jesus says is law. We do not vote on His law. We either obey it or we do not.

The fourth commandment does not change because men say it does. Look at a worse case scenario - Let's say not one single person in the church kept the Sabbath after Jesus died. So?

Paul explains in Romans that God entrusted the Jews with His oracles, including the revelation of the Sabbath in the Word. The fact that the Jews were unfaithful does not change the faithfulness of God. "What then? If some did not believe, their unbelief will not nullify the faithfulness of God, will it? May it never be! Rather, [God is] found true, though every man be found a liar..." (Rom. 3:3-4).

God even has a plan for such an eventuality: "...For truth has stumbled in the street, And uprightness cannot enter. Yes, truth is lacking; and he who turns aside from evil [God calls Sabbath breaking evil] makes himself a prey...And He saw that there was no man, And was astonished that there was no one to intercede;

Then His own arm brought salvation to Him, And His righteousness upheld Him" (Isa. 59:14-16).

Church fathers have been known to lie. But not God. "God is not a man, that He should lie, Nor a son of man, that He should repent; Has He said, and will He not do it? Or has He spoken, and will He not make it good? Behold [says Balaam], I have received [from Jesus] a command to bless; When He has blessed, then I cannot revoke it" (Num. 23:19-20).

In other words, when God blesses something, He cannot take back the blessing, nor can man take it back (Isa. 45:23; Rom. 11:29; I Chron. 17:27). Jesus pronounced a blessing on the seventh day (Gen. 2:2-3). No man has the right to take away that blessing. Not Constantine. Not the pope. Not your pastor. Nobody -- not even God.

But men have tried to do just that. They have changed the Sabbath from Saturday to Sunday with no biblical authority whatsoever. Church authority perhaps – but not biblical authority. No matter who it is who changes God's law, He says to obey Him rather than men (Acts 5:29).

In one sense, therefore, it makes no difference what church history says about the Sabbath. In another sense, it is instructive to see where the Sunday leaven began to rise in the church.

Good Guys or Bad Guys?

My wife loves to watch Westerns. I sometimes watch them with her when I'm not writing books, counseling and preparing sermons. In those old Western movies, it's easy to tell who are the good guys and who are the bad guys. In church history, it is not so easy. Let's face it: no one is completely good or completely bad. It is true that a person either has the Holy Spirit inside them or does not, has accepted Jesus or has not, is born again or is not born again, in the same way that a woman is either pregnant or is not. You cannot be partially pregnant.

That being said, Jesus said tares or false Christians would exist in the church until an end-time separation He would orchestrate. Paul warned about wolves in sheep's clothing that would draw naïve members to follow them in error. Then again, compromise starts small and leaders may be in different degrees of compromise at various times in diverse areas of belief. Moreover, history does not tell us everything and is not always totally accurate.

It was with this Bible basis and with these warnings to myself that I began to do some research into church history regarding the Sabbath and Sunday. This is a truthful work; it is not, however, a scholarly one. The statements I do make regarding history are based on reputable works. The only difference is that I base my understanding on the clear Bible proof of the Sabbath.

I actually started my search with the erudite works of a modern advocate of Sunday. Willy Rordorf surprised me with some startling admissions[1]. He admitted that the early church in Jerusalem and the surrounding area was primarily Jewish, which was not the surprising statement. The interesting confession was the following acknowledgment, shared by other historians and leaders who wrote about that early period: the Judean church, including the Gentiles, continued to keep the Sabbath and holy days. As other writers readily admit, ***had the Sabbath been changed to Sunday, it would have caused gigantic upheaval in the church and we would have read about it in the Bible.***

It didn't happen.

This change did not occur even at the destruction of the temple in A.D. 70 -- destroying the argument that the Sabbath and/or holy days were somehow ceremonial and would be abolished with the temple. It was only when Roman Emperor Hadrian came to power in A.D. 135 and imposed his rule on the area that compromise could gradually begin to take root. It did.

Religious writer Jess Lyman Hurlbut states: "For fifty years after St. Paul's life a curtain hangs over the church, through which we strive vainly to look; and when at last it rises, about A.D.120 with writing of the earliest church fathers, we find a church in many aspects very different from that in the days of St. Peter and St. Paul."[2] Very different. Hurlbut also writes: "As long as the church was mainly Jewish, the Hebrew sabbath was kept; but as it became increasingly Gentile the first day gradually took the place of the seventh day."[3] Since when does God change His law "gradually" -- or at all? Many other historians admit that in the early church both Jew and Gentile kept the Sabbath and holy days.

Of course! The New Testament church is founded on the Hebrew Scriptures (Eph. 2:20; II Tim. 3:13-17). Christianity's root are Jewish. The Sabbath and holy day keeping element of the church was the dominant factor in the church for at least a generation.[4]

---

1 Willy Rordorf, Sunday: The History of the Day of Rest and Worship in the Earliest Centuries of the Christian Church, translated by A.A.K. Graham from the German edition of 1962 (Philadelphia, 1968).

2 Jess Lyman Hurlbut, *The Story of the Christian Church*, p. 41

3 Hurlbut, *The Story of the Christian Church* p. 45

4 Samuel Bacchiocchi, in *From Sabbath to Sunday*, p. 151, quotes Davies work, *Judeo-christianisme*, "Paul and Jewish Christianity," 1972, p. 72: "Everywhere, especially in the East of the Roman Empire, there would be Jewish Christians whose outward way of life would not be markedly different from that of the Jews. They took for granted that the gospel was continuous with [the religion of Moses]; for them the New Covenant, which Jesus had set up at the Last Supper with His disciples...did not mean that the covenant made between God and Israel was no longer in force. They still observed the feasts of Passover, Pentecost and Tabernacles...the weekly Sabbath and the Mosaic regulations concerning food. According to some scholars, they must have been so strong that right up to the fall of Jerusalem in AD 70 they were the dominant element in the Christian movement."

What *was* gradual was that "evil men and impostors will proceed from bad to worse, deceiving and being deceived" (II Tim. 3:13). Paul warned that "from among your own selves men will arise, speaking perverse things, to draw away the disciples after them," not "declaring the whole purpose of God" as Paul did (Acts 20:27,30). The false Christians were abandoning the church's foundations.

A move is underway today to bring the church back to its Jewish roots. It is not only a cute observance to add Jewish spice and culture to our modern worship, as some believe. It is God's command.

The Jewish beginnings of Christianity, especially the Sabbath covenant, are the bedrock -- the very foundation -- of the Christian religion. David wrote in Psalm 11:3, "If the foundations are destroyed, What can the righteous do?"

The answer is: not much. The Bride of Jesus today is limping. The answer? She has rejected the foundation of the Sabbath day. The Sabbath covenant is the very first covenant on which all the others depend.

The 10 Biblical Covenants

1. ***The Sabbath Covenant*** – Jesus made this covenant of intimacy with Adam, and we see it developed throughout the Bible with Israel and the church. In essence, Jesus said to Adam, "If you keep your feet off my day, which belongs to Me and over which I am Divine Master, you will have dominion over everything else, including the earth and the heavens (Isa. 58:13-14; Ps. 8:5-6)." It promises an intimacy and oneness with Jesus that leads to an eternal Sabbath rest with Him.
2. ***The Adamic Covenant*** – Adam and His descendants would be fruitful, multiply, and rule over the earth, if they obeyed God (including and especially the Sabbath). Having been freed from sin by the last Adam, Jesus, we are indeed Sons of the God of increase, ruling as Gods over the earth in the name of our Brother and Savior Jesus.
3. ***The Marriage Covenant***- God establishes marriage and invites husband and wife to covenant with Him and make Him a part of the trinity of marriage. Jesus' marriage covenant with Israel and later with spiritual Israel, His Bride, is foreshadowed in this covenant.
4. ***The Noatian Covenant*** – All mankind comes under the bow of God, the rainbow being the sign that He will never again destroy the earth by water. God saved all of Noah's family from the flood, so we can claim this covenant for family salvation and protection. Noah's small family became a righteous seed that brought forth a harvest in the earth, so we can claim this covenant with any financial or other seed we sow. Noah found favor with God, so we can claim favor under this covenant. As the world's sins and all the evil of the past were washed away in the flood, we can claim the same for us in this covenant. God's grief at the pre-Flood evil caused Him to shorten man's life span to 120 years (Gen. 6:3), a lifetime longer than most today and one we can claim in this covenant.
5. ***The Abrahamic Covenant*** – As children of Abraham by faith we receive all the promises made to Abraham -- including prosperity, eternal inheritance of the earth (Gen. 12,15,17), and defeat of all our enemies (Gen. 14:20). Abraham was favored of God, so we can claim favor under this covenant.
6. ***The Circumcision Covenant*** – As we are circumcised in our hearts, we complete the process of the death of the old ways and the reality of the new life begun when we accepted Jesus. We receive peace, joy, and God's graces that overflow in our lives (Gen. 17:10; Jer. 4:4 Acts 7:8; Rom. 2:29; Col. 2:11-12), rolling away "the reproach of Egypt [sin]"(Josh.5:9). When claiming freedom from bad habits, we can claim this covenant.
7. ***The Sinai Covenant*** – "Now then, if you will indeed obey My voice and keep My covenant [referring to the first covenant, the Sabbath covenant, and includ-

ing the covenant God was about to make with them] then you will be My own possession..." (Ex. 19:5). This is the essence of the covenant Jesus made with Israel – the believers. Although the covenant itself is no longer in effect, the laws and the principles of that covenant are still alive since they are in the Word of God to be claimed. When we obey, we receive all the blessings of the believers and more (see Deuteronomy 28).

8. ***The Davidic Covenant*** – God promised that David would always have a descendant to sit on his throne, culminating in Jesus Himself sitting on David's throne to rule with us over all the earth (Jer. 33:21-26; Psalm 89). God promised to defend David and his descendants. We can claim today this covenant of defense against our enemies (Ps. 89:22-23).
9. ***The New Covenant*** – We accept Jesus and agree to obey Him, and by His blood He offers us freedom from sin, sealing the covenant of peace in His blood – the covenant of eternal life. We can claim every word of God and seal it in Jesus' blood. Also, we can now ask anything of our Father through Jesus (Jer. 31:31-33; Heb. 8:10).
10. ***The Everlasting Covenant*** -- The Father will make a tenth and final covenant with His Sons and Daughters when He comes to rule forever over the New Heavens and the New Earth (Ezek. 37:26; Rev. 21:1-5).

The God who cannot lie promises to fulfill His part of the covenant (Heb. 6:13-18; Ps. 111:5,10; Eph. 2:12-13). Let's do our part and boldly remind God of His covenants (Neh. 1:5-11; Ex. 32:11-14; II Sam. 7:28: "...You are God [Love], and Your words are truth, and You have promised this good thing to Your servant [son/daughter]").

Jewish Christianity?

An archaeological find of an ossuary claiming to contain the bones of James joined the chorus of cries to cast doubt upon Jesus' credibility. It caused a news magazine to focus on an aspect of early Christian theology of which most believers are totally unaware.

The magazine wrote: "As leader of the mother church in Jerusalem, James was the key proponent of a brand of Christianity that retained strong ties to Judaism … practicing a form of the religion, says James D.G. Dunn, professor of divinity at the University of Durham, England, that 'we today would scarcely recognize – ***Jewish Christianity.***[5]'"

Another fact that escapes many is that most of Paul's early Gentile converts were uncircumcised "God-fearers" and synagogue attendees who were already familiar with the Sabbath and the holy days (Acts 13:16,42; 18:4). They had already forsaken the pagan ways and days and were eager to follow this new Christian way rooted in the Hebrew Scriptures.

An ironic modern twist to this scenario is the fact that many Jewish people became Messianic during the charismatic renewal of the 1970's and summarily rejected the Sabbath for Sunday. What began as "Jewish Christianity" has become a baptized paganism, rejecting the days Jesus, John, James, Peter, and Paul observed. Other Messianic groups are somewhat shy about the Sabbath, not wanting to impose it on other Christians. Being called to repair the Sabbath breach, we are not shy.

We rejoice to see more and more Christians discovering their Jewish roots. What must happen, however, is more than a cute cuddling up with the holy days in a casual manner based in curiosity of fascinating customs. The discovery must involve recognizing that refusing to honor what God calls holy is sin. Breaking the fourth commandment is sin. Faithfulness involves obeying all God's commandments.

Day Based in Love? – or in Hate?

We find one shining example of faithfulness to the teaching of Jesus in Polycarp, a disciple of the apostle John. One of the early church writings[6] gives some interesting details about which days Polycarp kept, with my comments in brackets: "Con-

5 *U.S. News and World Report,* "A Discovery and a Debate," Nov. 4, 2002, p. 50.

6 *The Encyclical Epistle of the Church at Smyrnam,* excerpts from Chapters VII, VIII and XXI on the subject of Polycarp's martyrdom.

cerning the Martyrdom of the Holy Polycarp [considered by most to have taken place in the middle of the second century – thus those who wrote this were still keeping the Sabbath, as we shall see by what they say.]... His pursuers then, along with horsemen, and taking the youth with them, went forth at supper-time **on the day of the preparation** [note says this was Friday]...they set him upon an ass, and conducted him into the city, the day being that of **the great Sabbath**... Now, the blessed Polycarp suffered martyrdom on the second day of the month Xanthicus just begun, the seventh day before the Kalends **of May, on the great Sabbath...** The great Sabbath is that before the passover."

Even though over 80 at the time, Polycarp traveled to Rome to oppose Anicetus in the Roman bishop's insistence that the church should keep Easter rather than Passover. Polycarp stood fast.

When Polycarp was martyred, the leadership of the Eastern church passed to Polycrates. He also traveled to Rome to face the anti-Passover, anti-feast (and thus, ultimately, the anti-Sabbath) heresy espoused by Victor I, then bishop of Rome. Victor threatened to excommunicate Polycarp's successor.

Polycrates didn't budge. Of the Passover, He wrote [Roberts-Donaldson translation]: "As for us, then, we scrupulously observe the exact day, neither adding nor taking away." Referring to great luminaries in Asia who had died, including John, Philip, and Polycarp, he added: "These all kept the passover on the fourteenth day of the month in accordance with the gospel, without ever deviating from it but keeping to the rule of faith...[his relatives and he, Polycrates] always observed the day when the people put away the leaven...Better people than I have said, 'We must obey God rather than men.'"

Historian Will Durant recognized the difference between the early Judean and Roman churches. He noted that while the church at Rome adopted their moral values from Judea, their theology came from Greece (Justin bolstered his arguments with quotes from Plato!) and their organization from Rome (*Caesar and Christ*, p. 618). The "faith once delivered" was not bequeathed to the *pontifex maximus* who became the Roman pontiff. Most of his doctrines and practices came from ancient Rome and Babylon. The faith of Jesus and the apostles in Judea came straight from the Word -- unstained and unadulterated.

The bishop of Rome eventually excommunicated these staunch Sabbath keeping leaders in the East, including initially Judea and later Asia Minor. But in God's Book, might does not make right. He says it is not by power or might, but by His Spirit that we are to live our lives and establish our doctrine (Zech. 4:6).

His Spirit is characterized principally by love. John was more intimate with Jesus than any of the other apostles. He spoke eloquently of love and practiced what he preached. He taught his disciple Polycarp to keep all the commandments of love, including the Sabbath and the feast days. He laid down his life in martyrdom because he dared to keep and teach the Passover and all the days motivated by love.

On the other hand, what motivation do we see in the first church writings recommending Sunday as the day of worship? God says we are to discern the truth of a church leader by how much his words agree with Scripture and by the fruits of his life (Isa. 8:20; I Thes. 5:21; Acts 17:11; Mat. 7:20).

My Teen Challenge

This issue was a challenge for me early in life. When I received the seed of Sabbath truth in my heart in 1967, Satan came quickly to try to steal that seed. He sent a believer friend of the family, a journalist and author, to try to convince me I was wrong. He twisted some of Paul's verses in his epistles, which we will deal with later. He also cited verses from the Acts trying to prove that the early Christians in the birthplace of Christianity kept the first day of the week.

Much of his argument was based, however, on the words of men. He quoted church fathers who taught and practiced the observance of Sunday as the Christian day of worship.

As I look back on this turbulent period in my life, compounded by the pressures of the teenage years, I wonder why he did not quote the historical sources I quote above. Had he examined those sources, he would be faced with a dilemma. This is an important point that many have missed. It is so important that I will put part of it in bold type.

Those of you who claim evidence for Sunday keeping in the Acts, answer this question: If you are right, then ***why does no historical record exist of the early church in the Jerusalem area keeping Sunday?***

These arguments stand naked, revealed for what they are: dishonest excuses for keeping a day God never ordained. It may be easy for such Sunday defenders to forget that their champion Paul was a part of that early Judean church leadership. While he traveled to Gentile areas to fulfill his commission, he maintained contact with the leaders in Jerusalem and kept feasts there (Acts 20:16).

These Sunday protagonists pretend Paul kept the Sabbath in the synagogues to win the Jews, not because he truly believed in the Sabbath. Yet he preached on the Sabbath in Gentile areas. In Gentile Philippi, he went to a "place of prayer" by a riverside in order to properly keep the Sabbath (Acts 16:13).

Paul believed everything that was written in the Hebrew Scriptures, including the Sabbath (Acts 24:14), and no historical evidence exists to show he ever changed. He even said he had kept that same faith at the end of his life (II Tim. 4:7).

But all this doesn't matter for people who have set their wills against the truth. In France I had to deal with a lady who as a child sat on Hitler's knee. For her Adolph was a kind man who loved children, and the notion that he sent Jews to gas chambers was a propaganda ploy by his enemies. Nothing would convince her otherwise.

At 19 in 1970 I encountered another lady, a cab driver in Munich, Germany. I wanted to visit Dachau, and in my naiveté I accepted her answer to my request: "Dachau? There is no such thing as Dachau!"

In trying to justify Sunday, theologians are rewriting history. They thus ally themselves with the liars who rewrite Jewish and German history by saying the Holocaust never happened – which brings us back to the subject of motivation.

Are their teachings based in love? Are they showing how much they love Jesus by annulling His commandments?

Polycarp gave up his life in a loving sacrifice to abide in Jesus' love by keeping His Sabbath day. What about those first voices that spoke out in favor of Sunday? What was their motivation? Was it love?

A Day Birthed in Hatred?

One of the quotes our family friend used was in the writings of a man named Justin Martyr (A.D. 100-165). A former Gentile philosopher living in second-century Rome, he was the first to write about Sunday and denigrate the Sabbath. In his *Dialogue with Trypho*, the title of Chapter 21 is: SABBATHS WERE INSTITUTED ON ACCOUNT OF THE PEOPLE'S SINS, AND NOT FOR A WORK OF RIGHTEOUSNESS." He begins, "Moreover, that God enjoined you to keep the Sabbath, and impose on you other precepts for a sign, as I have already said, on account of your unrighteousness, and that of your fathers..."

False and hateful words such as these were behind the change from Sabbath to Sunday. Justin's words bear no resemblance to what the Bible says, and they are certainly not characterized by love. Why should we believe a man who bears such evil fruit? Why should we believe any man who changes God's Sabbath to Sunday with no biblical authority?

Ignatius, bishop of Antioch, while condemning a Jewish approach to Sabbath keeping, showed in his writings that the East was much slower to abandon the Sabbath than the West. He writes: "Let us therefore no longer keep the Sabbath after the Jewish manner...But let everyone of you keep the Sabbath in a spiritual manner, rejoicing in the meditation on the law [so it was not done away]...admiring the workmanship of God..."[7]

As Egypt represented sin in the Bible, it is interesting that the leaven of Sabbath hatred rose early in Alexandria. Barnabas, the bishop in this Egyptian city,

7 Pseudo-Ignatius, *Epistle to the Magnesians* 9, ANF I, pages 62-63

even denied that the literal practice of the Sabbath had ever been the object of a commandment of God. In Chapter 15 of his epistle, He called the Jewish people "the wretched [Jews], wandering in error…"

Will You Heed the Voice of Truth?

God in His Word does not refer to Rome and Egypt in praiseworthy terms. Is it any wonder that the voice of Sabbath truth began to be swallowed up in Sunday error in these areas? And the voice these bishops used to denigrate the Sabbath was a voice fuelled by hate rather than love. They spoke against clear Bible truth and their voice of hate was a noisy gong that clanged in the ears of the visible church (I Cor. 13:1). It virtually deafened the voice of truth.

The song, "The Voice of Truth," contains a phrase I love: "and the voice of truth tells me a different story…" The voice of truth tells a different story from the loud gong heard in virtually every church throughout the land.

Will you hear the voice of Jesus? Or will you prefer to have your ears tickled by Justin Martyr of Rome or Barnabas of Egypt? Or perhaps the present bishop of Rome? Listen to the voice of love. Listen to the Word. Listen to your heart as the Holy Spirit speaks to you according to the Word.

Paganism Baptized in Christian Waters Still Stinks

The justifications given by early church fathers for introducing Sunday were based in compromise. Israel did not abandon their adoration of God for Baal worship. All they did was mix the two. History repeats itself. God clearly said not to mix paganism with Christianity, but that is exactly what these fathers did.

Here is Justin's explanation: "But Sunday is the day on which we all hold our common assembly, because it is the first day on which God, having wrought a change in the darkness and matter, made the world; and Jesus Christ our Saviour on the same day rose from the dead. For He was crucified on the day before that of Saturn (Saturday); and on the day after that of Saturn, which is the day of the Sun, having appeared to His apostles and disciples, He taught them these things, which we have submitted to you also for your consideration.[8]"

His first reason has nothing to do with what God expressly commanded.

8 *The First Apology of Justin*, Chapter LXVII, Weekly Worship of the Christians.

It is totally irrelevant. The second reason, only to become a major justification for Sunday later in church history, is an excuse we have proved to be false.

Other historical evidence upholds Justin's statement that Sunday was recognized as the "Day of the Sun" and that the week named after the planets was already in place at that time. While church fathers for obvious reasons do not openly admit that they borrowed a pagan day and baptized it Christian, it is evident that is exactly what they did. Constantine's edicts in the fourth century remove any doubt.

Yet God was clear. Mixing pagan ways and days with true worship is partaking of the tree of the knowledge of good and evil (Deut. 12:28-32; Gen. 2:17). It's a miserable mix -- a putrid porridge that eventually kills. The party line in Constantine's time was basically the same as the reason the church chose the date of the birth of the sun, December 25, to celebrate Jesus' birth instead of true date of the autumn Feast of Trumpets. The justification, paraphrased, was this: "if you can't beat 'em, join 'em. Since we cannot suppress the popularity of these pagan days, we must purify these customs." Far from purification, it was pollution. You don't purify sewage by piping it into your house.

If you want to know what the real Jesus thinks of this mess, read Malachi 2:3. This is not the "sweet baby Jesus," but the Lion of Judah who speaks here: "…I will spread refuse [the word in Hebrew is stronger than our four-letter word for excrement] on your faces, the refuse [garbage] of *your* feasts…"

They had changed God's feasts for pagan days. Jesus loves those who worship on Sunday. He has a fierce hatred, however, of the rejection of His days of intimacy and celebration with His people. He hates compromise.

Eusebius' Bias

Transferring the sacrifice of Sabbath praise to the "true day of the sun" as Eusebius suggests is not pleasing to Jesus. He prefers obedience to sacrifice. With no biblical authority, this historian wrote: "All things whatsoever that were prescribed for the Sabbath, ***we*** have transferred them to the Lord's day, as being *more authoritative* [than Jesus?] and more highly regarded and first in rank, and more honorable than the Jewish Sabbath. In fact, it is on this day…that God said: 'Let there be light and there was light.' It is also on this day that the Sun of Justice has risen for our souls.[9]"

Heavenly-sounding hogwash! God calls forth a Sabbath blessing only on those who "call…the holy day of [Jesus] honorable, And honor it…" (Isa. 58:13) – not choosing the day *they* decide to honor, using *their* authority rather than God's.

9 Eusebius, *Commentaria in Psalmos* 91, PG 23, 1169-1172

We acknowledge that neither the early Christians nor the Sunday keepers of our day had or have the intention of worshipping the sun. They applied the sun analogy to Jesus. But they might as well have been worshipping the sun! In an unmistakable reference to the Days of Unleavened Bread that early Christians were keeping until Justin of Rome, Barnabas of Egypt, and Constantine came along, Paul says that a little leaven of sin leavens the whole lump (I Cor. 5:5-8).

The commandments are so interwoven, that when you break one, you break them all. Sabbath breaking is idolatry, taking the name of Jesus, Divine Master of the Sabbath in vain, dishonoring our heavenly Father, expressing hatred toward Him, bedding down with falseness, stealing time from God, living a lie, and coveting a gift from Satan.

Sins vary in their degree of evil and their physical consequences, but they all end in death when they are knowingly committed and repeated calls to repentance are ignored. In any case, they produce the ways of death in the life of the disobedient. Sin kills.

You can pick and choose whom to believe in the annals of church history, or you can choose to believe Jesus. Don't be deceived. Church history can confuse you and give you a muddled story of compromise and human reasoning. The voice of truth beckons you to hear a different story, the true history of the Sabbath – **His**-tory. Don't believe the lies and half-truths. Believe ***His*** story.

Sabbath *Selah's*
Blue Laws: Closed on Sunday

Why would you go shopping when the store is closed? All treasures of wisdom and knowledge are stored up in Jesus (Col. 2:3), who made the Sabbath holy by pouring Himself into this day. The spiritual store is open on the Sabbath so we can receive all that is stored up in Jesus. God commands us to stop our normal shopping on His holy day and to go to His store when it's open. Jesus' "store" is closed on Sunday, like many of the shops shut down by religiosity on that day. The true "blue law" is that, sadly, Sunday keepers will not be able to benefit from the fullness of the joy of Jesus released to His people on the Sabbath day. "Jesus' joy is our strength" is a truth rooted in an annual Sabbath day (Neh. 8:10). Soon the weak will say they are strong, for Jesus "will have compassion on His servants, When He sees that their strength is gone" *(Deut. 32:36-38) because of idolatry. His people will no longer have "the blues," but* "will call the sabbath a delight" *and* "will take delight in [Jesus]" *(Isa. 58:13-14). As an added bonus of seeking first the Kingdom on Kingdom Day, they will even receive financial blessings (Mat. 6:33). As with Adam in the garden, no sweat, no toil, no sorrow -- only sweet rest in the Sabbath, the gateway to God's blessings. Selah.*

Poverty is a curse, not a blessing. Yet many Christians believe it's more righteous and humble to be poor. This false doctrine has locked the treasures Father Love is waiting to pour out upon them.

CHAPTER NINETEEN

Don't Read This If You Don't Want to Be Rich and Generous -- The Race for Riches versus "Manna-fold" Provision

Millions of people – even Christians – are in the proverbial rat race. It's a rat race for riches. The winner is the one with the most toys. They work and work and work by the sweat of their brow to get ahead to keep up with the Joneses and even surpass the Joneses. They're in a manic rush to amass wealth.

Something's missing. They don't understand that the key to wealth is in Jesus. And the key is not working more or scheming more. The beginning of wealth – the beginning of provision – is ***resting in Jesus.***

But not just any kind of rest. We have to rest from our works as Jesus did.

That includes the how and the when. He tells us rest exactly as He did (Heb. 4:10), which means on the same day.

Many Christians are looking for manifold provision – but by mega works in the flesh. They don't understand the lesson of the manna that God gave Israel, a lesson we aim to teach in this chapter. They do not understand their purpose or "manifest destiny." Why? They don't know who they are.

Again we ask why? It's simple. They don't keep the day of rest that Jesus said set them apart as His people. The Sabbath is a sign that Jesus is Creator and that we are His special, favored people (Ex. 31:13).

A Freedom-from-poverty Party!

It is also a day of freedom. Egypt represents sin. So God's command to the believers 3500 years ago applies just as much to us today: "You shall remember that you were a slave in the land of Egypt, and the [Eternal] your God brought you out of there by a mighty hand and by an outstretched arm; therefore the [Eternal] your God commanded you to observe the sabbath day" (Deut. 5:15).

The Sabbath was given for the purpose of remembering that Jesus brought the believers out of the land of sin. Do you remember how He brought them out? He brought them out victoriously – with a high hand (Ex. 14:8, KJV; Ps. 105:37,43). He brought them out with silver and gold!

That has powerful implications regarding the Sabbath and the Sabbath covenant. Jesus gave the Sabbath not only to commemorate our covenant with the Creator of all things, a covenant that gives us dominion over all things – including wealth. God also gave it to keep us in remembrance of His covenant of provision.

It is indeed a celebration of freedom from sin. But it is also a freedom-from-poverty party! Just as Jesus brought the believers out of sin and poverty when they left Egypt, so He brings us out of both sin and poverty when we accept Him. Like Israel, we may decide to go around the mountain a few times before we realize our heritage and destiny, but He has already given us the freedom. We must simply claim it in faith.

The Heavenly Window-openers

Certain keys -- the heavenly window-openers -- are essetnial. They allow God to "open for you the windows of heaven and pour out for you a blessing until it overflows" (Mal. 3:10). What opens heaven's windows?

First, we must be givers like God. We must tithe – and give offerings. Giving is the foundational key to provision. Giving pays.

God was showing Israel through Malachi how to begin to return to God (Mal. 3:7-8). They were presenting defiled food on God's altar, but at least it was God's altar, on the right day. They were keeping the Sabbath, albeit with a lousy attitude and mixing Baal in with it.

So the other window-opener, Sabbath keeping, was already in place. Keeping the Sabbath covenant without tithing cancels the first covenant's financial blessing.

Here again, giving is the opener. We give money -- and time. Actually, in the cases of both the tithe and the Sabbath, it is in reality *God's* time. He set aside the tithe and the Sabbath as holy – something you don't touch with your hands or trample with your feet.

But the Sabbath/provision connection is more than about simply giving up the one day of the week God calls His. Both the tithe and the Sabbath are sacrifices that don't seem like sacrifices at all when we begin to respect them. Keeping them blesses us in so many ways, including financially.

God is saying, "Give Me back My tenth and I will bless your nine-tenths more than if you kept it all – much more. Respect the one day out of seven I have chosen as Mine to meet with you and I will make your other six days more productive than seven days of your work would have produced. I will not only redeem the time; I will bless you financially much more than you could have been blessed by working on My day."

Deceived by the Devil's Day

It's too bad Satan has so deceived the church. He doesn't want us honoring God's time and observing Jesus' appointed times. He has two-timed the bride of Jesus, robbing her of her weekly date with her Bridegroom and tricking her into spending time, in too many cases, praising "the Lord" instead of Jesus on the wrong day. He has convinced God's people they should keep the *devil's* day. After all, Satan is the one who introduced Sunday to keep God's people from the Sabbath dynamite that would blow him to smithereens. The devil led the church go to the pagans to learn how to worship God. Instead of keeping God's day that celebrates and produces miraculous provision, Christians have, in effect, praised and worshipped Satan by keeping the pagan days that glorify him.

As John 10 explains, the Good Shepherd gives to the sheep. He provides for them, giving them green pastures in which to graze. David said: "You prepare a feast for me in the presence of my enemies...My cup overflows with blessings" (Ps. 23:5 -- NLT).

Why has that not been the case for the modern church? One of the main reasons may surprise you. Instead of keeping the day of the Good Shepherd, most of today's sheep have kept the day of the thief, the murderer, the devil of destruction (John 10:10).

When you cozy up to the one who kills, steals and destroys, what do you think will happen? We reap what we sow. If we are following the destroyer, are we following the Shepherd? When Jesus has prepared a luxuriant green pasture for us, a fabulous Sabbath feast, why go after satanic, Sunday stubble?

That may sound harsh and blunt to sincere, Christian people who have blindly followed tradition and ignored what God's Word actually says. We don't condemn you. It is nonetheless the truth – a truth we are appointed and anointed to share (Isa. 58:1) so that change and blessing can come.

Remember, Jesus is the Judge. He will not judge us according to the precepts of men, but according to His Word. He never ordained Sunday. Men did.

You will not be judged according to the Council of Nicea or the catechism. God's Word will judge you.

The good news is that God is the Father of mercies. He loves mercy. He forgives easily. He knows most have been deceived. Jesus' blood cleanses us from all sin, if we knew we were sinning or not.

Just as repenting of not tithing allows God to rebuke the devourer for us (Mal. 3:11), so beginning to keep the Sabbath enables Him to rebuke the destroyer and thief. Shepherd Jesus has come to give us life more abundantly (John 10:10) – and that includes prosperity.

Preachers who expound God's covenant of wholeness and prosperity have indeed been abundantly blessed. Men like Creflo Dollar, Kenneth Copeland, and Bill Winston have blessed us as a church with their inspired teachings. If they think their cup is overflowing now, wait until they reap the blessings provided under the Sabbath covenant!

While The Message is a free translation, it does convey the Sabbath blessing of Isaiah 58:13-14:

"If you watch your step on the Sabbath and don't use my holy day for personal advantage, If you treat the Sabbath as a day of joy, God's holy day as a celebration, If you honor it by refusing 'business as usual,' making money, running here and there -- Then you'll be free to enjoy God! Oh, I'll make you ride high and soar above it all. I'll make you feast on the inheritance of your ancestor Jacob." Yes! God says so!

The promises of Sabbath blessing in Isaiah 58:14 include prosperity. Modern translations emphasize this: "I will feed you with the best from the land..." (NLV) and "...cause you to ... feast on the inheritance..." (NIV). To "ride on the heights of the earth" certainly indicates power and prosperity.

God's intent for Israel was that they worship Him and Him only on His days, which they did at first. He said they would "ride on the high places," which included "the finest of the wheat" (Deut. 32:12-14).

The Ark of the Covenant and the Sabbath Covenant

It was no accident that Jesus placed manna in the Ark of the Covenant. It is not only a reference to the fact that He is our Manna, that we have eternal life when we eat of Him in communion and are hungry for His Word. It is also a reminder not to forget the only commandment He said to remember.

In fact, all three items in the Ark have a Sabbath link. The Sabbath was the centerpiece of the Ten Commandments, also placed in that box. The rod of Aaron represents God's authority and miracle-working power. Many Christians defy His authority today by rejecting His Sabbath. They thus deprive themselves of the authority Sabbath keeping brings and the wonder working anointing of that day.

Sabbath Manna

That Sabbath anointing also inspires the dispensing of quality spiritual food or manna. It's a special anointing that can often cause the same wonderment the Israelites experienced. When they beheld the manna, they looked at each other and exclaimed, "What is it?" They had never seen such a thing before. The name "manna" is Hebrew for "What is it?"

The Holy Spirit is smart and amazing in the inspiration of Sabbath sermons. Even the preacher stands in awe at what is coming out of his mouth. His reaction is often, "Wow! What is it? I've never seen this before!"

The audience is in awe, and so are the angels! As they protect the church on the Sabbath, and join in the praise, they stand in amazement at what God is revealing through His Sons and Daughters. Peter speaks of "these things which now have been announced to you through those who preached the gospel to you by the Holy Spirit sent from heaven – things into which angels long to look" (I Pet. 2:12).

They marvel at the truths revealed through men and the awesome destiny of mankind -- a destiny revealed in the Sabbath food or "manna." That future is assured as God's people reach greater intimacy with the Manna or Bread of Life – Jesus Himself – by keeping His appointment time.

The Sabbath is the key to the "manna-fest destiny" and the "manna-fold" provision of the believers. It all revolves around the lesson of manna.

It even involves seeking the Kingdom first by indulging in a weekly "manna-feast." When we seek the spiritual manna of the Word of God preached under the Sabbath anointing, God can add to us all the "other things" of Matthew 6:33.

The Manna Test

Exodus 16 tells the story of the manna miracle, a story richer in spiritual food than you may have realized. Israel failed the manna test. That Sabbath-manna test in these last days will make manifest the true spiritual Israelites (the believers) who will inherit the spiritual Promised Land. You don't need to die in the desert. You can enter the Sabbath rest if you pass the manna test (Heb. 4:1-11).

Notice the attitude of the rebellious Israelites. They complained that they at least had bread in Egypt (Ex. 16:3). Like many in this world of sin, they slave away "24/7" to make a living. They get their provision under the rule of Satan, the financial Pharaoh of this world. It's all in the flesh – by the sweat of their brow.

When Christians find out about the Sabbath, they often, as with tithing, try to close the window-opener immediately. The "I can't afford to…" or "I'm gonna die of starvation" reaction to tithing is similar to their excuses for not keeping the Sabbath and probably as ludicrous as the theological excuses: "You're going to kill us." "How can we possibly obey Your Sabbath? This world works on Saturday. We gotta keep slavin' away or we won't survive. We don't want this stupid manna. We want Mammon!"

It wasn't that God did not want His people then and now to do any work. We work, but we don't toil. God adds no "sorrow" or painful toil to His blessings (Prov. 10:22). We are gatherers who cease gathering and rest on His day. Working diligently to pick and prepare the manna each of the six days of the week was part of the test, "whether or not they will walk in My instruction (Ex. 16:4)."

Jesus chose the fourth commandment to be a major test for Israel (the believers). It's the same for the believers today. The only difference is that we have God in us and live by faith. Our faith is in the power of the body and blood of Jesus. The connection between communion and "manna-fold" provision may surprise you.

The "Manna-fest' Meaning of Communion

Israel saw with their eyes the double portion of manna that came on Friday. We believe we have a double portion based on the Sabbath covenant we have with God.

When we take communion, we break the blessed Bread of Life from heaven (the body of Jesus) into two parts.

They represent the Alpha and the Omega. Jesus is the A to Z. Nothing is missing. No lack. He is our Source, our Provision, the Author and Finisher of our faith. He promises to provide and even gives us the faith to trust in His provision.

Furthermore, all the promises of His Word – including provision – are available in His body, since it was broken for us, so that we could receive all the good things He has for us.

If you read *Why Doesn't God Heal Me?* you may recall the link between the two parts of the body of Jesus and the figure eight loop Jesus made with Abraham as they walked through the two parts of the covenant sacrifice. That loop of love – the symbol of infinity -- signified God's guaranteed faithfulness to fulfill all His promises.

We claim the promises in the Omega part in our right hand, including the promises of provision of the Sabbath covenant. On the left or Alpha side, we pledge to Jesus that we will obey Him to fulfill our part of the covenant. The Sabbath test commandment is an important part of that pledge.

But there's more. We hold in our hands the body of Jesus – manna from heaven. That's exactly what He called Himself in John 6:41-58. We have in our hands not one piece of manna – but two.

What does that signify? Double provision! Double blessing!

Here we see confirmed that the Sabbath covenant is the basis of all biblical covenants. This communion celebration of the New Covenant takes us back to the beginning as we celebrate the double portion of manna Jesus gave to the believers in the desert.

Not only does Jesus' body give us physical strength and spiritual strength as the manna nourished the believers in the desert. That double portion of the manna from heaven gives us the promise that Jesus is our abundant provision – spiritually, physically and financially.

Manna Miracle

The Sabbath manna was a miracle. It should have gone bad, but "…it did not become foul nor was there any worm in it" (Ex. 16:24). The Sabbath is the day that celebrates and enables miraculous provision!

That miracle shows another aspect of our Manna. Jesus is also our Sustainer. He sustained Israel with the manna as He sustains us. He preserved the Friday manna to be just as good on the Sabbath.

We are the birthright people – the first fruits. The firstborn received a double blessing. We have a double spiritual and physical blessing.

If upon learning about the Sabbath, however, we rebel and refuse to obey Jesus, we are saying we don't love Jesus (John 14:15). Jesus even said that if we rebel against His law of love, we could not enter the Kingdom (Mat. 7:21-23). We cannot be part of the covenant people and have the blessing.

Our obedience to our part of the Sabbath covenant, along with tithing, giving, and walking in love and wisdom, is our guarantee of supernatural provision.

We are a Sabbath keeping church and God has blessed us with abundant financial provision. We have received money in the Bible to provide for our needs – even on one Sabbath eight 1954 thousand-dollar bills! The Sabbath covenant is powerful.

The wealth of the wicked is stored up for the righteous (Prov.13:22; Mic. 4:13; Isa. 45:3; 60:5; 61:6), but unless you understand and keep the Sabbath covenant, you cannot be fully established in righteousness. Proverbs 8:20-21, speaking of wisdom, or the Word, makes that righteousness/wealth connection clear: "I walk in the way of righteousness, In the midst of the paths of justice, To endow those who love me with wealth, That I may fill their treasuries."

Full Obedience – Full Provision

How can the end-time church receive the fullness of wealth to preach the gospel unless we are fully walking in the way of righteousness, keeping all Ten Commandments?

As a father, would you release huge sums of money to a son or daughter who was not willing to fully obey you? God is not going to release abundant wealth to sons He cannot trust. If they are already deciding they know better which day to keep than their Father, how will He know they won't follow their own whims as well in spending the money He gives them?

When it comes to giving out money, our Father dishes out lavishly and extravagantly to His own. But He's not a pushover. We must come in line with His covenants, the last nine of which depend on the first – the Sabbath covenant. Ten covenants. Ten commandments. Ten is a number of completion. If you don't keep all ten of the commandments, you can't expect to enjoy the benefits of all ten covenants.

When we knowingly compromise regarding any of God's instructions, we open the door to Satan to eventually pollute our entire walk with God. Paul did not say for naught that a little leaven leavens the whole lump. Sin grows.

Righteous King Josiah pleased God. He burned the idols of Baal, ground them to dust and disposed of them. He smashed the altars of Baal and threw their dust into the brook (II Kings 23:6,12).

God "strongly support[s] those whose heart is *completely* His...(II Chron. 16:9)." He will support them in every way – even financially.

Modern Josiahs, like in Israel's history, are a rarity. In their role as kings and priests, most Christians act like the kings of old.

It's striking to read how the kings of Israel and Judah so often did everything right, except one thing. Remember reading that familiar phrase, "He did right in the sight of the [Eternal]...." The problem comes in the following verse that keeps repeating itself: "Only the high places were not taken away..."(II Kings 12:3; 14:4; 15:35).

Classic compromise. And curious coincidence. Although cleverly disguised by Satan as popular feast days, the days of Baal today strangely find their roots in the very practices of pagan worship on the high places of Israel. When we even innocently mix true worship with pagan days, to be unveiled in the sequel, and we dress up Ishtar's sexual revelry in a pretty "Ishtar bonnet" and the day of Baal in its Sunday best, the fullness of blessing can't come. Not spiritually. Not financially.

My wife in her early days on the farm fed the sheep. She would go around with a pail of grain as she heard the grateful chorus of "baahs." God's modern sheep are calling out for the wrong shepherd as they look to "the Lord" for their grain. Baal is pronounced in Hebrew "Bah-ahl." We sheep today need to change our tune, or we'll only be getting "toonies" (Canadian two-dollar coin) from "Ba-al" rather than "God-zillions" to preach the gospel.

The *wealth* of the heathen cannot come to us if we're keeping the *days* of the heathen!

Jiving with Jehovah-Jireh

The Sabbath is linked to every major biblical principle. No surprise, then, that it is closely tied in with the prosperity principle. The very prophetic meaning of the day points to the greatest time of abundance ever – the Millennium. The release of the wealth of the wicked to the righteous will only come in its fullness in the seventh millennial day. The most wicked generation that has ever lived will forfeit all its wealth to the most righteous rulers ever – Jesus and us, His co-heirs.

How does that wealth come? Does it come by a feverish, rodent-like race for food? Or by resting in Jesus?

Deuteronomy 8 says a great deal about how Israel got the wealth of the Promised Land. Verse 3 reminds us of the manna miracle, emphasizing the lesson to be learned: "...man does not live by bread alone, but man lives by everything that proceeds out of the mouth of [Jesus]." Jesus repeated this lesson: obedience is the most important thing. We must keep the commandments (8: 6). We can't do that alone.

Did they enter the land by their own efforts (8:7)? No. God brought them in. Even the manna test was to show Israel they had to depend on Jesus – the Manna Himself that came down from heaven.

What about prosperity? Where does the "power to make wealth" come from? Jesus gives that power (8:18) so "that He may confirm His covenant…."

Remember, the Sabbath was the very first covenant made with mankind. It was also the first covenant of which God reminded Israel when they came out of Egypt. He gave them the manna lesson as a covenant lesson.

Have we learned the manna lesson? Are we manna-fed or flesh-fed? Do we race like rats after food, doing everything in our strength? Or do we know who our Provider, our Provision – our manna from heaven -- is?

He is Jesus. He is Yehovah-Yireh – the Eternal One who sees ahead and knows exactly what we need and will need. Jesus knew Abraham would need a ram in a nearby bush to replace Isaac (Gen. 22:13-14).

Jesus used His name Yehovah or Yahweh here – the name that embodies His relationship with His covenant people. But He can't fully confirm His covenant by giving us the power to get wealth if we aren't keeping the very first covenant – the Sabbath covenant.

Set Apart to Prosper

God calls the Sabbath a sign. He says that it's a "sign between Me and you throughout your generations, that you may know that I am the [Eternal] who sanctifies you" (Ex. 31:13).

Signs identify. The Sabbath was intended by God to be a sign to show who were the believers. It set the believers of the Old Covenant apart to show they were God's special people. It set them and it sets us apart from the fleshly strugglers in Pharaoh's sweat pits. It sets us apart to prosper.

We identify ourselves with our Father -- Love. Consequently, we receive all the blessings from Love -- "every perfect gift…from above, coming down from the Father of lights…"(James 1:17).

Even though modern believers have for the most part not accepted the sign of Love embodied in the Sabbath, it is an important mark of identification to God.

But notice the emphasis here. "Between Me and you" implies a mark of intimacy. It is an intimate sign between Jesus and His bride to show that the bride takes dates with the Bridegroom seriously. Grooms don't like being "stood up." No-shows don't make good mates.

Jesus realizes that Satan's deceptions have caused His belle to be pretty ugly

– and poor -- for many centuries. Time is short, and He's not going to put up with it anymore. He wants a bride who sets herself apart from the Sunday suitors. She can't be holy and set apart if she isn't willing to submit to her Beau.

Whom Do You Choose as Your Provider – Jesus or Baal?

Jesus will not take that kind of bride in marriage to provide for and nourish. The handsome, billionaire "Bachelor" would not choose her as the blessed bachelorette if she were to compete as some have done on American TV. Why would He lavish her with extravagant gifts, even before marrying her, if she shows up for dates on the wrong day?

Jesus let His Old Covenant bride go and sent her away into captivity because of Sabbath breaking (Ezek. 20:12-26). He left her "desolate" (20: 26) – without provision.

Like the bride of the last 2000 years, she had once kept the Sabbath. Both brides quickly abandoned the Sabbath and holy days for the pagan days of Baal. In so doing they lost the blessings – including financial blessings.

On today's TV we see the pitiful, shameful sight of preachers begging for money, browbeating guilt-ridden contributors to cough up the cash. Why? One of the main reasons may surprise you.

They have forsaken Jesus' appointed times, showing up instead on Baal's day. They've dated Baal! Jesus gives a baleful warning to His "Baal-full" bride. You can read it in Hosea 2:8-13.

We have also in the past done Baal's bidding, sincerely keeping days that God never ordained -- days that find their origin in the gods of Canaan, as we will explain more fully in the sequel. No condemnation. Our prayer is that you feel convicted -- not condemned -- by the strong words in this book, and in *the* Book.

Jesus' words against believers keeping days He did not ordain are strong (Hos. 2:6-13), but because He is Love He follows His stern words by gentle ones: "Therefore, behold, I will allure her, Bring her into the wilderness And speak kindly to her" (Hos. 2:14). We are speaking strong words in Jesus' authority and according to our commission (Isa. 58:1), but we also speak kindly for we have been where you are, and we don't condemn you personally. We want you to experience the joy of the Sabbath that God has graciously revealed to us. Please take Jesus' words in Hosea to heart.

Don't allow the "that's Old Testament" heresy to deceive you. It's full of … *Baal*. Baal was associated with an earlier object of worship named Nimrod, was called "lord of heaven" and was often symbolized by the *bull*. The popular theology that rejects God's days for Baal's or "the Lord's" are full of both "b" words.

A Bunch of Baal

Maybe – just maybe – if the bride began to read the *whole* Bible, she would get rid of her bull and her Baal. God be merciful to her and help her. It's time.

Playing footsy with Baal won't put you under the winsome wing of a billionaire Boaz -- a Provider bigger and richer than Ruth's husband.

Jesus said He "lavished on her [His bride, Israel] silver and gold, Which they used for Baal. Therefore, I will take back My grain at harvest time And My new wine in its season…I will also put an end to all *her* gaiety, *Her* feasts, *her* new moons, *her* sabbaths And all *her* festal assemblies" (Hos. 2:8b-9a, 11).

Heretical hermeneutics notwithstanding, these were not God's Sabbaths! They were Baal's days. You will discover in the sequel the surprising connection between the popular holidays we celebrate today and the days of the Canaanite god called "lord of heaven."

This deception foisted upon sincere believers is a major reason the bride is made up today of "poor, humble folk." "Humble" is good; "poor" is not. Jesus wants to lavish silver and gold on His bride, but He can't if she's unknowingly bowing to Baal!

No More Loss When We Obey the Boss

But don't despair or be offended. ***God meets us where we are***. He leads us patiently and gently to where He wants us to be, never forcing our will. He wants us all blessed and rich (III John 2).

When the bride – or a large part of the church – began to abandon the Sabbath in the second century and sealed their fate in the Quartodeciman (Passover-Easter) controversy, she began to bow in a poverty posture to Baal. Poverty is rooted in penance, the idea we must pay for our sins and be punished for them.

Oh, Satan does provide, but then he punishes. He simply proceeds to steal what he gave you. Look at the lucky lottery winners who quickly become losers. Lady luck will kiss you while she's picking your pockets. Satan is a sore loser who loves company.

Jesus is a Winner who wants us to be winners. He is not a tyrant. He is our Divine Master, and Master of the Sabbath, the day in which He reveals Himself. He is also our Provider who wants to bless us. So let's look at the "bottom line":

today's bride is riddled with lack and loss because she's not obeying the Boss!

Visit the Bible history "check-out counter." Check out the apostasies and revivals of Israel. Most all of them involved Sabbath breaking followed by repentance. They involved being scattered and poor because of taking God's days lightly. When they paid Satan's bill at his till, they found themselves broke and broken. But when they refused to shop on the Sabbath (Neh. 13:15-22) and rested in Jesus, He paid all their bills and then some!

As Nehemiah sums up Israel's history of disobedience to God's laws, he zeroes in, as Jesus always does, on the Sabbath and the resultant, supernatural provision (Neh. 9:13-15).

Solomon's Sabbath keeping reign brought the greatest prosperity the world had ever seen. It pictured the seventh millennial day of abundance. It was *Shabbat shalom* par excellence.

The Sabbath – Redemption from Mediocrity to Excellence

The Sabbath is indeed a day of excellence. It is a celebration of the excellence of God -- the heartwarming story of the "rags-to-riches" redemption of His people. He takes the weak things of the world and turns them into prosperous kings and priests. "He raises the poor from the dust And lifts the needy from the ash heap, To make them sit with princes…"(Ps. 113:7-8b).

Sounds a lot like the Sabbath covenant promise of Isaiah 58:14: "Then [when you keep the Sabbath] you will take delight in [Jesus], And I will make you ride on the heights of the earth; and I will feed you with the heritage of Jacob your father, for the mouth of the [Eternal] has spoken."

What a mouthful! When God speaks, that's it. It's settled. It's sealed in Jesus' blood. God would have to do the impossible to break that promise. The Eternal One would have to lie – and die!

What a precursor of Matthew 6:33! Being the test commandment and the covenant sign and centerpiece, loving God by keeping His day holy leads us to put His Kingdom and His righteousness first in all things.

Time is precious. When God sees we put Him ahead of our time (it's actually His time), He knows He has our hearts. Then He can pour out the blessings and adds "all these things" that add more joy and peace to our lives.

Who Will Receive the Wealth of the Wicked in the Last Days?

Time is becoming more and more precious as humanity races towards the end of this age. We have seen that the wealth of the wicked will accumulate until it is released into the hands of the righteous. If you are not set apart to prosper, the wealth coming to you will be limited.

James 5:3 describes this wicked and greedy generation that worships money. "It is in the last days that you have stored up your treasure!" They have robbed and stolen and God is going to judge them. The cry of the used and abused "has reached the ears of the [Eternal] of Sabaoth [hosts, which includes the angels]"(5:4).

God is about to release the angels to fulfill His Sabbath covenant. He will dispatch them to make sure that the wealth of the wicked reaches those who have a right to it, the persecuted righteous who have waited patiently for justice. Those who have planted good seed, including financial seed, and have claimed the Sabbath covenant in communion, will be rewarded (5:7).

But once the Sabbath has been fully revealed to the believers, if they reject it they do not classify as the righteous. It will take more than patience (5:8). Receiving the vast sums to come will require obedience.

Paul's prosperity passage shows who will receive the wealth (II Cor. 9:6-15). The obedient givers "will be enriched in everything for all liberality" (9:11) with "an abundance for every good deed" (9:8). To prove it, he cites a verse from – perish the thought! – the "Old Testament."

Paul knew his prosperity verses. This one comes from Psalm 112, major proof that believers are supposed to prosper. In this psalm the righteous man gives freely to the poor. So he can't be poor, then, can he? "His righteousness endures forever; His horn [prosperity, power, authority] will be exalted in honor" (112:9). That's exactly what God promises Sabbath keepers.

Who is blessed? It's the man who "greatly delights in His *commandments*" (Ps. 112:1). Notice the plural. That means all. "Wealth and riches are in his house…" (112: 3).

Do you know who gets all upset when they see the prosperity of those who keep all of God's commandments? We'll give you a hint. Would you be mad if your wealth was taken away from you and given to someone else?

"The wicked will see it and be vexed, He will gnash his teeth and melt away; The desire of the wicked will perish" (112:10). The sinners of Egypt lost all their wealth to a bunch of slaves. The Sabbath was a celebration of that prosperity.

Jesus redeemed those slaves with the blood of the lamb that prefigured His sacrifice. The Sabbath celebrated that victory too. It was the supreme triumph.

Israel came out with a high hand. But they could not continue to ride on the heights of the earth unless they kept the Sabbath.

After pocketing all those millions, God led them out from their prison walls into a land with no malls. He wanted them to build Him a sanctuary with that wealth, putting Him first. Instead they built an idol and worshipped the gods of the sinners they left behind, the same way they would turn aside later to Baal and his days.

God gave them the blessing, but they failed to be responsible. We are set apart to be blessed and prosperous, but a great responsibility comes with it.

The Birthright Blessing

Joseph's two sons received the greatest blessing of all the tribes of Israel (Gen. 48:9-22). They were the birthright boys. The name "Israel" was to live on in them, not in Judah or any other tribe. They got a double portion – a double blessing. Though not the eldest, they got the blessing of the eldest.

Israel (the former Jacob) set them apart by laying his hands on them and blessing them. He thus sanctified them, setting them apart as special. He set them apart to prosper.

He set them apart for the blessing – and with it a great responsibility. God had high expectations of excellence for them. But without the Sabbath they could not achieve or maintain that level of quality and prosperity. Sad to say, they failed. They lost sight of the Sabbath and thus their identity.

We are the birthright people of *spiritual* Israel. We alone have been given God's name as His very sons and daughters. Even now, we rule as kings and priests in heavenly places with Jesus. But we cannot rule in excellence and full prosperity until we come into the blessed bonds of the foundational Sabbath covenant. The full power to get wealth will not come in these last days to those who choose convoluted, human reasoning and tradition over the pure and simple Word of God.

We can only come into that fullness of blessing when we take the unleavened manna, the body of our Savior, and claim the Sabbath covenant promise in the two parts of Jesus' body in communion. We must be willing to walk with Jesus through the figure eight loop of love. Loving Jesus means we promise to keep all His commandments. Otherwise, the loop is not eternal. A gap – a breach -- breaks the loop. Are you "in the loop?"

The Breach

The movie *Breach* relates the true story of an American spy who betrayed his trust and caused a breach in U.S. security. Selling secrets to the enemy opens us to attack and thus can affect the prosperity of the nation.

The account of Uzzah (II Sam. 6:1-11) is a similar story and a microcosm of the history of the church. The words *Shabbat shalom* in their Hebrew pictorial meanings signify "destroying the authority that causes chaos by returning to the covenant." In Uzzah's story the opposite occurred.

If you read the account, you will see that Israel was seeking first the Kingdom by rejoicing in love and unity with all their might in songs of praise as they carried the ark toward Jerusalem. But when Uzzah touched that which was holy to God, everything abruptly changed. The place where the breaking of the law occurred was called "Perez-uzzah" or Uzza's breach, a word that derives from the concept of breaking both in Hebrew and English. It is a breaking of the law and creates a break in trust and in the wall of love's protection around us.

This breach disturbed David's peace and brought in fear, doubt, chaos, and confusion. It also delayed God's perfect will for Jerusalem by causing the holy ark to make a detour. The house of Obed-edom was blessed and prospered by the holy presence of God, but not the capital city symbolizing the church.

God had clearly commanded His people not to touch the ark but carry it by poles inserted into it (Ex. 25:13). He warned even the priests who carried it that if they touched it, they would die (Num. 4:15). Why? In the same way Jesus poured Himself into the Sabbath, He poured part of Himself into the ark. He is a consuming fire and human flesh cannot stand His glorious presence without falling dead.

The situation is a bit different when He pours Himself into a day, but the ultimate result is the same. Because Jesus is in the Sabbath, when we trample on His holy day, we are stepping on Him!

Carting Away the Holy Sabbath?

In David's time the people had forgotten the instructions God gave. They had begun to carry the ark on a cart. A little leaven permeated the whole lump until judgment came suddenly. The breach in the church's history was also gradual, but judgment comes more slowly to His people today.

Beginning in the second century A.D. some began to touch that which was holy to God, His Sabbath. Constantine made the breach complete, "carting away" the Sabbath, followed by a dark time in church history. The church ceased to prosper, birthing a false churchianity that worships poverty and sin. Unity disappeared. A church emerged that was divided in competing denominations.

Self-proclaimed watchdogs that believe we should be poor bring forth unjust Senate investigations of those ministries that prosper. All because centuries earlier we trounced on God's holy day of love. We caused a breach in the wall of love around us, abandoning the day that promised us unity and prosperity.

Some of us are called to repair that breach (Isa. 58:12-14). It's no coincidence that the Sabbath covenant promise follows the "repairer of the breach" verse. When a breach occurs in the wall, the enemy can come in and conquer. He has. But his days are numbered.

God is calling you from a weakened position evidenced by a hole in your spiritual wall of protection – the Ten Commandments. If Jesus redeemed you from being the weak ones into His strength by His blood, He can do it again. He can make the weak ones with the breached walls into strong ones whose walls are complete and strong.

If you are among the many new believers hungry for the intimacy and power the Sabbath brings, come to Jesus and find rest for your souls – and blessings in abundance.

If you are one of those who doesn't know Jesus, the Divine Master of the Sabbath stands ready to rescue this world's weak who eek out a living in Satan's pit of miry clay. As the Holy Spirit leads them to begin to tithe, and to rest on the Sabbath, God's blessings flow. They come to the point of "rolling in the dough" of financial prosperity because their dough is unleavened. They are no longer sinning by breaking one of the most important of the Ten Commandments. They are intimately attaching themselves to the God of excellence so they can show forth His excellencies.

Sweating for Satan or Resting in Jesus?

God offered this choice of excellence and prosperity to all mankind through Adam. God made the Sabbath covenant with the entire human race through that first man Adam. But the human race chose the "rat race" to riches and men have tempted God with their unholy greed for the duration of their history on earth. Rats scrounge. Restful Sabbath keepers feast.

The four benefits Adam had in the Sabbath are available to those who keep it today. The Sabbath gave Adam *identity* in his *fellowship* with Jesus on that day. His *purpose* of ruling over the earth was also bound up in the Sabbath. If he trampled the Sabbath as unholy, he could not "ride on the heights of the earth" (Isa. 58:13-14). Just as Israel had to pass the Sabbath manna test, so Adam's *provision* for His Kingdom purpose was based on the fact that he rested in Jesus on the Sabbath day.

Forty is a number signifying man and the trials he experiences. Israel tested Jesus' patience ten times in those forty years in the wilderness. Only for the sake of

His name did He continue to provide manna when they rebelled against the Sabbath (Neh. 9:21; Ezek. 20:9-26).

Those forty years represented man's six millennial day's journey under Satan's sway and provision. Sweat pours from man's brow as he labors for Satan.

But what most ignore is that Jesus made a Sabbath covenant of provision for *all* mankind, represented by Adam. One branch of Jewish tradition says that Adam thrived in Sabbath provision in that lush garden for forty years.

Instead of man's forty years of Sabbath provision with perfect obedience in the garden, man tested God for forty years in the desert. According to this likely scenario, Adam would have abandoned God and His Sabbath after forty years and lost out on the "Promised Land" of eternal life in Edenic bliss. And as Israel did for the symbolic forty years, man has tempted God during the time of man's testing period on earth.

Mankind has writhed in the pit of poverty during his earthly journey. Why? It's because Adam ceased keeping the Sabbath. As with Israel, since he had the same covenant with Jesus, Adam lost that sign and seal of intimacy.

The Sabbath is God's ***point of access*** to man. Through the intimacy of that day, Jesus channels all of His blessings, including the financial ones.

Mankind swapped masters. Instead of resting in Jesus on His day of prosperity, man began to sweat for Satan. Sweat stinks. So does poverty.

Israel also exchanged masters, Satan being personified in Pharaoh. Jesus gave Israel the Sabbath to show His people they were now free from their cruel taskmaster.

Satan is the thief and the abuser. God's people today have been enslaved to Satan's days and His thievery. It's time the church broke free from the vicious, sweaty-brow "*sin*-drome." It's time to begin celebrating the day of freedom. It's time to rest in Jesus.

Every Sabbath day we are doing more than praying the prayer "thy kingdom come." We are *living* that prayer! We are foreshadowing the time of Jesus' rule on earth when financial prosperity will be the order of the day – the millennial seventh day. As we celebrate our Sabbath covenant with God, we are opening the windows of heaven to receive the fullness of prosperity here and now on earth. Celebrate the Sabbath! Celebrate your prosperity – now and forever!

The Million-Dollar Question

In 2001, Adventist Pastor A. Jan Marcussen began by publicly offering $50,000 of his own money to anyone could produce a Bible verse proving that God commands us to keep Sunday holy rather than the seventh day. In this Sunday versus Saturday contest, Marcussen increased his reward by $25,000 per week for forty consecutive weeks until the figure reached one million dollars.

An article on the web site WorldNetDaily.com by Joe Kovacs, posted on October 13, 2001, quoted James Efird, professor of biblical interpretation at Duke University Divinity School: "I am afraid that you are not going to find an exact Bible verse to counter the good pastor's challenge and collect. As far as I know, there is no verse which specifies that Sunday is the day for Christians to observe the Sabbath."

The article quotes Marcussen: "There's a fear factor among preachers on why churches don't have their members look into this issue. They're afraid their sheep will start reading the Bible, and they know they'll lose their sheep."

Canadian Bible scholar Grant R. Geffrey has written that the most frequent Bible question involves the reason the day of worship was changed from Saturday to Sunday. Why is this the most asked question? Simply because Christians who do read the Bible see the Sabbath throughout and never see Sunday as the day of worship. They end up believing the theologians and the pastors, but they are disturbed because of what they read daily in the Word of God.

As evangelist Jesse Duplantis says, "It's so simple you need a theologian to help you misunderstand it." While Duplantis was not referring to the Sabbath truth, his saying applies most appropriately to the simple words of God: "Six days you shall labor and do all your work, but the seventh day is a sabbath of the [Eternal] your God...the [Eternal] blessed the sabbath day and made it holy" (Ex. 20:8-11).

The church has betrayed its followers just as parents have betrayed their children by telling them the Santa Claus lie. One boy, after having realized his parents had lied to him, said: "I think I better look into this Jesus Christ business!"

Face the truth: we've been lied to. Satan has lied to us and stolen one of God's greatest blessings. Keeping the Sabbath can even open the door to prosperity. It is no coincidence that a man who keeps the Sabbath had a million dollars to give. The Sabbath blessing, however, cannot be measured in dollars.

Sabbath *Selah's*
If God Was Incensed about Holy Incense...

...how much more would He be concerned about His people not recognizing His holy day that He placed as a moral law within the Ten Commandments?

Aaron's sons, Nadab and Abihu, each took his fire pan, put fire in it, and put special perfume on it. They gave a fire that was not holy to the [Eternal] because the [Eternal] had not told them to do this. So the [Eternal] sent out fire that burned them up and they died before the [Eternal]. Then Moses said to Aaron, "This is what the [Eternal] meant when He said, 'I will show Myself holy among those who are near Me. I will be honored in front of all the people'... You are to know the difference between what is holy and what is not, and between what is clean and what is not (Lev. 10:1-3, NLV).

God had given specific instructions as to the ingredients He wanted in this holy incense (Ex. 30:37). This incense foreshadowed our prayers today, which are to be holy, presented to God according to His instructions in His Word. The Sabbath, on the other hand is a moral law and a perpetual covenant (Heb. 4:9; Ex. 31:13). While Jesus will not show His anger in the same way today as He did to those who did not agree with His definition of holiness, He is indeed grieved that many believers today have tried to sanctify a day He never made holy. As the tithe belongs to Jesus and is holy to Him, in the same way the Sabbath belongs to Him and is holy (Lev. 27:30). We are to keep our hands off His tithe and our feet off His holy time. How can our feet be shod "WITH THE PREPARATION OF THE GOSPEL OF PEACE [the gospel of the Kingdom]" (Eph. 6:15) *if we are stealing the tithe that finances the gospel thrust and trampling on the holy time that prophesies the coming of the Kingdom of peace? Selah.*

Are you dancing to deception's tune? Many Christians are dancing a dangerous dance, twisting the truth into a lie. Satan's doctrines of demons have covered their eyes so that they have not yet been able to see the simple Sabbath truth. Take off the shade and begin to dance with Jesus in His day of joyous celebration!

CHAPTER TWENTY

Dancing the Twist

Unscrupulous people have always twisted the Scriptures (II Pet. 3:16). Nowhere is this more prevalent than on the subject of the Sabbath. Paul warned that wolves looking like sheep would enter the church and deceive many. They have.

People love deception so much that their itching ears love to hear how these wolves twist the truth. These deceived Christians welcome these wolves and dance to their tune, not to the lyrics of Jesus. Cuddling close to these wolves, they dance around the truth.

Whose fault is it? It is the teachers' twist. God places the main blame squarely at the feet of leadership (Hos. 4:6), who "have forgotten the law of your God...." They have rubbed God's holy day into the ground (Isa. 58:13). Instead of dancing with Jesus on the day He inhabits, they have stomped on His head. We are supposed to be dancing on the devil's head, not on the head of our Savior. How true the words of Isaiah: "...truth stumbles in the public square..." (59:14, NRSV).

This treacherous twisting of truth waters truth down into a comfortable lie.

You may have seen or heard clips in the media where leaders are quoted but only partially. They take only parts of what the leader said and it makes for hilarious comedy. The way religious leaders twist the Bible is not so funny.

Buffeting the Bible Buffet

They take only what they want in the Bible buffet. They are adept at taking two of their favorite vague verses to twist the truth of the entire Bible. The Bible truths in this book defy these twisters.

God decries this scenario: "O My people! Those who guide you lead you astray And confuse the direction of your paths" (Isa. 3:12).

Listen to what the world's wisest man (before Jesus) said regarding God's Word: "All the words of my mouth are righteous; there is *nothing twisted* or crooked in them. They are all straight [straightforward, NASB] to one who understands and right to those who find knowledge" (Prov. 8:8-9, NRSV).

Nothing twisted. Nothing crooked. When it comes to the Sabbath, God's Word is about as straightforward as you can get. But Satan has taught theologians the terrible twist, and the Christian world has joined in a dangerous dance with the devil.

Nowhere is the twist more evident and blatant than in the demonic dance religious people do around a couple of verses from Paul. One of their favorite dances is the Colossian Twist, which we shall see shortly. Let's look first at the Sunday shuffle, a popular dance around the truth in Acts.

The Sunday Shuffle

In light of the overwhelming proof we have seen that the Sabbath is a command of God and unchangeable, it seems superfluous to even consider the feeble attempts by Sunday espousers to find some justification for keeping the first day of the week. They grasp at slender, slippery straws in the Gospels and Acts to find some excuse to keep Sunday.

In John 20:19 the disciples were assembled "for fear of the Jews" when Jesus appeared to them after His resurrection. Sorry. No Sunday service here.

Acts 20:7 is the only text that clearly shows a meeting on the first day of the week, but the preceding verse clearly indicates that Paul and his team did not leave Philippi until after the Days of Unleavened Bread. He had to be an observer of the Sabbath and feast days, or he was a liar. He claimed that he had never broken any law of the "Old Testament" (Acts 25:8; 24:14; 26:22; 28:17).

His reference to the feast days also shows that Luke used the biblical reckoning of days, the day beginning at sunset. No Sunday meeting here. It was a Saturday night gathering – and an extraordinary one at that. It was Paul's farewell. He had a long journey the next day, a trip that would have been inappropriate for the rest day of the Sabbath. Rather than prove we should rest on Sunday, this example shows that Paul considered Sunday as a regular workday on which tiring travel would be appropriate.

Moreover, "gathered together to break bread" does not necessarily mean they had communion. Even if they did, what does that prove? The indication from the Word and historical tradition is that the early disciples often had communion several times a day because of the curses that came against them (Acts 2:42; John 6:53).

Paul walked for about twenty miles to "celebrate" Sunday and several days later "was hurrying to be in Jerusalem, if possible, on the day of Pentecost" (Acts 20:16). He traveled long distances on Sunday and hurried to be at the right place at the right time to observe God's "appointed times" (Lev. 23:2). Rather than a Sunday support text, Acts 20:7 is an affirmation of God's holy days.

The "Sixteen Shuffle" and All Sabbath Sidesteps Stop Here

The "Sixteen Shuffle" (I Cor. 16:2) is the next dance in praise of the devil's day. Once again, the bomb they try to use to destroy the Sabbath explodes in their face. No mention is made of corporate worship. It was a private, individual act. The phrase "lay by him" (KJV) is the Greek *par heauto titheto*, meaning to put aside at home. Any proof of Sunday worship here is contrived.

We have seen that the apostle John mentored Polycarp, who kept the Sabbath. Yet people try to say that John kept "the Lord's day," meaning Sunday. The Holy Spirit transported John in a vision into the "day of the Eternal," the end-time day of God's wrath (Rev. 1:10). "The Eternal's day" is a reference to this future time. It's that simple. John was not keeping Sunday.

The Sunday shuffle is a dangerous, potentially deadly dance. The twist must stop.

Sabbath *Selah's*
Some Like it Hot

Remember the sabbath day, to *keep* it holy (Ex. 20:8).

Can you keep ice hot? How can you keep Sunday holy? God never made it holy, and only God can make something holy. Constantine couldn't. The Pope can't. Religious people have tried to make holy what God did not make holy. Like Cain, they are telling God what kind of offering and worship He should require -- telling Him how to "run His show." A child who thinks he knows better than his parents is disciplined by godly parents. Father Love's correction is coming. It's time for the church to quit pretending the Sabbath is not in the Bible, time for pastors to stop hiding their eyes from the truth they know in their hearts.

Her priests have done violence to My law and have profaned My holy things; they have made no distinction between the holy [Sabbath] and the profane [Sunday], and they have not taught the difference between the unclean and the clean; and *they hide their eyes from My Sabbaths*, and *I* am profaned among them (Ezek. 22:26).

Treating anything God makes holy as unholy is the same as considering Him *unholy. He demands respect of His holiness, and He has been known to assert Himself. Remember Sodom? Remember the Red Sea?*

'By those who come near Me I will be treated as holy, And before all the people I will be honored' (Lev. 10:3).

In these last days some will like it hot. God has warmed the Sabbath with the heat of His anointed presence. Will we keep it hot? If not, will we eventually feel the heat by experiencing the fire of God's judgment (Jer. 17:27)? God is a consuming fire. Which part of the fire do we want? On fire for Jesus? Or will the fire that tests "the quality of each man's work" *(I Cor. 3:13) cause our work to be* "burned up" (3:15), *suffering loss.* How *do we like it hot? Selah.*

CHAPTER TWENTY ONE

The Colossal Colossian Twist

The Colossian twist is a blatant attempt to give a private interpretation of Colossians 2:14-17. Assumptions abound.

One is that the heretics were Judaizers who preached the religion of the "Old Testament." We should know from the accounts of Jesus and Pharisaical legalism that Judaism is not the religion of the Old Covenant. Additions by tradition: that's Judaism.

Another false idea is that the heretical philosophy of Colossians was Greek or Phrygian since Colossae was Phrygian city. Neither of these philosophies, however, contained any knowledge of angels (Col. 2:18). Judaism did. Interestingly, angel worship developed in the second century schools of Gnosticism run by Cerinthus and Valentinus.

The phrase, "not holding fast to the head [Jesus]," (2:19) indicates the heretics had known Jesus but were departing from the truth, yet still influencing other members in Colossae. They were clearly ascetics who wanted to heighten their spirituality. Jesus was no longer sufficient. They taught you had to go through angels to attain to a higher spiritual level in the pure Gnostic tradition. While the church was predominantly Gentile (1:21; 2:13), these heretics were Jewish legalists with a large dose of Gnostic asceticism (2:21: "...do not taste, do not touch!") Referring to this heresy as "the philosophy" (correct translation of 2:8) fits with both Philo's and Josephus' allusion to Judaism as a philosophy. Paul was denouncing this specific philosophy, not philosophy in general.

These men felt you could not be complete in Jesus (2:10). Angelic intermediaries were necessary. They did not believe that the "fullness of Deity" dwelt bodily in Jesus. For these heretics, Jesus didn't "cut it." They had to cut their flesh by being circumcised and felt Gentile Christians needed to do the same. They had to abase themselves, neglecting their bodies in a self-righteous pursuit of spirituality. Believers who went directly through the Mediator Jesus needed humbling in their view, depriving themselves and going through the much lower angels to gradually ascend to the Supreme God.

Paul was showing the Colossians that self-righteous asceticism and esoteric, mysterious Gnosticism was empty. All "the fullness" (1:19) dwells in Jesus. Anything apart from Him is empty, even keeping God's laws and His holy days.

No Meat, No Wine, No Fun and No Potty – Essenetially Legalistic

We may not have known about such a strange mixture of Judaism and Gnosticism had it not been for an Arab peasant who found the Gnostic books called the Nag Hammadi in 1945 and the Bedouins who found the Dead Sea Scrolls in 1947. We now know that the extreme Jewish sect called the Essenes espoused Gnostic ideas.

Gnosticism did not diminish their Jewishness. They made the Pharisees look like liberals. Josephus tells us that on the Sabbath they did not "venture to remove any utensil or go and ease themselves."[1] Even the Pharisees went to the bathroom on the Sabbath!

The Essenes would not eat – or even touch – meat, wine or oil. The proper translation of 2:16 should be "Don't allow any man to take you to task in regard to eating and drinking…" In Greek the words represent actions, not entities, so the biblical teaching on clean and unclean meats was not in question. The basis of the heresy was "the commandments and teachings of *men*" (Col. 2:22).

Remember, Pharisaical Sabbath keeping was not biblical. It was based in ridiculous, exaggerated Sabbath laws invented by rabbis. Such was the case with the Essenes, except that the regulations were more extreme and picayunish.

While circumcision heightened their ascetic feeling of superiority, it was not the main issue, especially with the predominant Gentile population of the Colossian church.

We cannot deny that these heretics took the Colossian Christians to task about the Sabbath[2] and the holy days, which were calculated based on the new moons, a key to freedom we will explore in the sequel. The new moon, while not a holy day (Ezra 3:5), was a time where the Hebrews and early Christians laid down

1 *The Jewish War*, translation of G.A. Williamson, Penguin, Baltimore, 1959, page 373.

2 The word *sabbaton* is singular, referring to the weekly Sabbath. The Septuagint, the famous Greek translation of the Hebrew Scriptures, never uses *sabbaton* for the annual holy days but rather *sabbata sabbaton* (Sabbath of Sabbaths).

their long-term burdens and problems to God.

To assume, however, that Paul was summarily doing away with one of the Ten Commandments is unthinkable – that is, unless you have decided you're looking for a loophole to avoid obedience. Many are.

Paul was frequently misunderstood and accused of saying what he didn't say. Peter confirms this (II Peter 3:16). While the comparison is not exact, Paul had a similar accusation against him in Acts 21:21. The many new Jewish converts had heard that Paul was teaching "all the Jews among the Gentiles to forsake Moses, telling them not to circumcise their children nor to walk according to the customs."

Don't Twist Paul, and Don't Twist Jesus!

That was a lie. Customs based in the Hebrew Scriptures, including circumcision, were not forbidden for the Jews who came to Jesus. Gentiles did not need to be circumcised to be saved and be in right standing with God. But Jesus did say, in essence, "If you love Me, obey Me." And in case you've been deceived into believing in a "lovey-dovey" Jesus who did away with the Big Ten and said like the hippies, "Just love, man, just love," listen to Paul. That's right, Paul. The misunderstood guy who was supposed to have done away with the law.

"Hear, O Israel (of God, New Covenant believers)" what Paul said: "Circumcision is nothing, and uncircumcision is nothing, but what matters is the ***keeping of the commandments of God***"(I Cor. 7:19).

Notice that Paul did not say what mattered was the keeping of the commandments of Jesus in the New Testament. He said what mattered was the keeping of the commandments of **God**. That means all ten (James 2:10). That means the Sabbath. That means, as the sequel will show, the other annual holy days that were statutes of the fourth commandment. Holy is holy. We must keep holy that which God has declared holy, no matter when He declared it holy.

When you take Colossians 2:16 out of the context of the Colossian heresy, you can make it say what you want. Many do. And most Christians listen to their tune and hum along in a sad sing-along.

But think a minute. If you believe Paul contradicted his statement in Corinthians and that he was condoning breaking one of the Ten Commandments, you are not only saying Paul is a liar. You are saying that the Bible was written by an old, forgetful Father. But Jesus said the Scripture could not be broken (John 10:35). David, who loved God's Word, His law, His Torah or instruction, said: "The law of the [Eternal] is perfect" (Ps. 19:7) and His testimony "sure," not contradictory. It's *all* true.

Saying Paul did away with the fourth commandment here is like saying he did away with the commandment against adultery or murder – or lying, which is what we are doing when we twist this verse.

It seems the bigger the lie, the easier it is for the masses to believe. Pastors who should and often do know better feed this colossal, Colossian concoction to multitudes of naïve believers. If you were a sheep, would you swallow pig dung if your shepherd fed it to you? People come to pastors with questions about the Sabbath, and they simply spit out a few twisted verses they do not explain. It's time we sheep spit out the devilish dung and graze in green Sabbath pastures. Lies go unchecked.

History Sometimes Lies, But the Bible Never Does

The whole Bible is clear about the Sabbath question. It's not a question. It's the truth.

History agrees. Though some church fathers defended Sunday, we have seen how John's disciple kept God's days. Jerome, in *Illustrious Men*, writes: "Polycarp, disciple of the apostle John and by him ordained bishop of Smyrna was chief of *all Asia*..." The Sabbath was not kept in a corner.

Even as late as the fifth century, church historian Socrates Scholasticus Sozomen wrote: "For although almost all churches throughout the world celebrate the sacred mysteries [communion] on the Sabbath [Saturday] of every week, yet the Christians of Alexandria and at Rome, on account of some ancient tradition, have ceased to do this...The people of Constantinople, and almost everywhere, assemble together on the Sabbath, as well as on the first day of the week, which custom is never observed at Rome or at Alexandria."

We know that Sunday keeping did not begin in Asia Minor and Judea in the first and second centuries as it did in Rome and Alexandria. These areas were staunch in their refusal to let go of the Passover and the days God made holy.

The idea that the Colossian church kept any days other than the days God had ordained in Leviticus 23 has no basis in the Bible or in church history. In these areas of Asia Minor, Sunday gradually and much later crept in, but not initially as a substitute for the Sabbath.

The Colossian heretics sought to transcend Jesus. What Paul said to counteract this heresy in 2:16 could be taken in at least two ways. First and foremost, Paul was saying that no amount of law keeping or Sabbath keeping could replace Jesus. Without Him, law means nothing. The law can't save us. Only Jesus can, by His blood. Furthermore, the holy days and the Sabbath are only shadows that point to Jesus. Without Jesus in the Sabbath, it means nothing. This strong statement to counteract heresy does not mean that we can now forget the day Jesus Himself commanded us to remember.

We might as well throw the Bible away if we believe it undoes in one verse what it affirms and commands in many other passages. God is not a liar (Num.

23:19). "My covenant [the Sabbath is the first covenant of God with man] I will not violate, Nor will I alter the utterance of My lips" (Ps. 89:34). If God changes what He said in Exodus 20:8 and Mark 2:27-28 in Colossians 2:16, then He has altered the utterance of His lips. He has lied. You can't trust him for anything. Little wonder many Christians have little faith.

But our God does not lie. Jesus lived a perfect life as a man, never lying once. He died for us. He died to blot out all the sins men have done and all the lies men have said. That includes the lie that the Ten Commandments were nailed to the cross, a terrible twisting of Colossians 2:14.

Most people have sung the lyrics, "Forgive us our debts, as we forgive our debtors." It speaks a biblical truth. Sin is debt and debt is sin. The Greek word *cheirographan* is properly translated in the NASB as "the certificate of debt," the written record of our sins, our I.O.U. of sin that was cancelled at the cross. Jesus' blood didn't do away with the law of love. His death did away with sin – the breaking of the law (I John 3:4). Since Jesus commands us to grow into perfection like our Father (Mat. 5:48), why would He do away with the standard of perfection?

Many have complicated this verse, yet it is quite simple. What was the "certificate of debt [or sin] consisting of decrees [*tois dogmasin*] against us"? This is not referring to God's law at all. It is referring rather to God's decrees against sin, establishing the penalty of sin. God decreed, "For the wages of sin is death..." (Rom. 6:23). Paul wrote that verse, and he knew well Ezekiel 18:20: "The person who sins will die." Those decrees, although given by God, were conditional upon repentance. But even with a changed life, without Jesus the slightest sin committed at any time in our lives would require that we die. Thank God, Jesus paid the penalty! He cancelled the debt of sin and the decrees saying we must die because of sin.

Paul is saying, "You Colossians don't need to feel condemned by these ascetics who depend on the spirit of legalism to keep the Sabbath rather than accepting Jesus and letting Him guide them into the proper rejoicing on His day. Jesus has cancelled out all your sins and guilt."

Strong Meat and Drink Hard for Heretics to Swallow

It is hard to escape another possible application of Colossians 2:16, the aspect of festive celebration. Anyone who has kept the Feast of Tabernacles, as I have been blessed to do since 1969, knows that it is decidedly not ascetic. Essenes who could not so much as touch wine or meat would have recoiled at God's instructions for this feast: "You may spend the money for whatever your heart desires; for oxen, or sheep, or wine, or *strong drink*, or whatever your heart desires; and there you shall eat in the presence of the [Eternal] your God and rejoice, you and your household [Essenes even abstained from marriage]" (Deut. 14:26).

It's easy to see how Colossian believers could have been taken to task about celebrating God's feasts and Sabbath days. These days were fun! Too much fun for sorry sourpusses who were busy restraining their holy bowels on the Sabbath day.

Marcel Simon, in *Les sectes juives au temps de Jesus* (Paris, 1960, p. 62), adds an interesting detail. While the Essenes basically kept the same feasts as the Jews, Simon writes: "…others have been added which seem to be unique to the sect."

This only reaffirms the fact that Paul was not dealing with a controversy about whether to keep the Sabbath and holy days of God. He was dealing with a strict Jewish sect of holier-than-everyone church members who looked down their righteous noses at others who didn't keep as many days as they did, and didn't keep them the holy way.

I didn't always keep the holy days or the Sabbath to the liking of other members. Some took me to task about the way I kept the Sabbath, but not at all like those Colossian heretics. We do need to avoid offending others, if at all possible, without compromising our obedience to God. And that brings us to another devilish dance, the tricky two-step of Romans 14 -- a dance of desperation.

Sabbath *Selah's*
"A-Paul-ing"!

But this I confess unto thee, that after the way which they call heresy, so worship I the God of my fathers, believing all things which are written in the law and in the prophets…(Acts 24:14, KJV).

This is what Paul said to defend himself: "I have done nothing wrong against the law, against the Temple, or against Caesar" (Acts 25:8, New Century Version).

If Paul were still in the grave, hearing the lies using his name would make him turn over. It is truly appalling to see how people twist his epistles. He said to follow him as he followed Jesus (I Cor. 11:1). Religionists ignore the context and declare him a Sabbath breaker. They confuse his opposition to justification *by law with* keeping *God's law of love. Paul said he believed everything written in the Law, which obviously included the Sabbath. The book of Acts confirms this. If he did not keep the Sabbath, he would be a liar. People labeled his beliefs as heresy and accused him of being part of a cult. Sabbath keeping groups today are often labeled the same way. Who are the heretics? Selah.*

CHAPTER TWENTY TWO

The Romans 14 Contortion -- or "the Sabbath Side Step"

The terrible twists get worse. This is a desperate dance. It's also called, "Looking for a way out of keeping the Sabbath," a.k.a. the Sabbath Side Step.

Paul talks about days, but he never mentions the Sabbath in Romans 14. Yet many Christians believe that Romans 14:5-6 is proof Paul did not tell Gentiles to keep the Sabbath and that the days we keep are not an area in which we should be judged. The context is about eating meats or being vegetarian. The *Didache* supports the inference that specific days for fasting were involved. This early Christian guide to holiness says, "But not let our fasts be with the hypocrites, for they fast on the second and fifth day of the week. Rather, fast on the fourth day and the Preparation (Friday)" (Chapter 8).

Eating habits and the way and times that we fast are intensely personal matters. Paul did not and the church should not legislate in these areas. On the other hand, which day we keep is not a private matter, although in some circumstances it may be. It is a public decision practiced corporately and this was the case with the organized church at Rome. Church leaders make such a decision, preferably according to the Word.

Paul writes: "Now I exhort you, brethren...that you all agree and that there be no divisions among you, but that you be made complete in the same mind and in the same judgment" (I Cor.1:10). In this same letter Paul said, "Clean out the old leaven so that you may be a new lump [spiritually], just as you are in fact unleavened [already, because you have put away leavened bread in preparation for the feast]. For Christ our Passover has been sacrificed. Therefore let us celebrate the feast, not with old leaven…but with the unleavened bread of sincerity and truth"(I Cor. 5:7-8).

The same apostle that spoke of "the unity of the Spirit in the bond of peace" and encouraged the understanding that we are one body, one Spirit, with "one faith [set of beliefs]" (Eph. 4:3-5) commanded Corinthians to keep the Feast of Unleavened Bread. If they kept the high days or annual Sabbaths and were physically unleavened at feast time, they obviously kept the weekly Sabbath.

"Each person must be fully convinced in his own mind" (Rom. 14:5). Could this refer to whether we keep the fourth commandment or not? What about the sixth commandment? If you are not convinced in your own mind that it is wrong to murder, does that mean you can put a bullet in someone you don't like? Why do we sidestep the Sabbath but dance to the tune of all the other commandments?

None of the Ten Commandments, including the Sabbath, are directly in question in Romans 14. While it is helpful for a believer to be "convinced in his own mind" about the Sabbath truth before keeping it, obeying what you see in the Word will add greater understanding (Ps. 111:10). The Holy Spirit leads us into all truth (John 16:13) and it is His job, not ours, to convict you of the Sabbath truth. It is nevertheless the truth, agree with it or not.

Paul is giving guidelines here about matters that are private and not always spelled out in the Scripture. The Sabbath is spelled out. If the Holy Spirit doesn't tell us, would not common sense tell us what Paul was *not* saying? He was not saying that it doesn't matter which day we keep as holy to God. God never said all days were holy and that we could choose any day to keep, that all days were alike to Him as far as corporate worship is concerned. He said He made the seventh day holy – no other. He ordained holy convocations on the seventh day and on no other day.

We may wisely do our best to avoid offending others by the manner in which we keep the Sabbath day. The day we choose, however, is not up for discussion. It does matter to God. He did not suggest that we make up *our* minds which day was holy. He *commanded* us to remember the seventh day (Ex. 20:8,10). It is not called the day of the Jews but the Sabbath of the Eternal – the Sabbath of Jesus. And don't forget…He, Jesus, is the One who said, "Remember."

Everyone can be convinced in his own mind whether he eats meat or is vegetarian. Each Christian can decide to drink wine or be a teetotaler, to choose to fast on the first Monday of every month or every other Tuesday or simply fast when he feels the need. We don't judge our brothers in these personal matters. We don't condemn them for not keeping the Sabbath either. The question of whether Christians should or should not keep the fourth commandment is not a matter that is decided by any individual. God has already said it. His Word is law. He cannot alter the utterance of His lips. And He will not change the time of the Sabbath no matter how many twisted arguments religious people invent.

Answering the Skeptics

This might be a good time to share anonymously a letter I received from a gentleman I met at a pastors' luncheon. He is in ministry and has Bible school training. He had agreed to receive our church emails. When he read an email I sent on the subject of the Sabbath, he gave a reply that reflects the nonchalance of many pastors and others about keeping the Sabbath on Saturday. I chose not to answer his letter at the time, but I answer its italicized text here with his permission for all those who want to escape from religiosity and embrace Jesus.

OK brother, the Sabbath is another interesting topic and I simply can't resist commenting on your article. Please read Romans 7. We are no longer under the law bro!!! Pass me a porkchop will ya!!! Many people misunderstand Paul's teaching on the law. We are dead to the law as a means of making ourselves right before God. Paul was talking to people who knew the law (7:1) and who in typical legalistic manner trusted in the law for justification and salvation rather than in Jesus. While we now serve in the newness of the Spirit (7:6), Paul makes it clear in this chapter and elsewhere that the law is holy, righteous and good (7:12) and God expects us to obey the law. The law shows us in detail how to love God and our fellowman. Jesus is clear in saying that if we love Him, we will keep His commandments (John 14:15). Paul dealt with different audiences and spoke about the law in such a way as to be misunderstood by those who desire to fall into lawlessness (II Pet. 3:16). God has always spoken in a way to give enough rope to those who want to hang themselves in disobedience (Isa. 28:9-13). Paul was clear in saying we are not to sin because we are no longer saved by the law or under its penalty of death (Rom. 6:1-2). Sin by definition is breaking the law (I John 3:4). So Paul is saying we should not use our freedom as an excuse to break God's law (Gal. 5:13). Paul upheld the law, but not ceremonial laws fulfilled in Jesus (I Cor. 7:19). The Sabbath is as much a moral law as any of the other Ten Commandments. His day is as holy as His name (third commandment). We refrain from using His name in vain for the same reason we keep the Sabbath: we honor what He says is holy – not what we say is holy. God never made any day holy except the seventh day. Regarding the pork comment, why be so nonchalant about that which God calls unclean? Our bodies are the temples of God (I Cor. 3:16). Unclean meats pollute us from a health standpoint, Jewish stomachs not being different from those of the Gentiles. Furthermore, the sequel will reveal why God had to make all those laws that guarded His people from being polluted by the transgenic practices of the pagans around them who had worshipped the *nephilim* or giants that were on earth before the flood and to some degree afterward (Gen. 6:1-3). Our readers will have their eyes opened as to why God said what He did in His Word, and even why the Sabbath became so much more important in light of the need to be a holy people, untouched by the impurities of the surrounding nations.

Then read Romans 14, and of course temper it with Romans 12! Would you prefer red or white? Oh, wine offends you, no problem I'll abstain in deference! Would you be as nonchalant and flippant about committing adultery on your wife as you are with the fourth commandment? I don't think she would appreciate it. And I don't think your abusive boss would appreciate you killing him by gossip with your tongue and certainly not with a gun. You may think a difference exists between the Sabbath commandment and the others. God sees no difference. Stealing from God is quite serious. When we break the Sabbath, we are knowingly or unknowingly (and He has mercy for that) stealing His time – His time with us to bless us. We are also stealing from ourselves. Drinking wine or not drinking so as not to offend a brother is not in the same category as one of the Ten Commandments, although it is an act of love. Even if you consider the fourth commandment as a "least commandment," Jesus has strong words for those who teach others to annul even the least of His laws of love (Mat. 5:19).

Now it may be the reason Jesus did not restate this particular commandment in Lk. 18:20, Mk. 10:19 and also did a bunch of healing on that day is that it was no longer a MAJOR issue to Him, unlike murder, stealing, adultery, etc. If we follow your reasoning, we could bow down to idols and take God's name in vain since Jesus didn't choose to restate the first four commandments in this passage. Those four show how to love God. So we don't need to love God anymore? Yet Jesus said it was the greatest principle in the law (Mat. 22:36-38). You may be surprised to find out that 613 commandments tell us how to love God and others in the Hebrew Scriptures – and 613 commandments explain how to show love in the Greek Scriptures ("New Testament")! Laws aren't bad and legalistic – people are. Commandments are not bad. Breaking them is! By the way, stealing is one of the most important issues for God, as you point out. Breaking the Sabbath is stealing from the most important Person in the universe. Jesus did indeed do "a bunch of healing" on the Sabbath because it is the day of love, redemption, and deliverance, in which a greater healing anointing is poured out. It celebrates the day God delivered us from sin and sickness (Deut. 5:15). Jesus was showing us how to keep the Sabbath in New Covenant times.

And Paul seems to support this fact in Col. 2:16 "So let no one judge you in food or in drink, or regarding a festival or a new moon or sabbaths, which are a shadow of things to come, but the substance is of Christ." "Seems" is an appropriate word. Things are not always what they seem, as our readers will see from reading the chapter on Colossians.

What was of MAJOR issue to Jesus though, was the traditions of men Mt. 15:3 - 20 and Mk. 7: 1-23, which I think this issue may fall, whether we are stout Sunday-ists or Saturday-ists! Or like lobster! Or raising our hands! Or not! Or hymns or choruses or contemporary etc., etc., etc. It's ironic that you would put Sabbath keeping in the category of traditions of men. Talk about turning the tables! Sunday is a tradition of men. The Sabbath is not. The above comments trivialize the fourth commandment. It is you who put His holy day in your categories of minor issues. He does not place it there.

But in all our efforts, may we strive not to divide our love with walls of doctrine or tradition, but rather celebrate our minor differences like flowers in the garden, each one bringing its own glory, in a different way to Jesus from whom all were created. While of course all the time also celebrating our indisputable, non-negotiable creeds! Our creed should be the Word of God. Compromising with truth is not God's way of bringing unity. The ecumenical movement is an example of an effort to bring unity by compromise. When truth is not our goal, unity means nothing. It must be in "the knowledge of the Son of God," "...speaking the truth in love" that we attain unity (Eph. 4:13-15). Your flowery analogy has a bad smell to it: how can rejecting one of Jesus' commandments of love bring glory to Him?

But of paramount importance are the two commandments that sum all other aspects of the law: Love God with all your heart, mind, soul, and strength, and love your neighbor as yourself... in this sense every day should be unto God, including the day He made for us, whichever one that we choose... Lovely words of love, these, but they are characterized by a lack of substance and a dangerous twisting of the truth. You rightly say the two commandments of love, which Jesus quoted from His Word in the First Testament, are a *summary* of all other aspects of the law. They summarize. They don't abolish or replace. Jesus told us in Part I of His Words of Love how to love God with all our being. We show this love by putting no one above Him in our lives, not using images to worship Him, not taking His name in vain, and by remembering the seventh day to keep it holy. Why should we leave out the last one – the fourth commandment? You have no biblical basis for doing so. Only tradition supports your opinion. God never gave us the right to change the day *He* chose for us. He gave us the freedom to either choose His day or disobey. You are doing what the Scripture forbids in II Peter 1:20-21. You are giving your "own interpretation" of words that were not written "by an act of human will, but men moved by the Holy Spirit spoke from God." They wrote down what Jesus, the Word Himself, spoke from Sinai and wrote with His own finger. You cannot truthfully say that the Word of God supports you in your opinion that every day is holy and we can choose the day we keep. God gives His definition of love in 49 scrolls and 66 books. We can't presume to tell Love Himself what love is. Love says that love is the law and the law is love, and the law of love is not a burden (I John 5:2-3). You can't even use the excuse here that we only have to keep the commandments Jesus spoke in the "New Testament." The verses speak of the love of *God*, referring to the Father and to all that He spoke through Jesus in the Word.

Now in terms of the theology of the matter: Well, God didn't even create the sun until the fourth "day", and of course the rising and setting of the sun is the only possible way we can establish one "day" from the next! So maybe even our understanding of what He calls a "day" in Genesis 1: 5-31 may be skewed! Yikes, if the sun wasn't made until the fourth day, maybe what we call Sunday is actually Wednesday! A long explanation is required to prove from the Hebrew words and the context of Genesis that the days you speak of are days of recreation, not creation, and that the sun was already created billions of years before the events of verses 14-18. Jesus only allowed the sun to show through the earth's atmosphere and the moon to shine at night. But all this requires much more time to explain than space allows. The answer is amazingly simple. What you are inadvertently saying in the lines above is that you don't believe Jesus is your Savior. If Jesus had kept the wrong day of rest, He would have sinned and could not be our Savior. He had to keep the right day to be our Savior. And we know without a doubt that the Jews have kept the same day for 2000 years. We also know He kept the same day the Jews kept. Had He not done so, the Pharisees would have attacked Him for more than the way He kept Saturday.

And please remember the seventh day is simply the day after the sixth day... whether that be Wednesday, Saturday or Sunday! Of more import to God is likely that "Folks you're going to work six days in succession but ensure you follow those six with a day to rest... cause hey I made you guys and believe me, you're going to need a day to rest, especially after Lucifer gets cast down to earth!

Jesus commanded us to remember the seventh day, not one day in seven. If it were not possible for us to know which day was the seventh, He would not have ordered us to remember what it is impossible to remember. While all things are possible with God and He sometimes needs to open Red Seas for us, He says His commandments are not burdensome. Asking us to do something that is impossible is a burden He would not lay on us. He is Love. Putting words in God's mouth that He never said is not likely to please Him. He makes the rules. You don't. He lays down the law, not the Christian -- or sometimes not-so-Christian – churches. They follow Cain's example. They hate and murder with their words those who worship God exactly the way He stipulated, and they arrogantly impose their form of worship on Him. Because He is so loving, merciful, and patient, He has not withheld all His blessings from those who keep Sunday. The day is coming soon, however, when the full consequences of disobedience will fall on those who knowingly reject the Sabbath truth.

So I close with a novel thought: Instead of getting all bent out of shape on the specific day we rest, (since it was made for us, and not for God after all!!!) how about actually taking one day (any day) to really rest... how many are doing that? That in my mind might be a better campaign to start...

That's not the campaign God has given us as a church, and we choose to follow Him. He has called us to be repairers of the breach, which includes being among those who help restore to the church the day God said to remember (Isa. 58:12-14). We know that most sincere Christians, even those in ministry like you, have not yet been blessed as we have to understand this truth. We are judged more severely because He has given us this revelation. We are thankful that God meets us all where we are and lovingly leads us into more and more truth (John 16:13). While I prefer to walk in His grace or empowerment, many times I have need of His mercy. I did not "deserve" to receive this knowledge about the Sabbath in 1967, but God lovingly gave it to me. To be totally frank, I was for a short while deceived into believing that Sabbath keeping was not part of New Covenant teaching. So I believe I have some compassion for those who have been deceived by the prevailing view, even though it may not always sound like it when you read the forceful words I write. While this truth is simple, I allowed myself to swallow Satan's big lie, even after keeping the Sabbath for many years. We sometimes make "the simplicity and purity of devotion to Christ" (II Cor. 11:3) complicated. Satan has weaved his web of lies in such complicated deception that the simplicity of the truth of Jesus sounds complicated to those who hear it. This simplicity is summed up in this book's original title: "Remember the Seventh Day: It is My Sabbath." It's simple. It's biblical. Anything else is a twist of the truth.

Will you be deceived by those who twist the truth? Or will you walk the straight and narrow path that leads to life? Will you offer excuses – or obedience?

Sabbath *Selah's*
Sunday: Holy Day? Or Hitlerian Heresy?

But whoever denies Me before men, I will also deny him before My Father who is in heaven (Mat. 10:33).

But he is a Jew who is one inwardly …(Rom. 2:29).

And if you belong to Christ, then you are Abraham's descendants, heirs according to promise…And those who will walk by this rule, peace and mercy be upon them, and upon *the Israel of God* (Gal. 3:29; 6:16).

Part of denying Jesus is denying His Jewishness and the fact that He kept the days He gave to Israel, the believers, in Leviticus 23, and especially the day He gave to Adam for all mankind. It is an historical fact that Sunday did not become an addition or replacement for the Sabbath before the second century A.D. In the birthplace of Christianity, the area surrounding Jerusalem, both Jewish and Gentile Christians kept the Sabbath and the holy days. Early church history records that Polycarp, disciple of John, the apostle who was the closest to Jesus, faithfully kept those days. Much of the opposition to the Sabbath in early church history was based on decidedly unchristian sentiments. A vile, almost Hitlerian, hatred of the Jews and everything Jewish animated many of the Sabbath opponents, including Justin Martyr, a second-century hater of the Sabbath day. He believed God made the Sabbath because of the wickedness of the Jews as "a mark to single them out for punishment they so well deserved for their infidelities." It is a dangerous thing to condemn a whole race, especially when our Savior was part of that race. Our Jewish Savior called Himself Divine Master of the Sabbath. While He did indeed give it as a mark or sign, it is a not a mark of condemnation, but a sign of identity. Those who demean it as "Jewish" are denying Jesus and their identity in Him (Ex. 31:13; Heb. 4:9). Selah.

CHAPTER TWENTY THREE

Dances with Wolves: Twisting the Tarnation out of Galatians

Paul's farewell warning to the elders at Ephesus was solemn: "Be on guard for yourselves and for all the flock…I know that after my departure savage wolves will come in among you, not sparing the flock…" (Acts 20:28-29). He was right. The wolves in sheep's clothing saved their greatest attack for many years later. They infiltrated the church from the inside, since martyring saints didn't seem to work. Satan used these men to deprive God's people of one of their greatest blessings – the Sabbath day.

A Roman emperor who called himself Christian put the nail in the Christian coffin. He birthed a church that changed the truth of God into a lie, substituting the ways and days of Jesus for those of the pagans. Baptizing paganism in Christian waters only muddied visible Christianity. The pristine source that bubbled up out of the early springs of salvation became sullied in the sewage of compromise Constantine-style. God was grieved.

He foreknew it all, however, and had a plan to redeem it. In these last days He will rain down His truth and the pure waters will once again flow and refresh those who will receive them. The wolves will be chased out of the sheepfold where graze the sheep who hear the voice of the Good Shepherd.

Will you hear what Jesus is saying through His Word? Or will you continue to believe the twisted story brought in by wolves long ago?

Robbing Peter to Pay Homage to Paul's Prose

The evidence for the Sabbath is overwhelming. So why has 99.9 % of the Christian community not understood?

I think Peter gives us the answer. He speaks in II Peter 3:15-16 of "our beloved brother Paul." Peter spoke of Paul's writings, "in which are some things hard to understand, which the untaught and unstable distort, as they do also the rest of the Scriptures, to their own destruction" (3:16). The NEB calls these parts of Paul's writings "obscure passages." The Amplified adds the idea of twisting and misinterpreting. And remember, in the inspired order Peter and James come before Paul. They present the unmistakable truth before the student of Gamaliel enters with his convoluted arguments. Most theologians prefer Paul over the clear words of Peter, James, and John.

Most pastors would probably resent being grouped with the "untaught." Nevertheless, like it or not, they have not been taught about the Sabbath. They may not be as heretical as those Peter referred to, but their doctrines come from the same source.

The Sunday doctrine is none other than a doctrine of demons -- Baal worship pawned off as holiness. It is Satan's lie to deprive Christians of the Sabbath blessing.

Paul's writings have been twisted throughout the ages. "Greasy grace" led one prominent Protestant reformer centuries ago to call the Holy Spirit's words in the book of James "an epistle of straw."

Many put Paul on a pedestal, peddling a party line they put in his mouth. Millions have swallowed that line. The party's over.

Do You Really Think Paul Would Throw Out One of the Big Ten?

Let's begin by asking a simple question. If you saw in Galatians some verses that seemed to say that the sixth commandment was no longer binding on Christians, what would you choose to believe?

Would you believe that it now okay to murder and hate? Who would you choose to question – Paul, or the words of the Holy Spirit in the rest of the Bible?

Would you take Paul's word over the word of the Holy Spirit and Jesus? And even if Paul's words seemed clear, would you not question them? Would you not question the fact that Paul seemed to be doing away with one of the commandments of God?

Would you think you could now get away with murder?

We have proved that Jesus talked the Sabbath talk and walked the Sabbath walk. So did Paul. So how could he be so hypocritical as to say the Sabbath and holy days were done away? How could he do away with one of the Ten Commandments with one sweep of his plume? How could one or two verses of Paul destroy the rest of the Bible teaching on the Sabbath?

It shouldn't. But it has. About 99.9 % of Christians seem to believe Paul did away with the Sabbath.

We may not be able to decipher in every detail what Paul meant. But we should understand what he could not have meant. He could not be doing away with one of the Ten Commandments. If he had done so, he would be destroying all the law of God, as James says.

A Serious Heresy

If you played a tape of a sermon I gave over thirty years ago (pretending you know French) to a church in Paris, France, it would be easy for you to misunderstand my words. It may have been a message trying to correct a situation of which you had no knowledge. It may have been directed to a particular problem known only by the people I was addressing at the time.

Paul does not give us a detailed picture of the heresy he attacked in the churches in Colossae and Galatia. But he does give us a few indications. Until I began doing some research for this book, I did not know what Paul was specifically addressing in Galatians 4:10. Before I explain it as well as possible, being removed from the historical situation by 1900 years, we shall briefly examine the context of this epistle.

This heresy is so serious it is difficult to see how anyone could conceive that the heretics were heretical because they kept the Sabbath and the holy days. Paul calls it "a different gospel" (1:6), accusing the heretics of wanting "to distort the gospel of Christ" (1:7). He even goes so far as to call these twisters of the gospel "accursed," repeating this judgment in successive verses almost verbatim (1:8-9).

We have seen how Paul himself kept the Sabbath and even some ritual laws he didn't have to keep other than as a pubic relations gesture to opposing Jews. He would have been calling *himself* "accursed!"

Paul says that he did not receive the gospel he preached from man (1:12). Catholic and Protestant theologians openly admit that the Sabbath is biblical and that Sunday is a tradition of men. They frankly state that Catholic leaders have more authority than God! While millions swallow the popular lie about a man being infallible in official pronouncements, God says that only He is infallible.

Most people ignorantly equate Judaism with the religion of the "Old Testament." But Paul distinguishes the ridiculous add-ons of the rabbis with Judaism and tradition, not with the true religion God gave Israel (1:13-14).

Even a cursory reading of this epistle shows this controversy was not about the Sabbath or holy days but about circumcision and the traditions of Judaism (2:3-4). False brethren were trying to bring the churches in the region of Galatia into bondage. We have seen that the commandments of God are not burdensome, so this could not be referring to the Sabbath, a day God declared to be a day of freedom celebration (Deut. 5:15).

Paul – the Misunderstood Man

The key point in this discussion is repeated throughout the epistle. It's the same old misunderstanding of Paul's approach to the law. Paul always praised and supported the law of love. He believed Christians should live a moral life in obedience to all the Ten Commandments, which he himself observed. He did *not* believe that *any* law, whether moral or sacrificial, could save or justify anybody. Only Jesus' blood could do that. Whether you sacrifice a bull or keep the Sabbath, that act cannot save you or justify you.

The proponents of the anti-law crowd hardly ever cite the many verses where Paul establishes the law (Rom. 7:12,16; 6:1-2,14-15; 8:4; I Cor. 7:19, and many more). They put their devilish twist of lawlessness on the verse where Paul condemns the law for purposes of ***justification***. Can you see the difference?

Gone Fishing – for Excuses

The anti-Sabbath establishment is such a divided camp that it should be evident that they are fishing for excuses. One group says the whole law is done away in order to get rid of the Sabbath, but they agree we're not "under the law" and "in bondage" if we don't cheat on our wife and shoot our boss. Cussing is bad and idols are wrong but that Sabbath is just terrible. Another group says Sunday replaced the Sabbath, an idea so unfounded that any competent scholar would refute their claim. The Catholic Church has essentially told Protestants: "Don't lie and pretend you got this Sunday stuff from the Bible. You got it from us, and we invented it." The Protestants couldn't protest that.

Please reread Peter, James and John as God intended, and then ask God to help you understand Paul. ***Justification*** by law is the issue here (Gal. 2:16,21; 3:10-12,18).

It's amazing how the epistle the lawless swear by traps them in their own excuses. Paul explains that a "covenant previously ratified by God" (3:17) cannot be done away by a law that Jesus codified with the addendum of a sacrificial system and rituals hundreds of years after said covenant was made. While Paul is referring specifically here to the fifth biblical covenant, the one Jesus made with Abraham, the principle also applies to the very first covenant made with man – the Sabbath covenant.

No laws added when Jesus made the Old Covenant with Israel at Sinai or shortly after can change the validity and permanence of the Sabbath covenant. And since Jesus made the Sabbath covenant and repeated it before He made the Old Covenant with Israel, the conclusion is evident: ***no covenant or law established before the Old Covenant can be done away when the Old Covenant was done away.***

Old Covenant people without the Holy Spirit had nothing to rely on except their own fleshly works. They fell under the curse of self-sufficiency (Jer. 17:5; Gal. 3:10). The law was a tutor to show them their need for a Savior, who was foreshadowed in the many sacrifices they brought (3:24-25). The heretics of Galatians did not realize their need for Jesus even though He was now available to be their Savior. They trusted in the works of the law (not to be confused with good works by God's grace or empowerment) to justify them. Paul encouraged the Galatians to do as he did, to be justified by faith in Christ and revitalized by Jesus' own faith inside him (2:20; 3:26-27).

Chapter 4 brings us closer to understanding the true nature of this heresy. Being "held in bondage under the elemental things of the *world*" (4:3) has nothing to do with keeping the Sabbath or any of the commandments of God. Paul is warning the Gentile Galatians who "did not know God" and were slaves to those which by nature are no gods" (4:9).

Since it is clear that the heretics were Jewish, pushing circumcision on these Gentile believers, something seems a bit strange. Paul warned these Gentile Christians in these verses not to "turn back again to the weak and worthless elemental things, to which you desire to be enslaved all over again..." (4:9). Paul could not have been warning these Gentile Christians not to turn back to Sabbaths and holy days they had never observed before becoming Christians. He is referring to elements of paganism.

Judaism was a mixture of teachings from Hebrew Scripture heavily smattered with human and pagan traditions. The context makes it clear that verse 10 could not be referring to the days Jesus commanded Israel to keep as a perpetual covenant.

Bewitched

Certain important clues that would help unravel the mystery have been overlooked. One key is the phrase, "You foolish Galatians, who has *bewitched* you..." (3:1). Witchcraft was involved. It had to be a Jewish version of witchcraft, which was not uncommon during this period. Even today movie stars are fascinated with the Kabala, a dangerous version of Jewish mysticism.

Jewish groups were not unknown at the time to mix witchcraft with their legalism. In fact, witchcraft is based in the desire to control others. I've been in churches where leaders tried to control me through picky legalism. In the demonic realm, witchcraft, control, and legalism are partners. One of the first sins Paul warned them about was the sin of "sorcery" (Gal. 5:20), which is witchcraft.

Before we reveal the answer to what these days were, we shall continue to examine the text. Chapter 5 brings back the "yoke of slavery" represented by circumcision (5:1-2). Since circumcision is a ritual that is no longer a requirement for belonging to spiritual Israel, the need to keep "the whole law" referred more specifically to the ceremonial part of the law. James said we were to keep the whole law and not to neglect even one point of the law, such as the Sabbath (James 2:10). Hebrews 9:8-14 makes it clear that the sacrifices and rituals looking to Jesus' sacrifice are no longer necessary. Doing them to be saved represents "dead works" (Heb. 9:14).

The extremely strong condemnation of being "severed from Christ" and having "fallen from grace" (5:4) could not have referred to keeping the fourth commandment. In fact, nowhere is that mentioned in the epistle, except in an artificial twisting of 4:10.

Paul contrasts circumcision with "a new creation" (6:15) and "faith working through love" (5:6). God defines love as the keeping of His commandments (I John 5:3). Moreover, keeping the Sabbath is not sin or "leaven" (5:9).

Anyone who would think that Paul is doing away here with any commandment should read Galatians 5:16-26. What better way to get Paul's definition of that misused phrase, "under the law" (5:18). He tells us in the next verses to avoid sin, which is the breaking of the law. If we walk in love and in the Spirit, we break no law. Paul is encouraging law keeping, so "under the law" cannot mean obeying the law. These heretics were encouraging the Galatians to seek salvation and justification by circumcision (6:13,15), keeping the laws of *Judaism*. "Under the law" in this context means being under the curse of the law because of sinful, dead works. Dead works make you trust in yourself, which transgresses the laws of love.

Days of Jewish Astrology

So what is the meaning of this infamous verse that some say changes the whole Bible? "You observe days and months and seasons and years. I fear for you, that perhaps I have labored in vain" (Gal. 4:10-11).

Most scholars believe that the term "elemental things of the world" (4:3,9) refers to the personification of gods in the physical elements of the world, whether on the earth or in the heavens, even making gods of stars that control the destiny of humans. In fact, certain Jewish groups were known to mix their radical Judaism with the observance of certain days, months, and years that were based in astrology[1]. While we do not know the specifics, this gives us a sufficient idea. We don't have to know all the details to know that the popular perversion of this verse is patently false.

While the days may not be purely pagan, they are a blend of pagan ideas combined with Judaism in a heresy that denied the power of Jesus' blood to justify us. The phrase, "...a festival or a new moon or a Sabbath day" (Col. 2:16), is a reference to the days God ordained for Israel being polluted by an ascetic, radical observance based in Judaism. This is totally different from the unquestionably pagan aspect of the days mentioned in Galatians, which are days based in Jewish astrology borrowed from the pagans. While admittedly a mix of Judaism and paganism, they have nothing in common with the special mix of Judaism and pagan asceticism in Colossae. The Colossian heresy emphasized a bizarre, bowel-restraining, holier-than-the-normal, Colossian version of Sabbath keeping.

Galatian heretics espoused justification by circumcision and by reverting to Jewish astrological days birthed in the paganism the Galatians had renounced.

Paul renounced this heresy, but he never renounced any of the days God calls holy. It is our moral obligation to respect all that God calls holy, including His name and His days -- including the annual Sabbaths.

Freedom to Dance "The Jesus Jig"

Evidence abounds in Bible and church history of the observance of the divine calendar among early Christians. The verse many use to try to justify Sunday worship actually works against their argument. Paul called members to lay aside an offering in their homes "the first day of every week" (I Cor. 16:2). The equivalent *mia ton*

1 "From Second Temple Judaism there comes ample evidence of speculation about the universe and how the heavenly bodies were related to angels. The Book of Heavenly Luminaries in 1 Enoch 72-82, a work dating from perhaps the first century B.C., testifies to Jewish astrological ideas and the association of an angel, Uriel, with the stars. This is set within a context in which particular attention is paid to times and seasons" (*Dictionary of Paul and His Letters* (p. 231)).

sabbaton is used in Acts 20:7. The common pagan expression at the time for Sunday was *dies solis* or Day of the Sun. But Paul used the Jewish term based on God's calendar, *kata mian sabbaton*, which means "every first day from the Sabbath."

Why would Paul, moreover, exhort the Gentile Corinthians to keep the Feast of Unleavened Bread, even stating that they were already physically unleavened? The answer is simple. He had to have taught them about the sacred calendar and the holy days. It is obvious whose side he would have taken much later had he been alive during the Easter-Passover controversy (I Cor. 5:7-8).

We don't have to dance with wolves in sheep's clothing. We need to fellowship with our Shepherd on His Sabbath day. Why not dance with Him, doing "The Jesus Jig," rejoicing in His day of celebration as He dances over us (Zeph. 3:17). We want freedom to dance with Jesus in the joy of His truth. And it is in His Sabbath days that we will experience that glorious freedom.

Sabbath *Selah's*
Kingdom of Lawlessness? Or Kingdom of Love?

Let no one in any way deceive you, for it [Jesus' return to establish His Kingdom of love] will not come unless the apostasy comes first, and the man of lawlessness is revealed, the son of destruction (II Thes. 2:3).

"Because lawlessness is increased, most people's love will grow cold…This gospel of the *kingdom* shall be preached in the whole world as a *testimony* to all the nations, and then the end will come" (Mat. 24:12,14).

…not forsaking our own assembling together…but encouraging one another; and all the more as you see the day drawing near (Heb. 10:25).

As the establishment of God's Kingdom on earth draws near, Satan will attempt to establish his government on earth to prevent God's Kingdom of Love from coming. God's Kingdom is based on law, centered in the Sabbath, which every week prophesies the coming of the seventh millennium of peace. Satan's kingdom is based on lawlessness, which will abound in these last days. This system will revolve around Sunday keeping and will be personified by the "man of lawlessness." *"The law is done away" heresy, which began early in church history (II Thes. 2:7), purports today to do away with the law in general, but only objects to the Sabbath, which it personifies strangely as "the Law." Christians who do not heed the warning in this book will be ripe for the deception of this man of lawlessness. Selah.*

God is a divine family of love. We are the cherished children He wants to place on His knee in tender fellowship on His day of love. He wants to meet with His family of princes and kings in training, giving them both His hugs and His marching orders. Come into the warmth and security of God's family through the joy of the Sabbath.

CHAPTER TWENTY FOUR

Dominion Day - Day of Ruling Family Fellowship

Why is the Sabbath so important? Why has it been lost?

The answer lies in another truth that has been lost -- the knowledge of the true gospel of the Kingdom or ruling Family of God and the real King of that Kingdom.

While Jesus is the Door to the Kingdom of God, the only gospel He ever preached was the gospel of the Kingdom of God (John 1:14-15). No other. He even said it was His purpose on earth: "I must preach the good news of the kingdom of God to the other towns also, because that is why I was sent" (Luke 4:43, NIV).

While salvation and the cross of Jesus are definitely the openers to the Kingdom and are facets of the one true gospel, Jesus never asked us to be on a soul-saving campaign. Father Love is responsible for drawing those He chooses in this age to be part of the Kingdom (John 6:44).

We have missed it. We don't preach what Jesus preached. Why?

The answer is so simple it is astounding: as ancient Israel, we have forgotten the day that opens the understanding of the Kingdom. It is God's Dominion Day -- the day of the Kingdom. It is also the very first covenant God made with man. It is the missing piece of the Kingdom puzzle -- the powerful hammer blow that breaks the Bible code.

A few preachers are beginning to understand the utmost importance of the Kingdom concept. The ignorance of two essential truths, however, block them from full understanding. Those two truths will be God's end-time test for the believers. It is by virtue of those two truths that a last days shaking will rock the church. Reformation and revival (the latter impossible without the former) will come only to those who grasp both.

Those two truths are the keeping of God's Sabbath covenant and the speaking out of the name of Jesus, both bedrock principles of the Kingdom. Those who accept the mistranslation made popular by the King James Version insist on calling on "the Lord." Unless they start speaking out the name of the King of the Kingdom, they will not be able to grasp the Kingdom concept nor its foundational operating system embodied in the Sabbath day.

The Mini Mac used to type this manuscript employs the Mac OS X operating system. My wife's PC has XP as its operating system. The Macintosh will not work with XP, or the PC with the Mac system. It's the same with the Kingdom system. It simply does not work without its operating system, the Sabbath. All the principles of the Kingdom are embodied and find their origin in the Sabbath day.

More and more ministers are stressing the importance of the covenant. They make statements like, "Everything in the Bible, every promise, every blessing you can receive is based on covenant." They are right. But where they err is in missing this essential truth: the Sabbath covenant is the first covenant on which the other nine biblical covenants are based. Without the first the others cannot truly work.

Using the covenants and the names of Jesus unleash great power. "Lord" is not one of His names. Keeping Kingdom Day becomes even more powerful when we understand the power of the name of Jesus. Do we want the power of the King and God whose name is Jesus? Or do we want to face the end time onslaught of the "god of this world" calling on a lowly title?

If Jesus is Lord, Satan is Above Jesus!

God has truly anointed Dr. Myles Munroe to teach about the Kingdom.[1] Of the 26 Kingdom concepts Dr. Munroe explains, 25 are embodied in the Sabbath. The only one that misses the mark is the "Lordship principle." When King James had Jesus reduced to a lord in his 1611 translation, lords were five to seven levels below the king.

1 Myles Munroe, *Rediscovering the Kingdom,* Destiny Image, Shippensburg, PA, 2004, www.destinyimage.com

Britannica's 1911 edition includes this definition of lord: "It is thus not only a general word for a prince or sovereign, but also the common word for a feudal superior, and particularly of a feudal tenant holding directly of the king...." These lords owned their manors and collected taxes for the king, being allowed to keep some of the funds. They even had to pay taxes to the king. They were not, however, owners in the strict sense of the term. The king had that distinction, which is why King James was happy his translators referred to Jesus (God) as "the Lord."

One more important fact puts the nail -- or should -- on the "Lord" coffin: *lords were forced to submit their trained soldiers for the king's armies and were* ***obliged to enforce the king's laws.*** Do we realize what this means?

If Jesus is Lord of the earth, our church or our life, then Satan has to be God and King!

Lords are not on the top of the totem pole. Kings are. The Most High God calls Satan "the god of this world" (II Cor. 4:4). If Satan is the god of those who live on earth (with the exception of the saints) then he is definitely king of the earth as well. If Jesus is Lord, then He is under Satan, who is God and King.

While God is merciful and has not allowed the fullness of the consequences of calling Jesus "Lord" to fall upon sincere Christians, the implications are enormous. The power that will be released to Christians in these last days when understanding comes will be powerful. The Sabbath keepers who keep Kingdom Day and who choose not to call Jesus "Lord" will have the greatest results.

Satan and the demons are preparing a last-ditch attack to thwart God's plans. Their goal is total annihilation of the earth. Those who call Jesus by a title that puts him under Satan will not be able to withstand the attacks the devil is planning.

The King's Name Releases Revelation and Power

Dr. Munroe writes: "The name of the king is the essence of his power.[2] " Then why not call Him by His name? Why use a lowly title, and an uncomplimentary one at that, as we shall see in the sequel?

Anointed men of God are coming oh so close to grasping the Sabbath truth. They almost speak out the truth that we should be keeping the Sabbath -- until religiosity takes over to stop them. In the context of Jesus' defense (in John 5:16-19) of His healing people on the Sabbath as Sabbath "work," Dr. Munroe makes these surprising statements before turning in a different direction: "What did Jesus mean by this statement? Doesn't the second chapter of Genesis tell us that God worked for six days in creation and then rested on the seventh? Wasn't that day of rest commemorated and established as a standard for God's people in the Sabbath law?[3]"

The answer is yes, yes. It was actually the member of the Godhead who be-

2 Munroe, *Rediscovering the Kingdom*, p. 216

3 Munroe, *Rediscovering the Kingdom*, p. 202

came Jesus who rested on the Sabbath day in Genesis. And it was the Word, Jesus, who thundered out the unalterable decree on Sinai as King: "Remember the Sabbath day, to keep it holy."

This anointed Kingdom author also writes: "The laws of a kingdom are the way by which one is guaranteed access to the benefits of the king and the kingdom. Violations of kingdom law place one at odds with the king and thus interrupt the favorable position one enjoys with the king. The laws in a kingdom cannot be changed by the citizens, nor are they subject to a citizen referendum or debate. Simply put, the word of the king is law in His kingdom. Rebellion against the law is rebellion against the king.[4]"

God understands that some leaders in Rome and later Constantine, as people purporting to be Kingdom citizens, did change the Sabbath law for the church. He knows that most churches and pastors today do not keep the Sabbath because of Catholic tradition that the Protestants refused to protest. He realizes the sincerity of those people who keep Sunday and is meeting them where they are. Nevertheless, they still lose out on the breaking of the Bible code that opens the door to knowledge, intimacy, anointing and power. The King pronounced a blessing on the Sabbath day that He cannot revoke. Jesus has made the Sabbath a law in His Kingdom -- even a test commandment to see if we truly want to know and love Him the way He loves us.

Why can't the church understand this simple truth? Perhaps because the church is not calling on the name of revelation -- Jesus. Satan certainly does not want the church to call on Jesus' name to discover the Bible code breaker. The Sabbath is Satan's defeat day. The holy Day of Atonement is even more specific in prophesying his demise.

The two blockbuster truths of the name and the days of Jesus may seem inconsequential, even heretical, to those based in today's church tradition and system of religiosity. But God never intended man to substitute the Kingdom truth with the vain attempt to do it our way, aided by a demon called "religiosity."

If you think the above statement is controversial (and truth always is), the next idea may rock your boat. The truth will keep you afloat, but a certain demon wants to capsize you, or more accurately push you from ditch to ditch. That is exactly what he has done to the church and explains why we haven't been able to see the simple, oh so simple, truth about the seventh day.

Some truths are revealed by experience, provided they do not contradict the Word. We are in deliverance ministry and we have seen firsthand the truth we are about to relate. When affected people agree to bind up this demon and send him to the pit, they also see more clearly the truth and no longer struggle in their Christian lives. "Lord" is also the name Satan gave to one of his demons, also known as "quagmire," a demon who pushes Christians from one ditch to the other in a mire of failure when they pray to "the Lord."

---

4 Munroe, *Rediscovering the Kingdom,* p. 65

The truth, as you will see in the sequel, is that the word "lord" is connected to an entire system of holidays formerly belonging to Baal. They are holidays -- not holy days.

But that's what religion has taught us. We have swallowed it without examination. The very understanding of the gospel of the Kingdom has been blocked by its greatest rival, religiosity. So why not start praying to our Father in the name of Jesus? Why bring a pagan god or even a demon into the picture? Think about it.

Religious Losers? Or Kingdom Conquerors?

Religion makes us losers. As I write today I'm hearing in the background the rousing song, "Victory," sung by Yolanda Adams. For many Christians today the spirit of quagmire has made their songs of victory ring with a hollow tone. Something is missing. It's the Sabbath. It's the name and the days of Jesus.

Jesus has more appointed times than the weekly Sabbath, as you will see when you are ready for the meaty sequel(s). God set appointed times for everything (Eccl. 3:1-3) -- yes, even a time to heal. The Sabbath is a time to lay down to Jesus the cares and problems of the week. God also set a monthly time was for laying down long term burdens, fears, regrets, dreads and the like, and annual holy days for giving the bad stuff to Jesus to exchange for the blessings of the Kingdom.

Divine exchange cannot occur if we do not honor divine appointments. The Sabbath and the other appointed times of Jesus are special dates in both the chronological and "romantic" senses. They allow intimacy, the Father's greatest desire in His fellowship with His children and Jesus' passion for His relationship with His bride, the church. On the Sabbath we exchange "sweet somethings" with Jesus. And in brotherly exchange with Him, we give Him praise and worship and receive in return knowledge, tactics for our fight of faith, and strength for our Kingdom assignment. We also (on His various appointed times) exchange our burdens, cares, sins, fears, and weaknesses for His power. What a deal!

Indeed it is a deal. God calls it a covenant -- a covenant that began with all mankind and will once again soon, in the seventh day of 1000 years, be offered to all humans (Isa. 66:23).

Need power to overcome? To be a winner, a Kingdom victor rather than a churchgoer who only talks the talk? Meet with the most powerful King in the universe on Dominion Day. Your prayers on that day have dominion power, and Jesus will refresh and empower you to walk the walk.

Jesus has been patiently waiting for some 1700 years to pour out His Sabbath covenant blessings and power on His bride. But how can we receive the blessings and overcoming power of King Jesus and His Kingdom if we aren't meeting with the King on Kingdom day?

Will King Jesus' Own Finally "Receive" Him on His Day?

The religious world hates the Sabbath with a passion, yet Jesus' passion to meet with us on His day is much greater. Religiosity resists new understanding. Religion does not understand the conceptual nature of the biblical languages and balks at the idea of several meanings for one text. John was the apostle most intimate with Jesus. John kept the Sabbath and taught his disciple Polycarp to do the same. So John was able to keep the intimacy with the King on Kingdom Day long after Jesus died and rose again.

It was John who said that Jesus came unto His own and His own did not receive Him (John 1:10-12). This refers to His creation, all the people of the world, the Jews in Jerusalem at the time of His coming, but the meaning does not stop there. Jesus has come through the Holy Spirit (John 14:18) to His people today, but He has reserved a special part of Himself for intimate fellowship with His Family of co-rulers in His Kingdom.

The Greek word for "receive" in the above verses of John 1, *paralambano*, is pregnant with conceptual meaning. It implies an intimate fellowship, much as the intimacy between marriage partners on their wedding night, learning from an intimate one so you can assume an office prepared for you, accepting that person fully, taking hold of him, being taken up away with him as being enraptured, even raptured into his presence.

The same word is used for the Pharisees, who embraced religiosity as Christians are supposed to embrace Jesus and His Kingdom (Mark 7:4). Paul warned believers not to receive (*paralambano*) a gospel Jesus had not given (Gal. 1:9), and that's exactly what the church has done. Hebrews enjoins us to receive (same word) a Kingdom that cannot be shaken. Paul received (*paralambano*) the gospel He preached by direct revelation from Jesus, not from man (Gal. 1:12). He continued to receive Jesus' Kingdom teaching every Sabbath day throughout his life.

Paul encouraged the Colossians not to be disturbed by the heretics who wanted them to keep the days of Jesus in a legalism devoid of Jesus (Col 2:16-17). He also exhorted them to walk in the steps of the Divine Master (the correct translation) they had received (same Greek word).

It is impossible to walk fully in the steps of Jesus as Divine Master if we do not receive Him in intimate fellowship on the Sabbath day -- the day of which He said He was the Divine Master.

Jesus is also Supreme Commander. What reaction would an army general have if his officers did not show up when He summoned them? We are blessed that Jesus is not a harsh Judge. He graciously beckons those who are weary in their religious toil to come to Him. "Learn from Me," He says, "for I am gentle and humble in heart, and you will find rest for your souls [your mind, heart and will]" (Mat. 11:29).

Jesus went on to say, "My yoke is easy." Once again, multiple meanings abound. One of the yokes Jesus took on His shoulders was the Kingdom yoke. "And the government will rest on His shoulders…" (Isa. 9:6). Jesus is King of Kings. He is the great King and we are the smaller kings governing under His direction. He bears the brunt of the government of God. We, however, have been granted authority on earth even greater than that of the Father, since He gave *us* dominion here as He did Adam (Gen. 1:26-27).

As a pastor I often attended ministerial conferences to be refreshed and directed. Ministers of earthly government do the same. If you don't show up on time, you miss the camaraderie and the refreshing. The King of the universe calls an important conference of His saints or holy ones every Sabbath. He calls these meetings "holy convocations" for His holy kings and priests. It is His loving invitation to come out of the weekly "rat race" for a refresher course with the King.

Jesus calls us to come out of the "metro, boulot, dodo" routine, a rhyming French phrase, meaning literally, "take the subway, go to work, and then go to sleep." Our God of love wants us to come out of our routine to rest and delight every Sabbath in a gourmet Family "meal" prepared and served by Chef Jesus, the King of the ruling Family of Kings. As we revel in the spiritual delicacies of God, we receive a meal that foreshadows a millennial Sabbath meal -- the time when Jesus will "prepare a lavish banquet for all peoples on this mountain [symbolizing the government of God]" (Isa. 25:6).

We delight in Jesus in many ways on the Sabbath. We "eat" the Word, who is Jesus (John 1:1). As a prophet once said, "Your words were found and I ate them, And Your words became for me a joy and the delight of my heart" (Jer. 15:16). When we meet with Jesus on His day, we begin to delight in Him (Isa. 58:14), rejoicing in getting to know and love Him as He exults in song and dance over each of us (Zeph. 3:17).

Break the Book Code: Get to Know the Author!

The Bible code breaking secret is so simple. Some books are rather complicated. The best way to understand a book is a rare occurrence today: get to know the author. Sadly, while the Author of the Book of books has made His Sabbath invitation clear for 6000 years, His people have refused to meet with Him for a weekly encounter much greater than any book signing. God's heart is yearning for something we have not given Him. God has made the effort to know who we are individually in such an intimate way that it is hard for us to grasp. If He knows the hairs on our head, He also knows our insides like no one else. His greatest desire is for us to get to know and love Him as He knows and loves us -- intimately.

The result of our delightful Sabbath intimacy with Jesus is that He makes us "ride on the heights of the earth" (Isa. 58:14). Jesus wants to know His co-rulers intimately and He wants us to know Him.

We are called to rule with Jesus in His Kingdom -- now and in a fuller way, unopposed by Satan, in a 1000-year Sabbath in the Millennium. As Esther met with the King and had "come into the Kingdom for such a time as this," so it is with Jesus' bride today. We must not miss our important appointment with the King. He has summoned us every Sabbath day so we can get to know and love Him as He does us.

We are also ambassadors of the Kingdom. Myles Munroe says it best: "An ambassadorial representative is only as viable and legal as his relationship with his government.[5]" He goes on to say that God's first ambassador on earth needed to put fellowship and relationship as his priority. And that is exactly why Jesus made the Sabbath for Adam.

In fact, Dr. Munroe's education and worship principles belong in the Sabbath context. It is the day when the anointing is strongest and it is the King who *commands* us to assemble for the teaching of His kings and priests and for corporate worship.

Jesus comes to meet with His co-rulers on the Sabbath. But how many receive Him on His day? Jesus "came to that which belonged to Him [to His own -- His domain, creation, things, world], and they who were His own did not receive Him and did not welcome Him. But to as many as did receive and welcome Him, He gave the *authority (power, privilege, right)* to become the children of God, that is, to those who believe in (adhere to, trust in, and rely on) His *name* [Isa. 56:5]" (John 1:11-12, AMP.).

Sabbath intimacy is the door to knowing the real Jesus and in receiving Him on this day we open ourselves to receiving the authority and power of the Kingdom -- dominion power. And isn't it interesting that the Amplified Version refers to the chapter on the Sabbath covenant, Isaiah 56?

Notice that the two end-time keys to Kingdom power are included in John 1:12: the name and the days of Jesus.

How can we rule with Him if we don't know Him intimately? And how can we rule if we don't have time to rest with Him and learn about our unique Kingdom assignment?

Unveiling the Plan of Author "Love"

Before anything came into existence, God was. He has always been and always will be. He is the Eternal One who has no beginning and no end. Because he *is* Love, we as spirit beings existed in His genetic make-up. By His very nature, He had to share His love and His ruling authority with all of us -- all mankind. He made our unique personalities long before time began.

From the very beginning His great mind of love has envisioned and seen

5 Munroe, *Rediscovering the Kingdom*, p. 33

every detail of a Family Government that begins on earth and expands forever in love into the whole universe (Isa. 9:7). The plan is detailed even in the first verse of His coded Book of Family Love. "In the beginning, *God created* [*Elohim bara*]…" Volumes could be written from this short coded message.

Conceptual meanings abound as revealed by the qualifiers or terms that surround these two words in context. Here are a few: "God, in Family unity, as Supreme God, in full authority, created, spoke out, caused to exist, made out of nothing, established boundaries, set laws in motion, causing harmony and beauty to exist, chose in unity the universe to be manifested and then created the earth, selecting what is to exist forever, defined perfection and increase in order to bear sons for God, to rear sons, to give a beloved Son, to make pure, to make heirs, to establish obedience, to magnify the truth, to bring in a harvest, to give life, to bless for increase, and to produce seed for the God Family." What a mouthful!

How great is our God! God is the name of the ruling Family and therefore our name as well. As Adam, we are called to be Gods on the earth (we use capitals here to emphasize that it is a Family name) until such time as the Father comes down on the earth, when Jesus hands over all authority to Him (I Cor. 15:29; Ps. 82:6; John 10:34). We will remain as members of the ruling God Family under our Father Love, Jesus and the Holy Spirit, to whom we submit today as Governor of the earth.

God blessed the Sabbath day after He made man, making the Sabbath holy. The Sabbath will always be the regular and special time of intimate fellowship of the Father's mature Children to meet with Him, Jesus, and the Holy Spirit. It is an eternal covenant He has made with mankind who become "Godkind" (Gen. 1:26-27; Gen. 2:2-3; Ex. 31:13; Isa. 56:1-7).

How have we missed these colossal truths? Why do they seem unreal? The answer is simple: we have disobeyed the fourth commandment and missed out on the blessings of intimacy of the Sabbath covenant.

You can embrace these wonderful truths if you will simply follow the words of one commercial: "Just do it!" Start resting in Jesus on Friday night until Saturday sunset, and you will begin to know the Author of the Book of Love like you have never known Him. Ask God to bring another person to meet with you and Him in Bible reading and praise songs on Saturday, and you will have the two or three required for a Sabbath meeting. Perhaps you could ask God to touch your pastor with the spirit of repentance, not forcing his will, and you may end up with lots of Sabbath company.

The Author of the Book is waiting for you. He wants the Bible code to be broken in your life so His Book of Love may come alive for you.

Prophecy will come alive as never before. Most exponents of Bible prophecy today give scenarios that are 90% flawed, left behind in a quagmire of confusion, disagreement, and error. Sabbath keeping opens the door to understand what is going on in these topsy-turvy last days.

The Kingdom *Returns*

The first king on earth made in God's image was Adam. He was King under the direction of King Jesus and priest or teacher/intercessor in his god-like and god-class function. Jesus made the Sabbath for Adam and Eve, who spent every Sabbath for years getting to know Jesus in an intimate way. Jesus instructed them on that day in regards to their Kingdom assignment, watching over and embellishing the garden, and preparing to spread the Kingdom way of love throughout the earth.

After re-creating the earth for six days after Satan's rebellion had caused it to be in a state of confusion, Jesus entered into His first Sabbath rest that Friday night (which was also the Day of Trumpets, according to Jewish tradition). He thus created the Sabbath as the holy Kingdom time for us to get to know Him and the principles of His Kingdom and for His fellow Priestly Kings to get to know each other. After all, the domain (or King*dom*) of King Adam and Queen Eve was the earth, the same as it is for us today and will be in a greater way later.

While Satan's plan makes no sense, God's plan does. He made the first six days of the week for Adam (and us) to nourish the flesh and bring increase. The seventh day was for nourishing the soul and spirit by resting in God. God created a Family Day of refreshing and revival, the only vestige of which remaining today seems to be the acronym, TGIF, meaning "Thank God it's Friday!" Jesus made it holy, thus putting part of Himself in the day. He put it as an essential part of His program for mankind, revealing on this day His collective and individual purpose for His children. To reject anything God has made holy is to reject God Himself. His name, identity, and purpose are unveiled in the Sabbath. It is not surprising that most Sunday keepers today call more on "the Lord" than on Jesus. They sing praises to the Lord on a day Jesus never made holy.

Little wonder that the gospel of the Kingdom has been lost. The message that focuses on heaven is a false gospel. Heaven is only a happy, very happy, holding place for the holy ones until King Jesus returns with them to rule the earth. The "sweet bye and bye" emphasis is an escape theology foisted on the church by religiosity. It is a total contradiction of Jesus' Kingdom gospel. Those who want only heaven forever must consider themselves anything but meek and teachable, for it is to the those childlike believers Jesus promised the *earth* (Mat. 5:5).

In fact, the Kingdom on earth will not be established but reestablished. Adam lost his dominion on earth to Satan. Jesus won it back. He gave us the Kingdom keys even He did not possess before He took them back from Satan on His trip to hell. Moreover, He told us to use them with full authority to tell Satan where to go. While Satan is the god of sinners not yet called (II Cor. 4:4), we are gods under Jesus granted full authority in the name of the King of Kings and Supreme Priest or God. When we resist the devil, he has to flee (James 4:4). We command Satan. He doesn't command us.

Adam also had full authority on earth but lost it. That was not all that slipped from his hands. He lost four blessings that we can only regain in the Sabbath covenant: fellowship and intimacy with Jesus, identity in Him, provision rather than sorrowful toil, and a Kingdom assignment. When Adam sinned, Jesus cut him off from Sabbath intimacy with Himself.

Jesus, who never changes, reinstituted the same covenant with Israel *after* He made the covenant with them at Sinai (Ex. 31:13). It is not part of the Old Covenant. He reminded them of the covenant in Exodus 16, and referred to it again just before He made the covenant with Israel at Sinai (Ex. 19:5).

It is a covenant of identity. It identifies who God is and who His people are (Ex. 31:13).

Do we realize that none of the other commandments identifies who God is? Only the fourth identifies Him as the Creator God (Ex. 8:8-11). It is the center of the Decalogue, the transition (or *cross*over point) between the commandments showing how to love God and those showing how to love man. The letter *tav* in the word *Shabbat* means cross of covenant, and the Sabbath is indeed the covenant of the cross, the day to remind us that Jesus brought us out of Egypt (sin), redeeming us by the blood He shed on the cross (Deut. 5:15).

We get to know the Author of the Book in the Sabbath day, and in getting to know and love Him, we begin to know and love ourselves so we can love God and others. Our identity is established in His.

Crack the Code Completely -- Read the Sequel!

We have seen that God has written the Bible like a book with a hidden code that must be broken to understand it. The key to decipher the code is amazingly simple. The key? Obedience! Obedience to the Sabbath command. "The [reverence of the Eternal] is the beginning of wisdom. A good understanding have all those who *do* His commandments..." (Ps. 111:10).

Many Christians are beginning to discover the richness of some of the other annual days of celebration in the Bible. These annual Sabbaths and feast days are statutes of the fourth commandment. The depth of biblical understanding and joyous celebration and refreshing these days afford far surpasses the emptiness and falseness of this world's holidays.

Yes, there's more. God calls us to live by His every Word (Mat. 4:4). In a prophecy for these last days, God says: "Remember the law of Moses [given to Moses by Jesus] My servant, even the *statutes* and ordinances which I commanded him in Horeb for all Israel [the believers]" (Mal. 4:4).

In the sequel to this book, we will not only explore the Sabbath in more depth to those serious about keeping it, but we will also explain how and when to observe the annual Sabbaths and all the appointed times of Jesus. Discover why more and more believers are rekindling their love for Jesus by keeping His feasts. It is a fascinating story you don't want to miss.

God is Waiting

God is waiting for us to meet with Him in His Sabbath so we can finally get to know who He is, who we are in Him so that we can do the job He has called us to do.

That job description is hidden in a prophecy that has not been fulfilled and should have been. It has not happened because we have not kept Kingdom Day.

It is interesting that this prophecy is found in the context of lawlessness abounding in these last days (Mat. 24:12-14). Another Bible mystery, that of lawlessness, had already begun in Paul's day, to the point that at the beginning of the second century some began to do away with the Sabbath (II Thes. 2:7-8). The man of sin or lawless one will proclaim Sunday as the Mark of the Beast. The spying mechanism to persecute those who keep the Sabbath could be the chip so many are focused on today.

Sunday and worldly feast days are feasts of Satan's kingdom, so they will become more popular as Satan tries to destroy God's Kingdom in these last days. But God is waiting on those who will restore His Kingdom Day, the Sabbath. In fact, without some of God's people embracing the Sabbath and all its Kingdom concepts, the desired end will not come, but a curse from God on the whole earth (Mal. 4:6).

Notice the message that must go out before Jesus can restore His Kingdom to the earth: "This gospel of the kingdom shall be preached in the whole world as a testimony [a witness, not to save souls for heaven] to all the nations, and then the end will come" (Mat. 24:14). Prophecy can fail (I Cor. 13:8) because of free will, and this prophecy has failed so far. This book is part of God's witness to the church to wake up and embrace the Sabbath so the real gospel can go out in power.

That cannot happen if we are not keeping the Sabbath, Kingdom Day. In fact, the church cannot have full provision to finance the effort without ceasing from human works and resting in Jesus in the day of provision, the Sabbath.

What excuse will we choose to follow lawlessness and break the Sabbath? One preacher, reflecting the majority sentiment, used the argument that God never intended us to be slaves to a strict and legalistic interpretation of the day of rest. But obeying the command to keep the seventh day by ceasing from our works and resting in Jesus, doing His works, is neither strict, nor legalistic, nor an interpretation. It is simply reading the Bible and obeying a clear and straightforward instruction from Jesus.

Doing so will open the coded Book that is the Bible. The secrets are opened when we obey the Sabbath law: "The secret of [Jesus] is for those who fear [meaning stand in awe of Jesus in love and obedience] Him, And He will make them know His covenant" (Ps. 25:14). None of the ten covenants of God are fully activated until we keep the first, which is the Sabbath covenant. When we make the step of faith to begin to obey the Sabbath, God then opens up the secret of His Sabbath covenant and all the others.

Even the church, however, will remain in the dark until we begin keeping the Sabbath as Jesus' disciples did (Mat. 13:11; Luke 23:56). God never intended the Kingdom to be a mystery for His people. He promised that we would have dominion on the earth, showing that we understand the Kingdom concept fully, if we keep *all* His commandments (Deut. 28:1). And by all He means all -- no excuses.

Sabbath *Selah's*
"Ce n'est pas catholique"

Every word of God is tested…Do not add to His words Or He will reprove you, and you will be proved a liar" (Prov. 30:5-6).

I had the blessing of living and ministering in France and Quebec for a total of fifteen years. I often heard the above expression, which is roughly equivalent to our English phrase, "That's not kosher." The French say, "It's not Catholic," meaning "not quite right, a bit fishy." Not adhering to Catholic doctrine in a European country called the eldest daughter of the church is definitely not seen as orthodox. In The Convert's Catechism of Catholic Doctrine, *here are some answers to questions regarding the orthodoxy of Sunday: "Saturday is the Sabbath day… We observe Sunday instead of Saturday because the Catholic Church transferred the solemnity from Saturday to Sunday… The Church substituted Sunday for Saturday by the plenitude of that divine power which Jesus Christ bestowed upon her. The Third Commandment commands us to sanctify Sunday as the Lord's Day. [The church conveniently took out the second commandment against images because they have images in their churches and divided the tenth commandment into two sections. The Sabbath is in reality the fourth commandment.]" The authority to change the Sabbath day did not come from God, and Daniel prophesied this blasphemous change (Dan. 7:25). The emperor I call "Constantly Compromising Constantine," the author of some 5000 false doctrines that he introduced into the visible church, established the first Sunday "blue law": " Let all judges and all city people and all tradesmen rest upon the* venerable day of the sun." *The Catholic Church Council of Laodicea in A.D.364 stipulated in Canon 29 that "Christians shall not Judaize and be idle on Saturday, but shall work on that day; but the Lord's day they shall especially honor…If, however, they are found Judaizing, they shall be shut out from Christ." This same council admitted that Christians in Ethiopia at the time were keeping both Saturday and Sunday, a common practice among Christians in the second and third centuries. To all this, I would add, "Ce n'est pas biblique!" This is not biblical! Selah.*

CHAPTER TWENTY FIVE

Rome's Challenge and God's Sabbath Challenge

This book is replete with astounding quotes from Sabbath and Sunday keepers alike about the biblical foundation of the seventh-day Sabbath. Some of the most amazing come from the Roman Catholic Church.

In the last part of the nineteenth century, the *Catholic Mirror*, with the full approbation of Cardinal Gibbons and the Catholic Church, made a remarkable confession. It was aimed at their Protestant daughters. While I take some liberty in the following paraphrase, this is the essence of what they said: "Why are you Protestants pretending that you derived Sunday worship from the Bible? Who are you trying to fool? You got it from us! We believe our church leaders have greater authority than the Scriptures, in which you will never find any evidence of Sunday observance. The Sabbath in both Testaments is unquestionably Saturday. Why can't you just be honest: you keep Sunday because of our Catholic tradition, established by papal authority."

This paraphrase is no more surprising than the actual quotes. It seems for once this ecclesiastical behemoth called Catholicism agrees with God's assessment of the situation. While He does not approve putting tradition ahead of His Word, He does not appreciate the Protestants lying about the origin of Sunday.

God is also from His Word facing each reader with a challenge. When you assimilate this material and the Holy Spirit convicts you of the Sabbath truth, you face a decision. You must choose the ways that lead to abundant life or the ways and days that lead to death.

They Admit It!

"You may read the Bible from Genesis to Revelation, and you will not find a single line authorizing the sanctification of Sunday. The Scriptures enforce the religious observance of Saturday, a day which we never sanctify." Catholic Cardinal Gibbons, in *Faith of Our Fathers*, page 111.

"There is nothing in Scripture that requires us to keep Sunday rather than Saturday as a holy day." Harold Lindsell, Baptist, former editor of Christianity in *Christianity Today*, November 5, 1976.

"Sunday is a Catholic institution, and its claims to observation can be defended only on Catholic principles . . . From beginning to end of Scripture there is not a single passage that warrants the transfer of week public worship from the last day of the week to the first." Catholic Press, (Sydney, Australia), Aug. 25, 1900.

God's Challenge to You

The famous draft poster, "Uncle Sam Wants You!" was a call and a challenge from the U.S. government for young men to join the army and fight for the defense of freedom. Jesus wants you free and to be an instrument for setting others free, not with a sword but with the Sword of the Spirit. He is calling you to commune with Him and rejoice with Him in His Sabbath because He wants all of you.

The seventh day is the test of your commitment. ***The Sabbath is the end-time litmus test of the believer***. It is the test of full surrender.

You have a choice: to listen to the complicated excuses for not keeping Jesus' day – or to accept the simple Bible truth.

Jesus was a Sabbath keeper. He definitely did not go to church on Sunday. He didn't keep it because He was a Jew. He kept it because He Himself rested on that day at the beginning and He blessed it and made it holy. He even said the Sabbath was made for ***man.*** That means all mankind – not only the Jew. He kept that day because He always honored what was holy. He kept it because He made it for man – and He was a perfect man and was to be a perfect example of keeping all of the moral law, summed up in the Ten Commandments.

Bottom Line: Do You Love Jesus?

The question is, in reality, simple: ***do we choose to believe our God is Love and believe His Word, or not?*** Do we believe He means what He says, or do we think God is a liar?

We must also answer another important question: Do I love Jesus? ***Do I really love Jesus***? If we truly love Jesus, we will love Him according to ***His*** definition of love – not ours. Some people don't believe the black letters of the Word – only the red letters some bibles use to show what Jesus Himself said.

Check this one out again. It's a hot, red-letter verse. Jesus said it, and we have emphasized it in this book. John, who taught his disciple Polycarp to keep the Sabbath days, recorded it: "**If you love Me, you will *keep My commandments***" (John 14:15).

Twist and Shove – or Walk in Love?

Unlike the song, "Twist and Shout," today's hermeneutical, theological tune is more akin to "Twist and Shove" -- twist the verses we don't like or simply shove them out of the Bible as if they were never in it. If we try to twist Jesus' words about obedience, beware lest we twist them to our own destruction.

We had a hard time ordering pens for Freedom Church of God. Our order was initially refused because someone in the company did not like what we put on the pen: "And Jesus said, 'If you LOVE ME -- OBEY ME." Too simple, perhaps? Too direct? Too controversial? Too true?

We must, of course, understand the concept Jesus expressed to the Pharisees when He said they were accountable because they knew better. Their eyes had been opened to the truth, but they refused it. God neither approves our Sunday-keeping nor does He condemn us for it at the present time. He has patiently endured the deception and disobedience that has characterized His church for some 1700-1800 years.

But His time has come. Jesus must prepare His spotless bride. What does He expect of us? He expects us to pray over these words, to "prove all things" and hold fast what is true, testing it according to the Word – not according to our pastor's opinion or the idea of some commentary. He wants us to get our face in the Word and study it. He wants us to "work out your own salvation with [godly respect] and [awe]"(Phil. 2:12).

Earthshaking Times

All hell is beginning to break loose. As I write these lines, seven prophesied years of sorrow have come to an end and tribulation has begun. The wise virgins who escape that unspeakable time will only be those who truly love Jesus according to His definition of love. Love=obedience. God is the merciful Judge of our predecessors who did not have this knowledge. He looks on the heart. But if we, after having received this truth and been convicted by the Holy Spirit, refuse to obey, we are saying that we don't really love Jesus. God even calls us liars (I John 2:4-6).

We are in the very last days. No time to coast. God said in Haggai He was going to shake heaven and earth. Hebrews says all that can be shaken will be shaken. This revelation of the truth about the Sabbath is part of that shaking. This is serious.

I'll never forget that morning when I was on my knees in a prayer closet in a dormitory in Pasadena, California in the early 1970's, studying a passage in the First Testament. It was in Samuel, and God was talking about how He holds the earth on its pillars. Just as I read that, the prayer closet began to reel to and fro. This South Carolina boy, who had known hurricanes, was about to feel his first earthquake. I remember lifting up my hands to heaven and crying out, "God, I know it's true! You hold up the earth on its pillars. You don't have to prove it!" I was shaken – in more ways than one.

The question is, will we be shaken by this truth, or will it take a Great Tribulation to shake us into obeying Jesus and acknowledging Him as Divine Master of the Sabbath? The choice is ours. My job is to tell you. Our anointing as a church and ministry is Isaiah 58, and that includes verse 1, crying aloud and showing God's people their sins. It also includes verses 13 and 14, telling God's people to keep their feet off God's holy day!

My colleague in this ministry was five years old when He accepted Jesus. He went to a Catholic school, and the priest who taught first grade was teaching Sunday. But my friend had read the Ten Commandments. He raised his hand and asked why this priest was not teaching what the Bible taught. It didn't go over too well. And the priest didn't change.

"All Shook Up"? – or Standing with Jesus?

What about us? Will we cling to the traditions of men and to the doctrines of demons? Or will we tremble before the Word of God?

We hear so many good sermons on the importance of obedience. And the same preachers who preach them have neglected to obey a simple command from God: "Remember the Sabbath day, to keep it holy."

The French simply say, "Pourquoi se compliquer la vie?" "Why do we complicate our lives or complicate things?" We have complicated our lives by choosing to observe a day God never chose, and observe it in a way He never intended.

We go to church on Sunday morning, but most Christians don't really rest in Jesus. And even if they tried to do so, they might rest, but they can't rest fully in Jesus because He poured Himself into the Sabbath – not any other day. We should indeed fellowship with God every day. But there is a manifest presence, an intimacy with Him that is not possible any other day. That's why He called it holy. He's in it. Let's meet Him where He is – on His terms, not ours. Jesus wants us to love Him the way ***He*** wants to be loved.

The shaking is coming. If we are found dancing with wolves who twist Scripture, we may be shaken.

Or we can choose to stand. If we stand with Jesus and avoid compromise, we have wonderful promises of blessings from God. God contrasts the curses of the law of sin and death with the blessings of keeping all His commandments (Deuteronomy 28).

An Invitation to Sabbath Blessing

On the positive side, God is extending an invitation. To the timid who see leaders and church members in large majority keeping Sunday and undermining the Sabbath, He gives encouragement.

Jesus even encouraged Himself with these verses when "...for the joy set before Him [He] endured the cross..." (Heb. 12:2). He persevered and did not give up because He saw in vision a group of end-time believers who would also persevere in keeping His Word (Rev. 3:8-10; 12:17; 14:12; Mat. 24:20), showing their love for Him by meeting with Him on His Sabbath days and feasts.

Jesus says He will gather those who love Him enough to want to keep His days (Ps. 50:5). After showing His ardent love for us by dancing in joy over His people and even comforting us in quiet love, He gives hope. This promise is not only for Israel in captivity in the 600 and 700's B.C. and in a time of tribulation to come, but also for those who desire to heed His Word before all hell breaks loose.

Here is His offer: "I will gather those belonging to you [those Israelites in captivity] who yearn and grieve for the solemn assembly [and the festivals], on whom [their exile and inability to attend services at Jerusalem have brought derision and] the reproach of it is a burden" (Zeph. 3:18, AMP.).

Satan has cast the Christian church into exile for some 1700 years. He has caused them to have no rest in Jesus by keeping the devil's day instead of the Sabbath. Those who do not heed this end-time warning to keep the Sabbath will go through much suffering to learn the lesson of obedience. Some of them will be literally taken captive in foreign countries before Jesus gathers them.

But He offers hope now to those who yearn for fellowship with Him at His feasts. He offers to gather them now in His loving arms and in His days of love. He calls them "My worshipers, My dispersed ones…" and says to them: "…I will give you renown and praise Among all the people of the earth…"(Zeph. 3:10,20).

The blessings await us. "How blessed is the man [or woman] who does this… Who keeps from profaning the Sabbath, and keeps His hand from doing any evil" (Isa. 56:2). Jesus says to those who "choose what pleases Me, and hold fast My covenant, To them I will give in My house and within My walls a memorial, And a name better than that of sons and daughters; I will give them an everlasting name which will not be cut off…Even those I will bring to My holy mountain And make them joyful in My house of prayer…The [Eternal] God, who gathers the dispersed of [the believers], declares, 'Yet others I will gather to them, to those already gathered" (Isa. 56:4-8).

To those who keep their feet off God's holy Sabbath, He gives this promise: "Then you will take delight in [Jesus], and I will make you ride on the heights of the earth; And I will feed you with the heritage of Jacob, your father, For the mouth of the [Eternal] has spoken" (Isa. 58:14).

In perfect accord with His Father and the Holy Spirit, Jesus, the Word, has spoken. He wants *you* to know Him and love Him more by intimately fellowshipping with Him on his holy day. He wants to bless you and yours, to protect you, to surround you in His arms of love.

Father Love is inviting *you* to enter the doorway Jesus has opened -- the Sabbath doorway. It's the doorway to intimacy with the Father and Jesus. He's reaching out His loving arms to you today, and He's saying, "Come, My son, come, my daughter, come sit on Daddy's knee and let me love you. Let me love you in a special way on My day, in a way you've never known. I love you. Come see how much."

Your Brother who died for you is also calling: "Come to Me, all who are weary and heavy-laden, and I will give you rest -- Sabbath rest."

The *rest* is up to you. The choice is yours. Choose life. Choose Jesus.

Appendix

Names of God: The Chapter, "Open Door to Intimacy and Power: Knowing God's Covenant Names" is an important one. Because of space limitations, however, we had to save it for the sequel (s). God's names are related to the Sabbath. They tell us who He is and what He wants from us. They show where we are falling short and help us to grow.

Names of Baal (Lord): We had indicated in *Why Doesn't God Heal Me?* that we would give more complete information about the use of the term "Lord." While we have done that to some extent, because of the strong nature of the chapter, "Lord Worship -- the Ways, Days and Names of Baal," we decided to place it in the sequel(s) to this book for those who want to go deeper. The story of how Satan has tried to recapture the adoration he enjoyed as Lucifer by using a King James term to demean Jesus and cause one of his demons to be glorified is a fascinating one. But it will have to wait.

Tithing and the Sabbath Connection: The chapter, "'Stop! Thief!' – Tithing and the Sabbath Stand or Fall Together" is also an important one, sowing the unmistakable link between these two laws, both of which came into effect long before the Sinai covenant. Many ministries understand the need to tithe, but they do not see why it is illogical to believe in one law established before the Sinai covenant and not believe in the other. Not tithing is stealing God's money. Not keeping the Sabbath is stealing God's time.

The Sabbath in a Nutshell

When God has given us the grace to understand the Sabbath truth, it seems odd and unfair to be put in a position of defending the Sabbath. It's biblical. In this summary, we give the biblical proof in resume form. Yet the burden of proof should rather be on those who have changed the biblical seventh-day Sabbath to Sunday with absolutely no valid biblical evidence. Why must we have to justify our obedience to God? Do we have to justify keeping the fifth commandment to honor our parents? The fourth commandment gets unfair treatment in the Christian world. Why single out that commandment as being legalistic? Is refraining from murdering your neighbor legalistic?

Why try to change the commandment? It is impossible to "remember the Sabbath" on "***the*** seventh day" by observing Sunday, the ***first*** day of the week. That's changing God's clear command – not obeying it.

Do we believe God wants us to obey the Ten Commandments, or not? We can't say the law is done away – Jesus upheld even "the least of these commandments" (Mat. 5:19). Furthermore, it is illogical to teach that Jesus did away with "the law" with the exception of all but the fourth of the Ten Commandments. Unlike God's Sabbath day, that argument is unholy – and full of holes.

James said that breaking one commandment was tantamount to breaking them all (James 2:10). Paul said that a little leaven (sin) leavens the whole lump, using an analogy based on one of the annual Sabbaths or feast days, which he kept.

The Ten Commandments are the foundation of God's moral law. And surprise! They are the foundation of both Old and ***New*** Covenants! That's right. Jesus wants the law He gave Moses to be written on our *hearts* (Jer. 31:31-33). This time, no stone tablets. Heart tablets. No new law here. It only takes on a newness because of keeping the law in the letter and spirit the way Jesus did.

Red-letter and Black Letter Proof

"That's Old Testament!" is not an argument (Mat. 4:4). Nowhere does actual Scripture refer to "Part One" of the Bible as "old." The covenant Jesus made with Israel is called old and is *replaced* by the New Covenant or agreement. Yet the agreement is based on the same law. What's more, when Jeremiah prophesied the New Covenant, the only Sunday worship was the worship of the sun god by believers in Baal on the first day of the week.

The New Covenant upholds the laws and Scriptures God gave to Old Covenant believers. The Old Covenant became obsolete (Heb. 8:13), but not the First Testament, and not the moral law summed up in the Ten Commandments!

Since some Christians will only believe "red letters," hear what Jesus says: "...if you [desire] to enter into life, ***keep the commandments*** (Mat. 19:17)." In the following verse He cites five of the Ten Commandments, showing that's the set of commandments to which He was referring.

Conclusion? The fourth commandment is New Covenant! Who do we choose to believe, God or man? The Word says that while men lie, God never does (Rom. 3:4).

Satan's Spin – A Web of Lies

This is not some clever "spin job." The Bible abounds in verses that clearly show we are to obey ***all*** of God's Word (Mat. 4:4; II Tim. 3:16) and ***all*** His moral laws, and many of them – in both Testaments – specifically uphold obedience to the fourth commandment.

The clever spin artists are those who distort God's Word. They twist two or three "New Testament" verses – a satanic spin that *contradicts* all of the remainder of the Bible. If they found a verse or two that seemed to do away with the commandment against murder or adultery, they would never understand those verses in a way that would contradict those commandments. Then why do they neglect the Sabbath commandment written by the very finger of Jesus at Sinai?

Why do they spurn one of Jesus' names? He calls Himself the *adonai* or *kurios* of the Sabbath (Mark 2:28), properly translated, "Divine Master of the Sabbath." That's part of who He is. We accept Him as Good Shepherd and Savior. Why not accept all that He is? Do we want all of Jesus, or only the Jesus we make in our image?

Jesus understands, of course, that the Christian world has been blinded from the Sabbath truth by false doctrine. But once He reveals it so His end-time bride can be spotless, His church will be responsible for keeping His day (James 4:17; John 9:41).

The Sabbath Made for Man

Has mankind been "done away"? If the Sabbath has been done away as many claim, then according to the following words of Jesus, man must have also been done away!

One of the strongest proofs of His day being the seventh day is in the Greek Scriptures, written in red! "...The Sabbath was made for ***man*** [the word means ***mankind – not just the Jew!***], and not man for the Sabbath."

Why of course! Jesus made the Sabbath just after having made man – mankind, Adam and Eve. Jesus rested on that first Sabbath, the ***seventh*** day, beginning on Friday at sunset and ending on Saturday at sunset (Gen. 1:31). "And God ***blessed*** the ***seventh*** day [not Sunday, and not just any day of the week] and ***made it holy***..." (Gen. 2:3, NIV).

What makes something holy? Moses had to take off his sandals in front of the burning bush because it was holy ground (Ex. 3:4-5). What made it holy? God's presence! God made all the other ground around it, just as He made all the other days. But notice this important fact: Jesus did *not* ask Moses to take off his sandals on the *other* ground. Jesus commands us to "turn back [our feet] from the sabbath" (Isa. 58:13, RSV). He does *not* say to keep our feet off the other days, including Sunday.

In this *last days* prophecy of Isaiah, Jesus speaks to this last generation of repairing the breach of the Sabbath day. He also tells us the wonderful blessings that come from obeying the fourth commandment (Isa. 58:14).

The One who says He never changes and is the same yesterday, today, and forever (Heb. 13:8) makes a similar prophecy for His end-time followers in Matthew 24:20-22, referring to the time just before the Great Tribulation, which is *now*: "But pray that your flight will not be in winter, ***or on a Sabbath***." If Sabbath rest on the seventh day were no longer necessary under the New Covenant, why would He be concerned about His end-time followers resting on the seventh day?

Jesus kept the Sabbath and prophesied that it would still be a command for Christians in these last days. He never kept Sunday, unless an annual Sabbath fell on that day, as did the Feast of First Fruits, later called Pentecost (Acts 2:1). Jesus obviously kept the same day as the Jews of His day. And the Jews have certainly not changed the day they keep since the first century.

Done Away at the Cross?

Some teach that the "Jewish" Sabbath was done away at the cross. If that were the case, Jesus surely did a poor job of teaching that to His disciples. His most faithful followers – the women – must have missed that important point. "Then they returned and prepared spices and perfumes. And **on the Sabbath they rested *according to the commandment*"** (Luke 23:56). Which commandment was that? The fourth.

Paul apparently didn't get the message either, even though Jesus dealt with him personally. Paul said to follow him only as He followed Jesus (I Cor. 11:1). Paul kept the Sabbath and the other holy days. Verses 4 and 11 of Acts 18 record no less than 78 Sabbaths that Paul kept.

In Gentile Antioch, Paul attended Sabbath services in the synagogue. He "sat down" and listened to the reading of the law and was then invited to address the people. "...As Paul and Barnabas were going out [of the synagogue], the people kept begging that these things might be spoken to them the next *Sabbath*. Now when the meeting of the synagogue had broken up, many of the Jews and of the God-fearing proselytes [Gentiles] followed Paul and Barnabas, who, speaking to them, were urging them to continue in the grace of God" (Acts 13:14-16, 42).

Here the grace of God included keeping the Sabbath. What is even more striking is what Paul did ***not*** say. Here was his big chance. He could have said, "Come back tomorrow. It's Sunday, 'the Lord's day,' and under the New Covenant we're not under that old law anymore. You Gentiles especially don't need to keep the Jewish Sabbath. We keep Sunday now." If he said that, then why does verse 44 say the " ***whole city***" assembled on the "**next *Sabbath?***"

All those who desire to follow Jesus fully should be keeping the same moral law Jesus, Paul and the other apostles kept. You can't obey a commandment to keep the seventh day by keeping the first day! No way!

This is Elementary

It takes a theologian to help us misunderstand such clear Bible teaching! Why is Exodus 20:9-10 so hard to understand? "Six days you shall labor and do all your work, but **the *seventh* day** is a **sabbath** of the [Eternal- the YHVH who was to be born later as Jesus] your God; in it you shall not do any work..."

What could be easier than reading the commandment and then looking at the calendar? The seventh day is Saturday. The dictionary confirms it. Only a clever deception from the devil could make something so clear be so complicated.

Sunday-keepers and those who claim all days are holy have made a gigantic assumption. They assume that "everyone" can't be wrong. If the vast majority of the Christian world teaches it and practices it, it must be right. The whole world, except a few fanatics, believed for most of history that the earth was flat. Yet the Bible had said all along that the earth was a circle or sphere. So who was wrong? The whole world (Rev. 12:9).

The Bible says to prove all things and hold fast that which is true (I Thes. 5:21). We're not asking you to believe us any more than the pastors and theologians who preach Sunday. We're simply challenging you to check up on them *and* us.

Freedom and Gateway to Intimacy with Jesus

The Sabbath is a day of freedom, celebrating not only the Creator but also being freed from the bondage of sin, symbolized in the First Testament by Egypt. The Sabbath is all about redemption through the blood of Jesus (Deut. 5:15). And since Jesus poured Himself into the Sabbath, it is a ***gateway to intimacy with Jesus.*** And since Jesus opens the way to the Father, we celebrate a great Sabbath blessing: ***all day with Daddy!***

Does that sound like legalism to you? You can get picky with any of God's laws. But the Holy Spirit inspires us to keep the Sabbath as a glorious day of celebration and release – release from the cares and burdens of the week.

As kings and priests like Jesus, we often perform our ministries on that day, especially those who conduct Sabbath services. Healing and ministry are part of the day. Spirit-filled Sabbath keepers don't fall into the Pharisaical exaggerations of Jesus' day.

Those who call the Sabbath a burden misunderstand this day of Love, Abba Love (I John 4:8): "For this is the love of God, that we **keep His commandments, and His commandments are *not burdensome*"** (I John 5:3). No, the fourth commandment is no more an "Old Covenant burden" than any other of the ten.

The Sabbath is no more Old Covenant than tithing. Both existed long before Sinai. Remember. God said, "Remember." That's because the Sabbath didn't begin at Sinai. Remember, Jesus said it was made for ***man***, and if Abraham kept "all" of God's laws (Gen. 26:5), that had to include the Sabbath. In a pre-Sinai verse referring to the Sabbath, Jesus tested Israel and said, "How long do you refuse to keep ***My commandments*** and My instructions [margin -- laws]" (Ex.

16:28). The test hasn't changed --only the excuses.

"What's the Big Deal?"

"But what's the big deal?" many will ask. The big deal is that God is a holy God and He expects His holy people to treat with respect those things He has made holy. Uzzah only touched the holy Ark of the Covenant -- and he perished. The two sons of Aaron made their own version of a holy sacrificial potion and it cost them their lives. Jesus' admonition to the priest was to "distinguish between [the] holy and unholy (Lev. 10:10)." We are priests of God today. Does He expect less of us?

A big difference exists between the ceremonial law and the moral law. Animal sacrifices are no longer necessary because of Jesus. Circumcision is now of the heart. Paul understood that circumcision was not the important thing, "but what matters is the keeping of ***the commandments of God*** "(I Cor. 7:19).

No one denies that the Hebrew Scriptures teach the Sabbath. What few realize is that the prophets show that the Sabbath and the holy days will be observed in God's perfect government in the Millennium. Isaiah 56 and 66 prophesy that Jew ***and Gentile*** will keep the Sabbath both in these last days and in the Millennium.

Jesus calls both weekly and annual Sabbaths "***My*** appointed times" (Lev. 23:2). They are Jesus' feasts – not Jewish days. Whether they come every week or during the year, God's holy days are just that – holy (more to come on this in the sequel). Zachariah 14:16-19 says there will be no rain for the ***Gentiles*** who refuse to keep the Feast of Tabernacles when Jesus returns.

Have you never wondered why Jesus, the same forever, would command Israel and the Gentiles among them to keep the Sabbath as a light to the surrounding nations under the Old Covenant, then keep it Himself when He was on the earth, teach His disciples how to keep it properly, command all nations to keep His holy days in the Millennium – and then tell His church *not* to keep the Sabbath for 2000 years?

It has been said that despots know the bigger the lie and the more often you tell it, the more people will believe it. How true when it comes to Sunday observance.

New Covenant Sabbath Rest

The Holy Spirit surely honored the Sabbath days. He came down in power in Acts 2 to start the New Testament church as they were gathered in unity keeping one of the annual Sabbaths of Leviticus 23. Yes, it was a Sunday, the only holy day that always falls on "the morrow after the Sabbath." It was kept, not because it was a Sunday, but because it was an annual ***Sabbath***! That doesn't mean that every

Sunday is holy.

This reminds me of a story: a man and his wife had enjoyed breakfast together and as he was slipping out the door, she said, "You remember what day this is?" Embarrassed, he lied, responding, "Of course!" "How could I forget our anniversary?" he thought. He proceeded to go all out with an expensive gift, flowers, and a pricey dinner at a fancy restaurant. At the end of the day as they relaxed in bed, his wife turned to him and said, "That's the best Groundhog day I ever had!"

The Sabbath is our day to celebrate our wedding with Jesus as His bride. But we've made a big deal about the wrong day. We've celebrated Baal's day. God says that idols are nothing, even less than a groundhog. We need to get it right.

Want New Testament evidence? Here it is: "So there remains a ***Sabbath rest*** for the ***people of God.*** For the one who has entered His rest has Himself also rested from his works ***as God did from His***." Four meanings apply to this rest in Jesus and in grace and they include the millennial Sabbath rest. This verse cannot be true, however, if we, the people of God, do not enter into a literal Sabbath rest every seventh day. Otherwise, we are not resting from our works ***"as God did from His"*** **(**Heb. 4:9-10).

The Holy Spirit spoke to one of our members who was hesitating about the Sabbath. God said to him, "If I cancelled the Sabbath, I would also have to cancel the Sabbath rest of the Millennium!" When we refuse to keep the Sabbath, we are saying in effect, "I don't want Jesus to come back. I don't want to see the Kingdom of God rule on earth." How can we pray the prayer, "Thy Kingdom come," and not keep the day that announces the coming of that Kingdom? Satan wants *his* kingdom to continue. That's why he lied to us about the Sabbath.

We all need to humble ourselves and come to rest on His day with the One who is "humble in heart," the One who says, "Come to Me, all you who are weary and heavy-laden, and I will give you [my Sabbath] rest" (Mat. 11:28-30)?

Childlike Teachability

Jesus said we should become like little children. Little children soon learn to count to seven. They can understand simple things like working six days and resting on the seventh – simple things like doing what Jesus did. We have become too complicated.

The record of the early church keeping God's Sabbaths is unmistakable (Acts 2:1; 13:13, 42-44; 16:13; 20:6,16; 27:9, referring to the Day of Atonement, and I Cor. 5:7-8.)

Romans 14, Colossians 2 and Galatians 4 do not contradict this gigantic mountain of proof we have seen. They can easily be properly understood in their context, and we explain them in this book. The Bible does not and cannot contradict itself.

Paul warned in Acts 20 that men would introduce false doctrines into the church. The first mention in church history of someone keeping Sunday is in the second century. It doesn't matter who began to change the day. What men have done, even in the early stages of the church, doesn't really matter. It was Jesus who said, "Sanctify them in the truth. Your Word is truth" (John 17:17).

There you have it – the Sabbath truth in a nutshell. We pray God's greatest blessings upon you, His *shelam* and *shalom*, as you enter into His glorious Sabbath rest.